GRAYWOLF FORUM 5

Open House

This is my first copy of the first book that includes something that I wrote. For Jim and Karen, because you're the ones I believed when you said that things like this could happen.

with much love and Thanks,

Michael

05.30.03

GRAYWOLF FORUM 5

Open House

Writers Redefine Home

Edited by
MARK DOTY

GRAYWOLF PRESS : SAINT PAUL

Publication of this volume is made possible in part by a grant provided by the Minnesota State Arts Board, through an appropriation by the Minnesota State Legislature; a grant from the Wells Fargo Foundation Minnesota; and a grant from the National Endowment for the Arts. Significant support has also been provided by the Bush Foundation; Marshall Field's Project Imagine with support from the Target Foundation; the McKnight Foundation; and other generous contributions from foundations, corporations, and individuals. To these organizations and individuals we offer our heartfelt thanks.

Andrea Barrett's "A Hole in the Wall" is reprinted by permission of the Wendy Weil Agency, Inc. and was first published in the *American Scholar* © 2002 by Andrea Barrett. Carmen Boullosa's "Seeing Is Believing" is translated by Alfred MacAdam and was first published in the *America's Society* magazine. Portions of Mark Doty's Introduction appeared in *Ploughshares* and *Gulf Coast*. Mark Doty's "The *Panorama* Mesdaq" appeared first in *Drawing Us In: How We Experience Visual Art*, edited by Deborah Chasman and Edna Chiang (Beacon Press, 2001). Paul Lisicky's essay is taken from his book *Famous Builder* (Graywolf Press, 2002). Carol Muske-Dukes's essay first appeared in *Married to the Icepick Killer: A Poet in Hollywood* (Random House, 2002).

The editor is grateful to the Center for Scholars and Writers at the New York Public Library for time to work on this collection, and to the Lila Wallace / Readers Digest Fund for their generous support. And to Bill Clegg, Fiona McCrae, and the staff at Graywolf for superb assistance, always.

Published by Graywolf Press
2402 University Avenue, Suite 203
Saint Paul, Minnesota 55114
All rights reserved.

www.graywolfpress.org

Published in the United States of America

ISBN 1-55597-382-5

2 4 6 8 9 7 5 3 1
First Graywolf Printing, 2003

Library of Congress Control Number: 2002111720

Series and cover design: A N D

Contents

. . . .

Introduction

. . . .

1. HOUSTON

It's a December afternoon in Houston and I'm stuck in traffic on West-heimer, in a strip of shopping centers—an unrevealing detail, since Houston mostly *is* a strip of shopping centers. There are more retail opportunities stretched endlessly along these roads than you'd think even the fourth largest city in America could ever make use of. To drive through nearly any part of town is to encounter a repeated string of terms that together make up a kind of local vocabulary: NAILS, COMIDAS, CELLU-LAR, AUTOS, ESPRESSO, FUTONS, TACQUERIA, BIG N' TALL, SUSHI, SHOES. (My friend Alan Hollinghurst, visiting from London, asked, "Is all of America so interested in *nails?*")

Some 15 percent of the cars registered in the United States are registered in Harris County, which gives some idea of the automobile's primacy here; this is a driver's place, developed over the last forty years or so on flat and swampy land an hour from the Gulf Coast. This urban world's designed—to the extent it *is* designed—for the convenience of the wheeled, and largely inaccessible by any other means. It's the only place I've ever lived where the homeless and the panhandlers work intersections by the freeways, standing out in the sun with handmade signs (HOMELESS, PREGNANT, NEED HELP PLEASE). They hope that drivers stopped at intersections will roll down windows closed up tight to keep the air-conditioning in, even this close to Christmas, and dole out their spare change.

I'm stopped this particular afternoon because a heavy orange piece of equipment is blocking the street, beeping and idling loudly. In its big metal claw is a peculiar, rough-textured stalk about twenty feet long, held horizontally in the air. It takes a moment to figure out what it is: a palm tree, trimmed at the top, almost rootless, about to be set into place in a row of matching trees along the edge of a particularly fancy strip of shops. The cordon this new palm will join is already decorated for the holidays: their trunks are wrapped in little white lights, and illuminated stars jut out into the air a dozen feet above the ground: a long row of Stars of Bethlehem, as if every one pointed to the location of a commercial miracle.

This is the sort of juxtaposition this city offers all the time, and in fact it's one of the things I really like about living here. I came to Texas a few months ago, for a new position in a wonderful creative writing program. I knew from my first week that I loved the job, and knew equally that this sprawling, unlikely town was going to take some serious getting used to. The skies were big and dramatic, full of towering clouds blown up from the tropics; the city was low slung and, at first glance, truly disorderly. Houston's never had zoning laws, which means that an adult bookstore sits next to a "luxury townhouse loft complex," a car wash by a cathedral, a museum by a bodega, an "erotic cabaret" by a RadioShack. What do you want to buy today? the town says. And if you want to build it, go ahead.

This lack of restriction seems metaphor for a larger kind of decenteredness. There's no real geographical center, no heart of things; a car culture makes everything a destination, nothing any more central than anything else. There is no dominant culture and just barely a dominant language; in some areas the street and shop signs are in Spanish, in others, Vietnamese. A teacher friend told me that there are some fifty-two languages in use here. In the classes my partner Paul is teaching, there are students named Gustavo, Batya, Senait, Jameka, Blas, Rogelio, Vonda, Mohammed, Chitra, and Bobbie Lee. Wildly disparate lives go on in the same city, entirely separate, occasionally overlapping. There are exclusive neighborhoods, of course, maintained by something called "deed restrictions," but even those are pierced by stacked freeways, and minutes away from collapsing apartment complexes. New corporate towers poke up randomly here and there among the ubiquitous shopping centers: FAX, BUFFET, QUIK LUBE, CHRISTIAN BOOKS.

What surprised me about all this, after the initial shock a Northeasterner feels on entering the rawly energetic Sunbelt, is the odd exuberance of it, the unexpected room, even in these endless asphalt acres, for individual expression. (What else are all those shops promising NAILS in big bright letters offering? Some sense of personal distinction, expressed as stripes and diamond chips, five-color lacquers, metallic two-tones.) I began to understand that this is what the future might look like; if America has a ready example of life in the twenty-first century, this is probably it: artificial, polluted, a little dangerous, and completely confusing, yes—but also

. . . .

interestingly polyglot, open ended, divergent, entirely unstuffy, and appealingly uncertain of itself. It reminds me of something Salman Rushdie said, in defense of his novel: "*The Satanic Verses* celebrates hybridity, impurity, intermingling, the transformation that comes of new and unexpected combinations of human beings, cultures, ideas, politics, movies, songs. It rejoices in mongrelisation and fears the absolutism of the Pure. *Mélange,* hotchpotch, a bit of this and that is how newness enters the world."

This understanding—the bracing impurity of the future—still startles me a little. I'm a child of fifties and sixties sci-fi; the future had a whole design ethos, which was about streamlining, a perfection of ideal solutions, sleek arcs of plastic and metal. The futuristic was, in other words, modernity, in a kind of idealized, chilly form. But postmodernity shows us that the old predictions of what was to come—a vision of the triumph of earlier avant-gardisms—isn't to be. I suspect this is true in literature, too. Distrust, dear reader, whoever says that the future belongs to the nonnarrative, or to new formalism, or to minimalism, or even to the kind of formal self-consciousness and quick juxtapositions we've come to call postmodern. Here in Houston, it looks like the future belongs to everything. What I first took as disheartening disorder begins to reveal an interesting richness and variety of life between the cracks, along the seams; there's much more to see in Houston than first meets the poor eye overwhelmed by all this visual information on the horizon.

That palm tree decked in its holiday finery, newly upright, looks both lovely and out of place; it's a stab at beauty and a sales pitch come-on; it celebrates life in the heart of winter, here where there isn't much cold. It reaches for the "natural" in an environment manipulated to the point where that term is an empty one. It is a gesture that plays on nostalgia, sure, but one so strange as to ultimately go beyond the cynical. Palm and star are far from home; maybe they represent the reinvention of tradition. Might this bright, tawdry new world display some loveliness, a strange kind of authenticity—its falseness complexified, if not exactly canceled out, by all these odd new conjunctions?

2. SAN MIGUEL DE ALLENDE, GUANAJUATO, MEXICO

We've been in this colonial hill town in the high desert north of Mexico City for all of half an hour—just time to set down our bags, wash our bleary faces after the long, scorching taxi ride over the hills, and find sweaters in our luggage to ward off the sudden evening chill. It would make sense to take a nap, but once we've opened the double wooden doors that lead out onto our room's terrace, it's impossible to even think of it. We look out over rooftops and gardens, a steep, stacked, tile-roofed welter of houses painted every shade of rose, terra cotta, brick, and ocher, with jolts of electric blue thrown in for good measure. Down the long decline of the hill, a wide, smoky valley opens out, distant trees and spires and the water of the lake, a hazy expanse like the miniature landscape in the background of some Renaissance painting. The world smells like burning mesquite, diesel fuel, geraniums, very old wood, sage, and dust. The street below us is alive: buses and cars threading their way between groups of people; children and dogs and adults strolling; vendors with dolls; a man with a tall stack of straw hats on his head; a table laid out with *helados* and *frutas* and golden round *empañadas*. We'll sleep later.

Out the hotel doors (every place seems to have these heavy wooden portals, tall, weather battered, armored with hinges and locks) we discover that the narrow street—Calle Canal, named for the founding family of the town—has filled with a parade. It's the eve of Three Kings Day, the Mexican feast of the Epiphany, and a succession of floats slowly makes its way down the street, each one a truck on whose flatbed is carried a display of children costumed to represent moments in the early life of Christ, though in fact it's the Virgin Mary who's the center of attention. In each tableau, she's portrayed by a serious girl wrapped in blue. Here she is, with Joseph, bent over the marvelous manger, receiving the attentions of the kings. Now she and Joseph are fleeing into the desert, perched on an amazingly cooperative donkey; now they are camped at an oasis, surrounded by boy angels and baby goats. And here they are settled at home, the boy Jesus receiving instructions in carpentry from his earthly father while Mary tends to the house. The angels look around, and even wave back at us when we wave to them, and one of the Josephs wobbles noticeably as the truck lurches a little on a pothole, but each Mary is radiantly fixed, entirely focused on the doll she holds in her arms.

This is a fine introduction to San Miguel, which turns out to be a town of remarkable complexity. There is a thriving expatriate community here, Americans and Europeans who've settled here for good, along with wealthy weekenders from Mexico City. These immigrants have brought with them coffee bars, Internet cafes, an ATM, a very good "fusion" restaurant that inscribes its name, Nirvana, on every slice of its delicious chocolate cake, and any number of elegant places to shop. There's a long-standing tradition of creative work: a Siqueiros mural in a former convent turned arts center, classes in silversmithing and life drawing. Various residents are involved, this week, in a festival honoring the work of Virginia Woolf. Some of the planned events seem of dubious merit, but it is a Virginia Woolf festival nonetheless.

But there is another San Miguel, with deeper roots and of much longer duration, one that seems very little affected by the newcomers, though it intersects, as far as I can tell, comfortably, and seems essentially indifferent to the new dispensations. In Provincetown, the resort town where I've lived on and off for years now, local culture has long since been essentially atomized by the money of the summer people and vacationers, by the shift in real estate prices, and the belly-up of the fishing industry. A coherent sense of community has been replaced, instead, by a multiplicity of communities, and by a steady influx of strangers. Newcomers with larger wallets displace older wash-ashores with Bohemian budgets; just this year the guys who own Abercrombie & Fitch remade their beach house into a brash, colonnaded monument to the success of their marketing campaigns. I am, of course, part of the problem, but since I arrived over a dozen years ago I am now something of an old-timer, and thus have acquired a special right to complain.

But in San Miguel the local is startlingly alive and well, and its particular character fills the senses. The parade that greets us (or, to be more precise, that we are lucky enough to encounter wending on its way, welcoming our presence but graciously indifferent to us) is alive with it, as will be tomorrow's parade, when the three kings ride through town on horseback, tossing pineapple candy to everybody along the street, followed by a delirious cast of celebrating characters: Bugs Bunny, Satan, Barney the dinosaur, Saint Christopher. Bells give out from I don't know how many churches all day, every day. People wander into mass and prayers and first communions, into the temples of the images: Virgins whose faces are lit by tenderness or transfixed by grief, boy saints who seem the incarnation of devotion, fiercely suffering Christs bearing their blazing wounds, the two thieves writhing in the air on crosses of their own. Each church is a treasury of carved and costumed emblems of the possibilities of human feeling. People wander out again to circle the square, or laugh at clowns, or sit in the benches in the lovely Jardín with its clipped laurel trees. This garden is so densely planted and ordered that it feels much larger than it actually is, a dreamy public space made both for social life and for private reflection, for festival and for respite. Ancient women, cowboys, the ubiquitous beloved children; the whole place pulses with a dense web of connection, the vital and burgeoning life of the streets. It is exactly the opposite of an American suburb, where few people are visible, where everyone's held apart in their privacy, and commingling happens by driving—either because we're all on the road together in our separate vehicles or because we've driven someplace, the mall or the restaurant or the church, where we can actually *see* each other. Here, people seem to be in the streets a great deal of the time, seeing friends and acquaintances and everyone else, selling and shopping, hanging out, consuming, enjoying. Once much of the world must have been like San Miguel, a place where so much is known and held in common. It feels like walking into a tapestry—that tightly woven, every corner abounding with life.

(Of course I realize that I'm a tourist here and constantly coming up against the limits of what I can know about the place. Do the citizens of San Miguel tolerate the gringos, accept them, ignore them? How much of a difference has it made that these expatriates actually contribute, actively, to hospitals and schools and libraries, services all the citizens of San Miguel can use? Have the expatriates who've settled here found a sort of paradise, or consigned themselves to lives of perpetual tourism, a permanent outsider status? It would take me years to understand. And wouldn't my own presence here help to undermine the very sense of locality I praise?)

A couple of days later—days of walking, drinking it in, sitting in the Jardín, talking to the helpful American expatriate who runs the Internet cafe—I'm walking on a steep side street when a woman comes from the opposite direction, leading three burros loaded with firewood. The beautiful animals are short, wide bellied. On their backs are woven serapes, and on top of those, canvas sacks filled with neatly stacked sticks. I think, good lord, this is like a *movie* of Mexico, such a perfect image out of another age. And then I look a little farther down the street and see on the corner the boom, the dolly that hoists a beetling black camera. It *is* a movie.

The next day we're walking on an angled street near the Parque Juárez—a tropical garden where dogs lope through the heat to drink from the stone fountains placed at each intersection of the shady paths—when along comes a fellow with three somewhat less photogenic burros, a little scrawnier and a bit less doe eyed, ambling up the street, and there's not a camera in sight. San Miguel manages to be both then and now at once, specifically itself and an image for tourists, both replica and original at once.

.   .   .   .

3.

If someone were to build a monument to my family, the motto inscribed on the lintel would read: THEY MOVED. We packed up, we headed to the next place; we kept the best and sturdiest boxes in cellar or attic or closet, ready to be brought out again. In my memory, moving is associated with particular smells: masking tape (scratchy sound as it's unrolled, sharp scent with a sick hint of sweetness to it), the volatile chemicals of Magic Markers (write on the box—*Mark's room / books)*. When the movers came with their long truck they put stickers on everything, boxes and furniture alike, and then I'd find the little yellow tags here and there for years: BEACON, MAYFLOWER. We lived in Sunbelt places— Tennessee, Florida, Arizona, California. My father's work, which drove our nomadism, was founded on the new: he built air force bases, missile silos, buildings for assembling rockets that would go to the moon. But our movers' names suggested sturdy old American stability and tradition. *Our* tradition lay in unpacking certain familiar things and setting them into place, emblems of home. It still seems a pleasure to me to open a box and discover, wrapped in newspapers gone inconsequential and out of date, the friendly aspect of some temporarily forgotten, familiar thing.

I didn't set out, as an adult, to replicate my family's wandering ways, but it turns out that the life of a writer and teacher is nearly as amenable to relocation as that of a civil engineer. I left my parents' home in Tucson when I was seventeen and spent much of my twenties in Iowa. Then a desire to reinvent my life sent me to New York City, and love brought me to Boston. Then five years in Vermont, until I found a home at the end of Cape Cod, in Provincetown, Massachusetts, surely America's oddest and most adventurous small town. I've kept my house there for more than a dozen years now, though in fact I am away for more and more of the time. Provincetown is a highly seasonal community, startlingly empty in the gray and blustery months at the beginning of each year, and my need to make a living also pulls me away. During the last seven years, "away" has included Iowa City, Salt Lake City, Houston, and Manhattan. Faced with an airplane conversation and the inevitable "Where are you from?" I am nonplussed. I realize the questioner doesn't want the whole elaborate story; it's just a polite inquiry. But how on earth do I answer it truthfully, without beginning a far more involved narrative than anybody wants to hear?

Although of course it isn't the listener I'm really worried about; my anxiety has more to do with the fact that I don't have an answer for my-self. It isn't surprising that a person who's moved around all his life would feel dislocated, and in recent years I *have* spent an awful lot of time in air-ports, those strange liminal zones, on the way to here and there. But I sus-pect my sense of homelessness goes beyond the personal. I have little sense of a locality—a specific geographical and cultural spot from which I and my people hail—because for all of my lifetime the local's been under siege, or at least under revision.

Fifty years ago, driving across America would have meant a meander-ing passage through regions clearly demarcated by evidences of particular-ity: regional architectures, locution and cadences and patterns of speech, cuisines, sartorial preferences, ways of viewing the world. The cloverleafs and arterial passageways of the interstate highway system changed all that, just as the advent of television did. Just as the triumph of the fran-chise, that arm of global capitalism has. America looks pretty much the same from one end to the other, unless you go digging around; sure, there's a sign advertising alligator viewing on the freeway outside of New Orleans, and on Interstate 90 through Wyoming you can watch antelope racing alongside the road when it isn't shut down by blowing snow. But the built landscape is frighteningly similar, from end to end, and the truth is that Burger King, Wendy's, and ExxonMobil don't care for alligators or prong-horns or the character of snow on the high mountain plains. We know how the new world feels: boxy, climate controlled, serene, with a sound-track of denatured rock and roll.

But isn't this the same world I was enjoying, a few pages back, when I was looking for life on the hot streets of Houston? Of course it is. I'm speaking now from what the poet Hayden Carruth calls "my customary umbrage with reality." How can I not? The world we've made is frighten-ing. Although it has the strange, untrustworthy calm of elevator music, it is probably a temporary, unsustainable construction, even if we behave as though we can drive our SUVs and go on eating factory-produced ani-mals forever. When I get in this kind of mood, I think of Carruth, who said it best:

> I felt the pressure of the house enclosing me,
> And the pressure of the neighboring houses
> That seemed to move against me in the darkness,
> And the pressure of the whole city, and then
> The whole continent, which I saw

. . . .

As the wild geese must see it, a system
Of colored lights creeping everywhere in the night.
Oh the MacDonald's on the strip outside Casper,
Wyoming (which I could indistinctly remember),
Was pressing against me. "Why permit it?"
I asked myself.

When I look at the world we've built, that's often exactly how I feel: why permit it? How can we live this way?

The new order isolates us, disconnecting us from the past and from each other. The noplace of suburban America feels as if the world just happened in the last twenty-five years, and it's impossible to see how we got to this particular point. We have lost our connection to our fellow species and have no use for animals save as pets, subjects of TV spectacles, or packaged foods. Other people sometimes seem to have as much reality as the electronically generated figures on video screens. Thus separated, we are easier targets; we need to be told what to consume, and we'll listen to the forces whispering in our ears about who we're supposed to be and what it is we want.

As soon as I write down that gloomy view of the way we live now, there's another voice in me calling for recognition. It's the necessary, corrective perspective: the other side, the strange humanity of even the crap we've made, the hopefulness it holds, the possibility of starting over. I start thinking about the kid sitting across the aisle from me on a plane the other day, a young Eastern European thoroughly Americanizing himself in huge pants, a soccer shirt, a backwards baseball cap, and gold chains. He was watching a movie on a little DVD player, with the sound cranked up so loud it leaked out his headphones, and I might have gotten annoyed save that he began laughing with such complete, evident pleasure that there was something contagious about it. He was working hard at being who he thought he was supposed to be in the new country but having such a good time at it that he was totally irresistible. So what if he seemed to buy into every cliché of mercantile American culture? He was laughing so genuinely he seemed to be laughing for us all.

Carruth corrects his own disdain for contemporary American culture, too. His poem continues:

It's a dreadful civilization,
Of course, but the pressure is yours.

And indeed it does belong to us, imperfect and brutal and vulgar as it is: the pressure is our own. The oppressive, ahistorical, untenable world out there is also the theater of human endeavor. The new world frightens, and yet the blurring of old boundaries excites, opens closed doors, complicates the story. Niels Bohr once said that "the opposite of a profound truth may be another profound truth." His statement suggests that something can be both awful and home at once, both anonymous and deeply personal, oppressive and full of possibility.

So where do I live? I don't have a ready answer, but I've realized there's something I *like* about not having an answer. Something of that spirit— a curious, open engagement with the now, in its slippery and uncertain character—animates this book. Some version of my question lies behind each of these essays; they are complex responses to a strange place and time in which to find oneself. Sometimes home is found in unexpected places: Honor Moore abandons a beloved country house for a city apartment with a view of a brick wall of inexplicable beauty, while Carol Muske-Dukes portrays an antiliterary, make-it-up-as-you-go L.A. that also somehow provides her with the necessary imaginative space to be a practicing poet. For Reginald Shepherd, displacement is itself a location. Paul Lisicky investigates his love for the hopeful promise of the suburbs of the early sixties and the inevitable betrayal of those prospects.

Home is betrayed, too, for Andrea Barrett and Carmen Boullosa, who chronicle the deeply revised experience of life in New York after September 11, the apparent solidity of the city compromised, a new space opened where something familiar once stood. Barbara Hurd also confronts a hole in the world, the deep silence and darkness of the cave, a place that invites the deepest confrontation with fear and somehow also comprises a sacred space.

There are other portrayals of refuge here: Terry Tempest Williams's desert defending itself against a ruinous drought, Mary Morris's welcoming subways, Bernard Cooper's imagined and longed-for Manhattan, capital of Art. Rafael Campo conjures a Cuba built solely from family stories and dreams. These refuges may be lost places, like Elizabeth McCracken's Jewish Des Moines or Victoria Redel's memory of a strangely comforting full-body cast. And lost places may be recapitulated: the safe havens of Kathleen Cambor's cemeteries and libraries recaptured in her work as a historical novelist, or Michael Joseph Gross's deep identification with his mother's powerlessness reconfigured in adult life.

This is a diverse, rangy book; these writers walk around the questions

· · · · · · · · · ·

at its core, deepening and enlivening them in the process. We're all trying
to make a home, as we always have, trying to fit ourselves to the world,
and the world to us. The heart of the matter is subtle, hard to name—
perhaps simply because of the difficulty of standing back and looking at
one's own times. But we can gesture in its direction: our sense of home,
our understanding of what location *means,* has shifted, in the last few
decades, in ways that trouble and invigorate at once.

MARK DOTY
New York City, 2002

GRAYWOLF FORUM 5

Open House

Houseful

. . . .

by
HONOR MOORE

1.

Yesterday I left while the buyers came to measure. On my return, there was a note: *We can't wait to hear more about your beautiful house.* Ahead of me are the painted floors, the eave where a swift nested. What will I say to these strangers about this house I've owned my entire adult life? That it was built in the eighteenth century, not as a farmhouse, but as a worker's cottage; that once it was sold for nonpayment of taxes; that in the 1920s two women lived here, one smithing ecclesiastical silver in the windowed alcove where I have written three books, the other keeping a tea house across the lawn. I will tell them where the old well is, how pachysandra grows under the scrub behind the ruin of the old tea house, and how you can't kill pachysandra. I will tell them the name of my friend the sculptor who designed the stone wall that replaced the ruin of a garage, and that deep in the wall there's a bottle with my name in it, and the name of the man who built the wall. I want to tell them that the weeping hemlock will grow back if it's protected with black netting from the deer, that I put a curtain drain across the south lawn, which used to be swampy, that there was once a pump house at the edge of the brook.

It is early morning now and I am still living here, writing in bed. Through all three windows, I see green, and the leaves of the maples are an enveloping through which I glimpse blue sky. Later in the day, gold will tinge the edges of the leaves. Once in a while, a car whooshes by outside, but at this early hour I hear just birdsong and percussive cawing. Some summer mornings, a gathering of crows makes its proprietary way across the lawn, beaks pecking insistently at the grass, and often in late spring a pair of wild turkeys lead a line of chicks around the circumference of the yard, their prehistoric-looking gangly necks jerking forward and back. What you see from the back of the house is a theater, its spectacle a shadowy reach up into the forest rising steeply from the brook's far shore. Sometimes deer slip between the trees, and in the fall all the leaves turn waxy, luminous yellow. On a rainy day years ago, a turtle the size of a hatbox perambulated the breadth of the lawn. Before I got my dog, I might look up from the kitchen sink at a family of deer, or a woodchuck on its haunches, munching something green in the middle of my vegetable garden.

2.

The house was built in the 1740s and added onto during the succeeding centuries. It sits on a sharp slope overlooking a road from which it looks deceptively tiny. The original saltbox had no cellar, and its foundation is boulders taken from the ground beneath it. When a second saltbox was slapped onto the back of the first, a cellar was dug and a stream runs through it, around its edges.

I returned to the house when I was in my twenties, walked up the overgrown driveway. White paint peeled from the clapboard and mildew greened the window frames. A woman whom my family had known, who had been twice widowed, had moved in after my father was transferred to the Midwest when I was eleven. She lived there more than a dozen years, raised three children there. Now she was leaving. The house needs new blood, she said. I was twenty-six, a year into my first enduring relationship with a man I'll call Tim. He was eighteen years older than I was, a writer. I was just starting to write. I was at the beginning of my adult life, and of my writing life.

We spent weekends there, leaving the city on Friday afternoons, crossing west on Twenty-third Street to mount the still-elevated West Side Highway, driving upriver in the failing light, across the Spuyten Duyvil Bridge and north for two hours until old Route 22 delivered us to country roads we considered ours alone. As we approached the house, timer-lit lamps glimmered, and as gravel crunched we came to a stop between two giant maples that had astonished me as a child. Last fall, when I decided to sell the house, the realization I would lose the trees as well as the house gave me a physical shock.

. . . .

We had been in residence just two weeks when the house began to teach me all I know about wood-frame construction. I learned that houses like mine rise from a sill, a heavy plank that rests on a foundation, and that a sill can rot. I learned that the siding on such houses is called clapboard and that you don't pronounce the P. I learned the virtues of oil paint over water-based latex, of wood shingles over asphalt, and when one winter the new paint peeled right off, I learned it was lead that kept old paint bound to wood. I learned, too, that a house has ways of communicating. Tim and I bought a grand piano, which he insisted on putting in the dining room. I didn't want to give up eating there, but Tim was in love with the piano, which he played badly but with passion. Not a month later, a vestigial pipe, cut off and left crazily poking from the back of an upstairs closet, gushed water through a nail hole in the dining-room ceiling. The piano was destroyed, and after the ceiling was replaced, dining returned to its rightful venue.

As years passed, I had bookshelves built, tore them out, and had more bookshelves built. One of the giant maples lost a limb, and so did the apple tree. I made applesauce and apple pie and thought of my mother canning pears in the same kitchen when I was a child, sweetening with honey rather than sugar but forgetting to adjust the quantity so the results were inedible. I had the roof replaced, stone walls repaired, chimneys pointed. Eventually Tim and I parted, and I fell in love with a married man whom I longed for one whole summer, writing naked on the new roof. When he went back to his wife, I fell in love with a black-haired woman and then a woman who wrote songs and sang them. I moved furniture in and out. I moved paintings in and out. The roof rotted, and I replaced it again. I fell in love with the woman from England who painted my hallway floor; she painted other floors and other walls, bright geometric shapes, repeating patterns, a buoyant chaos of color.

Some summers, I raised herbs and tomatoes, onions and carrots, zucchini and chard, and ate only my own vegetables. I kept roses and learned to kill Japanese beetles by squeezing them between my thumb and forefinger. After I installed outdoor lights to illuminate the maples at night, I could see, from the downstairs bathroom, the giant shape of an ancient woman looming in the bark. I tried every bedroom in the house. I have slept soundly here, and fitfully, have wept at the ends of love affairs and laughed on the telephone. I have picked Queen Anne's lace in August and in July arranged roses in red glass bowls, leaving them until they dropped their petals. My next-door neighbors told me that on a clear summer day my music often bounced across the ravine and was on occasion so loud they could identify both the opera, *La Bohème,* and the soprano, Victoria de los Angeles. I have had dinner parties on the back porch, lunches in the kitchen, teas in the living room. I have cooked here for friends and watched their faces around the dining-room table, thinking, This is happiness, how it is and how it should be.

3.

But it was mourning that married me to the house. Six months after Tim and I moved into it, my mother visited. She and my father had separated and she was alone, appearing in a white, rented car. She brought along a tin box in which there was a walnut torte she'd baked for my birthday, and a ring binder in which she'd pasted photos of roses she'd ordered to be sent in the spring, my birthday present. When she drove off, I wept, unaccountably, as if the world had ended. I believed I would never see her again. What was true instead was that she would never see the house again. On a Saturday in March, the bare-rooted roses came, and Tim and I planted them. That night I was waked from sleep by the telephone. My mother had cancer. Six months later she was dead, and after the weeks of vigil, of funeral and recovery, Tim and I returned to the house. Some weeks later, to bring back what could not be brought back, I planted a copper beech. It came to my shoulder and was no wider than I was with my arms outstretched.

The house was filled with my parents' furniture, antiques they had bought or inherited. Eighteen months after my mother died, my father married again and began to strip the house of that furniture. First the double bed went, then the secretary desk and the dining-room table. After another year, he decided to sell the house, and without much thought, I bought it from him. Even when I bought it, I understood it was not the house I wanted. I wanted my mother a young woman again, my brothers and sisters as children eating on the back porch, and me, the dreamy girl in the tiny room with its separate entrance, reading *Tanglewood Tales* and King Arthur as crickets and peepers drowned out the present.

Failing that, I would watch the copper beech grow, and Tim and I would be happy.

But, instead, two years after my mother's death, I fell in love with the married man and then with the black-haired woman. I made excuses to Tim and came to the house by myself. I wanted to take the walks alone

· · · · · · · · ·

that I had always taken in company. At first I was so frozen with fear, I could walk for only fifteen minutes at a time, and only on paved roads. I was not afraid of anything tangible, but the silence of my aloneness seemed as dense as any dark night in a strange place. When Tim and I walked together, we might talk or be silent. He might expound on Nadezhda Mandelstam or Ernst Becker or break into tears when evening turned the sky pale green and the mountains dense purple. Now I had chosen to look alone as the color of the mountains darkened to black, as the sun fell behind them, leaving a haze of gold. I would have to find my own accommodation to what rose in my silence. As week after week I walked the fields, what I looked at began to fill the quiet. Now it was my presence that disturbed the family of deer at the far end of the field, I who watched the scissor motion of their leaping, the fluorescence of their white tails in thickening dusk. I learned where I could swim and hike alone, and as I drove the countryside, what roads twisted into openings of apocalyptic beauty.

Eventually I brought my new lovers to the house, eventually I made friends who had lived in the country as long as or longer than I had, and eventually I abandoned New York altogether. By then I had no lover, and in the years I lived there year-round, I lived by myself. A decade passed, and then nearly another. I wrote one book and then another. I couldn't imagine living anywhere else.

4.

The decision to leave formed like a dream. It began one day at the river, the river at the foot of the mountains across the road, to which I have walked hundreds of times with people important to me, hundreds of times alone. To get there, I turn from the paved road that runs past my house onto an overgrown path and head downhill through a swath of forest, out into a vastness of field and sky. Each time I walk to the river, it seems as if instinct is leading me. I walk south through the field, then down a small hill into another field just as vast, then across the old railroad tracks and down into another. At the bottom of the fields, a path wends through a collar of forest that in summer opens first to an expanse of ferns, then to the water, which flows southeast, moving slowly toward the Atlantic. In autumn the water is either blue or gray-green. Toward spring it turns black. Most winters it freezes hard, and the ice is dove gray or white. In a cold January, I find the river broken, its thick fragments upended and stationary at the shore, as if a particularly violent process had been arrested. What was the sound as the surface cracked apart?

After years with women, I began to see a man who lived up the road, a weekender. I met him when a friend took me to dinner in his small house. I think I fell in love when he asked me to make the salad dressing. All winter, I whipped olive oil into tarragon vinegar, folding it into greens with my hands. All spring he cooked for me and we listened to music as I watched his face against the white of his furniture, scrutinizing it for desire. When desire came, his face was too bright to look at, and it burned itself out before we touched. But before it burned out, I went to dinner parties with him, and out to country inns where we sat at bars in rooms with fireplaces. We were invited everywhere that each of us had previously been invited alone, to the houses of people who had begun to build in the forests or at the edges of meadows, and to the houses of people who were bringing old houses back.

I was accustomed to the pleasure of entering lit houses from the dark, a dark broken by moonlight glancing off acres of summer meadow or illuminating autumn foliage, or, in winter, transfiguring snow ploughed to the side of the road into pale hulking shrouds. For a long time the landscape and I had made these dreams alone together. Now, perhaps, with a lover who had also left the city, that might change.

But something else was changing. During the 1970s, in my town, a former airline pilot made a fortune distributing Japanese kerosene heaters. After the heaters were found defective, his business collapsed and he sold the office building he'd built on a hill east of town to a chain of nursing homes. Soon he had bought the old general store, cut down the massive birch that had sheltered the old lumber yard, and built a yellow clapboard shop and office block. And then a bakery opened, and in the old station, an ice cream parlor, and in an old caboose, an art gallery. The small plant nursery became a big business, a graduate of the local prep school had a controversial television success, and a computer company built its corporate home in the lot behind the kerosene tycoon's yellow office block. I bemoaned this to my gentleman caller, and he told me he had yet to understand the landscape, and that he frequented a bar in his town because it was the only place to go. I told him that would change, and we kissed in my car in front of his barn until the automatic light turned off and the moon illuminated the dashboard. One night, he asked me if I would ever sell my house, and I surprised myself by saying, Yes, in a heartbeat. When he broke off our relationship, my new social life ceased. I turned off my telephone and spent the summer clearing out my basement, my attic, my shed. Old friendships curdled. I woke weeping; I thought I was grieving him, but actually I was grieving the future I had dreamed for myself in these hills.

That winter I took a sublet in the city

5.

In September, just after signing the contract to sell my house, I stood in a cemetery as my aunt was buried. My father, who is a clergyman, performed the burial for his older sister, dead at ninety. *In my father's house are many mansions,* he said, reading the scripture. When my aunt's son spoke at the service after the burial, his voice broke when he said how much his mother had loved her house, a great big house approached by a long driveway lined with old red pine that sits at the shore of a lake—a lake that is quiet, a bird sanctuary, without motorboats. When we went back to the house after the funeral, I saw, because my aunt was no longer there, how the high ceilings and formal spaces reflected her propriety, her sense of what was right, and how the lake, which she worked hard to preserve, represented the part of her that secretly painted. But I could also see in the profusion of photographs she had placed decorously across the top of the grand piano, that she valued her family. Outside, there was a swimming pool, turquoise in the style of the 1950s when it was built to keep her sons at home. She never updated it; that would not have been frugal. Ironic, since the only way to describe her house with its many rooms, its huge windows, its carpeting and pantry, its kitchen and alternative sets of china, is as a mansion.

That house is what my aunt made of her life, but the house came to determine her life. The kitchen and pantry were the equivalent of backstage; performances took place in the dining room, with its enormous table, and in the living room, where couches and chairs were set out in perpendicular arrangements. It was hard to get close, even in the library, the most intimate room in the house, where the seating was "cozy." When my aunt was in her forties, her courtly, handsome husband died, suddenly. Years later, married again and divorced, she told me that her heart still "leaped up" when she heard gravel crunch in the driveway, and then she would remember Freddie was dead. But the house remained, with her in it, overseeing her gardens, inoculating the two remaining elms, greeting children and grandchildren through sequences of divorce and remarriage. All her family, including her sons' former wives, stood at the grave as she was lowered into it, men in dark suits, women in summer dresses, my father saying the prayers as she was buried beside the husband she had grieved for all her life.

I come from a tradition in which the women were formed by making houses, houses it was hard for them to break out of, hard for them to transcend. My aunt may have painted waterfalls, but the angular force of her brush stroke was mitigated by how she framed the canvases. The manner in which she hung them, at proper intervals along the wide staircase, kept her secrets. I leave my house to move the force of my making into my body, to claim the form-bestowing energies that, in women of my line, have leached from creative imagination into wallpaper color, arrangement of furniture in a room, how pictures hang on a wall.

If it is so easy for me to see the character of my aunt in her house, my house must have presented my visitors with as accurate a portrait of me. If that is true, it follows that as I leave my house, I leave behind a self.

6.

The first winter I sublet in New York, I planned to stay three months, but I stayed six. I had been gone from the city nearly twenty years, and I saw those years in the faces of men my age whose hair had gone grey and thin, in the bodies of women my age whose torsos had widened, whose emotions marked their gait. As I walked and looked, I felt my years away from the city as loss. I must look and walk like they do, I thought. But as the winter passed and days lengthened, I began to feel optimistic. I was beginning a new book; I had enough money not to worry. The apartment I had sublet belonged to my sister, who had moved most of her things to another city. It was bare, with white floors, and high above Broadway. In the morning a blaze of orange pierced my sleep, and as I awoke, I watched the sun's reflection pulse from distant beaux arts façades, water tanks spread out like chess pieces on intervening acres of roof.

I made new friends and reconnected with people from the past. As I walked the streets, I began to understand that what was shifting had less to do with the aftermath of a love affair or a sojourn in the city than with the axis of my life. I walked my dog in Riverside Park, relearning the Hudson, its pale, ruminative surface, its width.

The next winter I sublet a tiny penthouse and the following fall a studio on Jane Street. I walked to my new teaching job through the exciting city

. . . .

darkness that begins in late November. In January, I moved to a friend's Soho loft, where I spent the spring of dot.com and cell phone, the spring that ended with the introduction of the tiny silver scooters.

I began to dream myself as houses. I dreamed my house overrun by unruly teenagers who ignored me as I protested their spray painting and banging, invaded by men in camouflage fatigues carrying assault rifles. I dreamed its walls collapsing and its rooms opening into rooms I had never seen. I dreamed the house submerged in water, wrecked, and perfectly finished. But when I got to my Connecticut house, it was always unfazed by my dreams, calm, substantial, itself. I came to think of it as a home, as doting parents, as an embrace. When I returned for those weekends, or for weeks in those last summers, it looked its most beautiful, most of my aspirations for it having been realized. It was a place I would always come back to, I mused. The painted floors sparkled in the sunlight when I crept out of bed, and the refrigerator and cupboards seemed supplied with whatever I might need for supper when I didn't want to shop.

My New York life was opening up. The teaching job became perennial, and new possibilities for romance, friendship, and work seemed to crop up at every party. One Monday in a favorite restaurant, waiting for a friend to join me for lunch, I called home on my cellular phone. The reassuring voice of Kathy, who takes care of the house and usually calls to let me know everything is okay, now vibrated a tinge of emergency. It's not good, she said. There's an inch of water on the living-room floor, water pouring in through the ceiling. When I got her on the phone, she said, You know the overhead light in the telephone room? Water filled it and it exploded, glass all over the floor. All the upholstery is soaking. . . . I called the plumber and the next morning drove to Connecticut. By the time I got there, the floors were no longer underwater, but they were still sodden. The plumber arrived, and then the heating company, and then the electricians and the phone company. The furnace-water feed had malfunctioned, pumping water into the radiators upstairs. Once the radiators filled, the water burst through their seams, releasing a torrent that pushed its way through cracks in walls, any little hole in the floor, bowing floorboards, underfloor, staining plaster and Sheetrock, newly painted woodwork.

Two months later, when I had nearly finished getting estimates for repairing all the destruction, a power surge laid waste my phone, toaster, microwave, fax machine, television, and VCR. Two months after that, the roots of the maples blocked the lawn drain, the basement flooded, and water destroyed the motor of the new washing machine. Any time I spent in Connecticut was spent with insurance adjusters, upholsterers, painters, plasterers, restorers, carpenters, plumbers, and electricians. New York became my refuge, the dot.com billboards along Houston Street a reassuring landscape.

In late June, the owner of the sublet returned unexpectedly from what was to have been a year away and I realized I needed my own place in the city. No sooner had I put the word out than I visited a bright, golden-floored, quiet one-bedroom tucked into the back of a vast, stolid door-manned building on Riverside Drive. There was no view of the river; the living-room bay window gave half on a sooty yellow brick wall, half on what a friend charitably called a *West Side Story* view. But the rent was reasonable, the rooms were newly painted and appointed, and the space had what I came to describe as a feeling of houseness.

I moved in that July, bringing along the things I'd moved from sublet to sublet, a new sofa, a few linens and dishes from the house. I found a dry cleaner, learned where to walk the dog, where to have breakfast. With as much pleasure as I'd had discovering shortcuts in the country, I found the quickest subway route to Union Square or Nolita. I noticed just going outdoors and keeping pace with everyone on Broadway lifted my spirits. One afternoon, moving through my living room, I burst into tears. Of happiness, I thought. A feeling that I had come, if not home, to a new place that felt right.

One October morning, my accountant called, and after we'd gone over the numbers, he suggested it was time to sell the house. Two days later, I called a realtor.

7.

Thirty years. Of papers, of books, of linens and blankets, of furniture, of candles and lightbulbs, of ornament, of chairs and tables, of paperweight and teapot, of vases and campaign buttons, of videos and cassette tapes, of rock and roll LPs, of childhood dolls and books, of flashlights and cushions, pillows for spare rooms, of empty jars and oil lamps with and without their glass chimneys.

And so I packed up. I removed books from shelves, organizing them into *keep* and *sell*. I tried on every piece of clothing, even the bright pink and gold *shalwar kameez* I wore in Pakistan when I was an exchange student there in 1962. Then booksellers came and made their selections and friends came to help pack the books, and the shelves were suddenly empty.

· · · · · · · · · ·

And the auctioneers came, choosing from among my tables, pricing them, scrutinizing the corner chair I'd bought thirty years before with Tim, the Windsor chair I refused to let go. One day the telephone room had no table and the room at the top of stairs with the orange and white and dark brown floor had no chaise lounge. The buyers wanted the dressers and so the dressers remained, along with one living-room table. I slept in my bedroom right up until the night before the packers came to pack everything not labeled *sell*. One of them was a man so tall he had to bend at the waist, as my father had when I was a child, whenever he went through a door or down the narrow stairs. Soon my house, where no angle is true and whose floors are rarely flush, was crowded with perfect cubes and rectangles of light brown corrugate, boxes of pictures tilted against the wall, boxes of books stacked, tall boxes of clothes and sculpture making a canyoned landscape of living room, kitchen, dining room.

And then the movers came, all Brazilian, speaking Portuguese as they carried a chest of drawers, as they boxed small chairs. It was the momentous autumn of 2001, but you wouldn't have known it watching us as the leaves turned yellow outside and the sky remained implacably blue. I am saving this sweater; I am giving this one to my friend Julia, who is helping me move. I am watching the movers shrink-wrap the chaise I've had re-upholstered three times: in 1973, bright purple; in 1981, a blue-and-brown weave; and after the flood, off-white crisscrossed dark red. It looks all new when they've finished wrapping it, polished. You can't touch it or lie down on it anymore. And then they pick it up as if it were light, a husk empty now of all the life lived on and around it, the life that gave it weight.

The shrink-wrap shone, and it began to seem that everything shone as the sun at a low autumn angle blasted the living room halogen bright. It occurred to me to imagine myself someone else, packing my house after my death; to imagine myself rendered separate and distinct, as if seen through cellophane. As I packed my papers, my life unreeled before me, from twelve years old on, it unravelled and unspun, was pruned, sorted and lined up in boxes. I'm dead now, I thought to myself, lain in a pine coffin, carried onto a truck. Now I will be driven through the yellow-leaved trees along with my furniture, my effects, like the final scene of a reassuring movie.

I ate chocolate to keep myself packing and sweeping, and that night, as the moon rose over the giant trees and I checked the empty house one last time, its gleaming floors, its walls marked here and there with the presence of something no longer present, I understood that I, too, was absent from it, that what had once expressed me so entirely was now gone from the house. Its arrangements of rooms, its architecture, even the architecture I had altered, had its own existence, and that existence was independent of mine.

I turned the tree lights on and turned them off. When they were on, I went into the bathroom and looked out the window at the old woman in the bark, the old woman bent and giant, who had remained there since I placed the lights that found her. I closed the blue back door and locked it. I put the key under the cement armadillo on the windowsill and walked toward my car, looking at the sky once more, the sky that had taught me a full moon can throw a shadow, the sky I looked at every time I climbed the lawn, green and warm, snowy and impassable, leafy, to the back door where I entered the house.

8.

It's three o'clock on a January afternoon and I have been houseless for two months. The dog is asleep on the apartment floor. I've been out to lunch with a neighbor, a new friend. Yesterday I e-mailed my buyers about the curtain drain and the brook in the basement. A family of carpenters from Staten Island is installing bookshelves. I am learning how to pay the rent on time. In a few weeks, the movers will arrive with a final shipment I left in storage in Connecticut. When I have unpacked the boxes and hung the pictures, this one-bedroom apartment with gold floors and high ceilings will be home, the house a fluid dimension of my imagination to be drawn on, which will shift, take on color or light as I summon one memory, then another: I was miserable there; no, I was happy. I forgot to say what the copper beech looked like. When my mother died and I planted it, it came to my shoulder. Now it is three, four, five times my height, and its dark, leafy branches form a perfect sphere. I have no plants yet in the apartment, and no curtains. I like looking at the sky. One morning when I returned from walking the dog, I was struck dumb by the beauty of the ugly, *West Side Story* wall. It was an illumination. In the sun, it glistened and glimmered, washed and pale, the dirty cement pointing a simple articulation, pulsing there in the white light.

A Hole in the Wall
(Brooklyn: July 20–September 25, 2001)

. . . .

by

ANDREA BARRETT

July and August

After living in the same house for fifteen years, my husband and I moved from Rochester—upstate New York, a small city surrounded by farms—to Brooklyn. Our plan was to live for a year in the city, during which time Barry would take a leave from his university teaching job, concentrating instead on his photography, and I'd take up a fellowship at the New York Public Library. Although Barry was excited and optimistic, I was mostly nervous: I'd written all my books in the same little room and feared my work might not weather the transplant.

Hopefully, foolishly, we'd signed a lease in May for a space behind a big hole-in-the-wall of an industrial building in Williamsburg. Windows had filled the hole by the time we arrived on a hot July day; a floor had been laid, wallboard was up, appliances stood in the kitchen. But the appliances weren't connected, and neither was the gas; there was no hot water and no way to cook; no screens, no key for the door, no way to get mail; no phone lines or radiators or shelves or closet poles; no lights in the bathroom nor stair rails nor a thousand other things. An apologetic trickle of electricity flowed through an orange extension cord strung from a neighboring building: not enough to power an air conditioner. Each time we entered or left we picked our way over rubble, unlocked a padlock, unwrapped a heavy chain binding the wire fence that caged us off from the street. At the stroke of eight each morning, the polyglot crew arrived and began working loudly everywhere at once. We showered at the public pool and ate in the local bars, moaning and groaning all the while. At first it was funny, and then it wasn't.

Later it was funny again. Our first four weeks in Brooklyn were preposterous, ridiculous, a giant cosmic joke. In the muddy back courtyard, three piglets appeared, wallowing and oinking and gaining weight until the night they were carried away, each one shrieking, to become someone's festival meal. By the end of that month—after the pigs and after the heat wave, which I spent largely immersed in a tub of cold water; after the bouts with no electricity at all and the weeks of jackhammering; after the arrival of the giant spinning truck that submerged the pigs' former home (a garden-in-the-making, we'd believed) beneath a sea of red concrete—we were dining out on our disaster stories, our first-month-in-the-city tales. We joked that we'd moved to a Third World country: it was like Bosnia, like Beirut. What did we know? New York is a pit, I said cheerfully. I could say that because it wasn't true, because I had no idea what I was saying, because the worst of it was over.

■ ■ ■

By the end of August, we had a home: we could shower, hang up our clothes, cook dinner, phone our friends. Most of the workmen were gone most of the time. I was starting to notice that, although our neighborhood was untidy and loud, I was interested in everything around me. My neighbors were people new to me, who'd come here from much farther than Rochester. Some were Polish immigrants, most of them elderly; they moved, talking under their breath, through a sea of recent young colonizers: artists, photographers, writers, and filmmakers. Construction sites all over the neighborhood brought in crews of workmen—Russian, Ecuadorian, Mexican, and Polish—until five or six languages rose from the morning streets. Our dog, an ill-bred, ill-behaved, somewhat scruffy pound-mutt disliked in Rochester, where the owners of poodles and borzois and Yorkshire terriers would cross the park to avoid us, here found herself a model of daintiness among a pack of pit bulls, Dobermans, rottweilers, Great Danes, and peculiar crosses.

The subway, I discovered, would take me safely anywhere, at almost any hour: what freedom! And there was music, too—on the L train platform, and also at the Union Square station I passed through each day, someone was always playing: bass and saxophone, solo accordion, a pair of percussionists, one on trap set and the other on white plastic buckets and big glass bottles. Both underground and above, I was surrounded by faces: so much emotion, so much expression, so many different countenances registering so many different things. In Rochester everything had been hidden. Here much was played out in public, before my eyes—and to my surprise, I liked this. There might be, I was learning to think (during those ten or eleven days of real life, during what felt like a kind of flowering) some reason to put up with the expense and inconvenience of living here.

Tuesday

What kind of a city was this where a plane—no, two planes—could crash into a building? I think I thought that; truly, everything that happened that day is muddled. I saw the second one hit while I was walking home from the dog-sitter's. The pilot had fallen asleep, the air-traffic system was down, someone had made an awful and clumsy mistake, and something I couldn't imagine had happened. A hijacking never crossed my mind. I was too naïve to think that thought. But in a city where it sometimes seemed that nothing worked—in Brooklyn, I had told my family, everything is broken—a mistake of even this magnitude seemed possible.

It was my upstairs neighbor, leaning out the window and shouting down to me—I must have run to our building—who first used the word "they": some "they" had attacked the second tower. But who were "they"? Nothing he said made sense. My husband, now framed in our front window, looked similarly puzzled; I ran upstairs and we turned on the TV. Somewhere during those minutes, we also first heard the words "terrorist" and "hijacking." We looked out the window again. Then at the TV. Then we ran up to the roof.

In our part of Williamsburg, the East River is only a block and a half away and the buildings are low, a mixture of warehouses, three- and four-story tenements, and industrial buildings. Nothing impedes the view of the jagged wall of stone and metal across the river, so near it seems one can touch it. The other tenants—two young Brits, a photographer and a filmmaker; a ballet dancer from Mexico and her musician boyfriend; the older French photographer who'd called down to me—were already up on the roof, staring at what had always dominated the sky. Smoke rose from the towers; flames began to shoot from the sides; by then we were crying. The builder and a friend appeared, also some neighbors from next door, while the Brits, who had cell phones, called their families in London to say they were alive. All over the world, I realized, this must be on TV; in Florida, my mother would be terrified. I ran downstairs to call her.

When I returned, what I saw was impossible. Someone tried to explain it to me—the south tower had collapsed while I was gone—but I couldn't hear it; I turned again and again to the sight and each time covered my eyes and turned away. Where had the tower gone? Soon the builder said, in a low, sad voice, "Shit. There goes the other one," and when I opened my eyes I saw the second tower unmaking itself, the sides curling away from the middle like skin peeling off a banana, the smoke spewing upward until everything was gone.

■ ■ ■

Why talk about the rest of that morning, the rest of that day? All of us were glued alternately to the desecrated skyline and the television, watching the same images again and again, each minute more deeply aware of the people who'd been inside those towers and what had happened to them. The trains closed down, the city closed down. No one knew what to do or say. At two that afternoon, the L train opened; Barry took his camera and went into Manhattan, working his way farther and farther downtown—so far that he was uncomfortably close to Building #7 when it came down. When he returned that evening to fetch more film, he convinced me to go back in with him. I should see this, he said. The way so much of daily life was still being lived; the tremendous social momentum that keeps us moving through the forms of life even after the heart has stopped. I would, he said, find the people and the sight of what still stood consoling. While I didn't believe that, I knew that if I didn't go into Manhattan soon I would never go there again. I'd put the dog and cat in the car and start driving and never stop—as if I could drive away from this, or that it would matter, now, where I lived.

■ ■ ■

Below Houston, then below Canal: closed streets, tired cops, an endless line of trucks and bulldozers and cranes and flatbed trailers mounded with lights and generators, machines whose names I don't know parked end to end with their engines running and their headlights on, a procession that stretched for miles and seemed to pulse with longing to get going, to do something, to move toward their grim tasks; prevented from that by the fires burning at what was already being termed Ground Zero. But also, among the tired firemen trudging toward the nearest open subway station at West Fourth Street, between the young police cadets and the Port Authority workers and the volunteer nurses and EMTs, we saw people walking dogs, pushing babies in strollers, sitting in bars and talking earnestly over supper and drinks. People on bikes. People holding hands. People unable not to do what they had always done, in the neighborhoods where they made their homes; people moving about, people living.

Where North Moore intersects with West Street, volunteers had gathered; meaning to see what we could do, we joined the crowd. Cots and stretchers filled a courtyard rimmed with face masks, bottled water, food, all sorts of supplies. No one walked or crawled or was carried from the rubble and there was nothing for the rest of us to do. We could see the fire burning, still. The smoke was lashing through the crowd, the trucks still waited helplessly. So did we.

Wednesday, Thursday, Friday
We watch the TV, we read the papers, we watch the TV, we read the papers. We talk to people on the streets and in bars and cafes. At dusk we stand on abandoned lots at the river shore along with everyone else. We used to walk the dog here at night, in the silent but pleasant company of others who, like us, had picked their way through the broken grass and the holes in the fence, around the garbage and over the rocks, to get a taste of the breeze blowing up the river and the sight of the city, so close. Now there are hundreds of people here, faces glimpsed before at windows or the subway platform or the park. In silent ranks, we watch the sun set over the smoking hole. The first night the cloud of smoke blew east, over Brooklyn Heights, and we could hardly smell it. But the wind has shifted since then and, as the sun sets, the smoke drapes Manhattan like a scarf and slides across the water into our nostrils.

It rains on Thursday night, after bolts of lightning first strike so close by that sparks fly and our next-door neighbor's television and amplifier are fried: a steady, unrelenting rain pushed toward us by a strong wind blowing up the river. Before I think to close the front windows (which face the bridge, and used to face the towers), the rain pours through the screens, all over the sill, and down the wall to the floor. I wipe up what I can. The next morning, I head for the sill with a rag, having learned during my first city rainstorm that each drop coming through the screens leaves behind a dot of the filth it has carried from the air. Now the entire sill is dark gray, six linear feet of grime. What I dab comes up like ash and as I back away, the rag still in my hand, I realize that's what it is: ash of buildings, ash of planes. The ash of people.

Everything in the apartment is gritty, I now see. Table, floor, pillows, and sheets; after that I can't stand to touch anything, and I can't sleep. Neither can Barry, who has processed his photos and is now obsessively editing them. He can't stop looking, and neither can I. We ought to stop looking, we ought to stop thinking like this, we ought to get in the car and go someplace, anyplace; we ought to do something to take care of everyone hurt, but we can't. We try to give blood and we can't do that either: for the moment, every place is full. On the TV, banners run across the screen saying no more volunteers are needed, please don't come to these places to help, stop stop stop.

■ ■ ■

The dog paces nervously, trying to understand why we're acting so strangely. If a dog can think, we think she thinks this: Why can't she run at the river now; who are all these people? Why do they have candles in their hands? The smells in the wind make her nervous too, along with our frantic comings and goings and the way that we're perpetually staring at glowing screens. The TV (we still can't stop watching). The screen at which Barry edits the digital versions of his photographs (he can't stop that either). The computers on which we try to retrieve and answer scores of e-mail messages, everyone either of us has ever known asking, Are we all right, are we all right?

We are, we write back. Knowing we aren't, exactly; and also that we've been extraordinarily lucky. We write and write and write and write, and the more we say the worse we feel until finally we decide we shouldn't say anything at all.

■ ■ ■

What, then, are we supposed to say to all those people who ask, "Don't you want to go back to Rochester? Are you going back? You must want to go back."

I did think of going back, sometime after the first minutes, during the first hour; I was stopped not by courage or a sense of shared community but by the physical impossibility of leaving. The dog, the cat, two people,

.   .   .   .

the car; I imagined us crammed with all the rest of Brooklyn onto the BQE, that narrow, broken-down, torn-up excuse for a highway. A sea of vehicles trying, like red blood corpuscles in a wounded capillary, to squeeze its way through the construction bottlenecks and across the bridges to the thruway. Who was I kidding? No one was getting out of here, I thought despairingly on that first day; if something else was going to happen, then it would just have to happen.

Now the roads are working again, some of them, some of the time. But now leaving seems impossible for other reasons, which I can feel but can't articulate, even to myself.

■ ■ ■

On Thursday, when I go into my office nervously—the library remains open, like the museums; much is made of getting back to "normal life," of "not giving in to them" (whoever they are)—we all try to pretend we're working. No one is very convincing; less so after someone notices that people are stampeding down Forty-second Street, in front of our windows, and that the street is now closed off. Uneasy minutes pass, during which we hear too many sirens and see too many police cars and too many running people, before we learn that Grand Central and the Condé Nast building have been evacuated due to bomb threats.

President Bush is scheduled to visit Ground Zero on Friday. Traffic will be blocked, the trains will stop, security will be crazy everywhere. Is going in worth it? I ponder staying home, feel like a coward, and solve the problem by waking Friday morning with an enormous migraine, which I blame, in my bleary and delirious state, on the ash we are breathing: what is on my sills is also in my sinuses. Whatever the cause, I am surely sick. Surely it's not my fault, then, that I don't go into Manhattan?

That evening, when I can see enough to walk, I return to the edge of the river with Barry, the dog, and a great many neighbors: the now-usual gathering. We stand and stare at the hole. Tonight we're joined by military transport helicopters flying low overhead, scanning us with their headlamps, and by fighter jets—four of them, F16s someone tells me—zooming back and forth in pairs, looping around the island. Since Tuesday the sky has been silent and empty, except for other ominous jets with their distinctive sound. These four extend their ellipses across the river and over us. Each time they pass us, I start to cry. Barry reminds me gently that they must be patrolling because of the President's visit; that they're American jets and won't attack us; that a war hasn't started, that the war hasn't started. A friend tells me I should welcome the sound: it means we are being protected.

Saturday

For twenty-four hours, what seems most relevant to me are the New York City newspapers from July 30 and 31, 1916, reporting the last huge explosion in New York: the munitions storage site at Black Tom Island, near Jersey City and the Statue of Liberty. For months I'd been meaning to look at these papers, as research for a novel I hoped to write. Now the stories seem to have an entirely different, and urgent, point. All day I hide in the library, reading microfilm, obsessed with this and determined to share it with others. How analogous, I think. German sabotage was blamed; a wave of anti-German hate crimes followed; the United States was not yet in the war but this would be one of the factors swaying public opinion toward participation. I print out sheaves of pages.

Later, this will seem crazy. Reading through those fuzzy copies, I'll notice that although thousands of people were shaken up, that windows were broken not only in Jersey City but all across lower Manhattan and Brooklyn, that businesses were damaged and warehouses burned, and that two hundred people were initially reported dead, only a few people really died. Property damage, not mass slaughter. The pages are meaningless.

Sunday, Monday

The jets continue, the helicopters continue; these start to seem almost normal. Months ago I accepted an invitation to visit a school a few hours north of the city and talk to the students about reading and writing. As the school has decided to go on with the planned event (miraculously, not a single student has lost a relative, and they're eager, the headmaster says, to "return to normal"), I gingerly board a train on Sunday afternoon. A few seats down from me, a firefighter who's clearly been working for days— his face is drawn, his clothes are filthy, his hat is covered with ash, or worse—falls asleep before we leave the station. Across from him, a man in his fifties thumbs through a news magazine, a special edition devoted entirely to September 11th. When I look at him next, he is weeping silently as he stares at whatever photo occupies the last page. Meanwhile the woman next to me, who clutches a bag labeled Baby Gap, keeps looking over my shoulder. (Of course I'm still reading about the events and staring at the photographs: Why can't I stop this?) When I offer her part of my

. . . .

paper, she accepts and then confides that she can't stop this either, indeed has been reading my pages surreptitiously. Russian-born, a recent immigrant, she lives in the suburbs and has a baby who, when the planes came, was staying with her father near Coney Island. Everyone is all right, but oh, she says, how terrified I was!

As we talk, the landscape beyond the window changes. Trees, lush green grass. Flowers, hedges, marshes, birds—it looks like paradise. White houses. How starved I have been, I realize, for a glimpse of nature. For a few moments, I am madly homesick.

And yet—although I stay in a guest room in a lovely house, although I walk across glistening fields that smell like hay and gaze at old and beautiful trees; although the school's faculty are immensely kind and the students are smart and attentive—as Monday passes I feel steadily odder, more disoriented, more unhappy. People here have seen the events on TV, rather than with their own eyes. They haven't smelled them or touched them or felt them. It's not their fault, they're not hard-hearted, they don't suffer from a failure of the imagination, it's simply that they are removed, and that their lives—of course!—are going on.

Don't I want them to go on? Don't I want the students studying, and necking in the corners, and worried about their boy- and girlfriends, and if they have the right clothes and how volleyball practice will go and what will happen at the dance?

I do, and I also don't. I want to shriek at them and am horrified at my desire to shriek at them. I understand how unfair I am being. But all I can think about, by the end of the day, is how much I want to go home.

■ ■ ■

By "home," I mean Brooklyn.

■ ■ ■

I can't sleep, I can't work, I can't think. I can't afford to live here, nor can I do without the life and friends I left behind in Rochester. And so how, exactly, have I come to think of this place as home? When I walk the block and a half to the river now I see, instead of the giant towers that once filled the skyline, a hole that continues to smoke. Everything that fell into that hole, and everyone still living their lives around it, is what keeps me here and makes me feel that I can't bear to leave.

Later

If this were fiction, I would have stopped with the line above, on that note of muted adaptation. But the truth is this: the second week is harder than the first, and the third seems harder still. One night the first thing Barry tells me when I arrive home is that our car has been broken into and the CD player stolen. Without thinking I ask, "Did they smash the windows?"

"No," he says.

"Then how did they get in?"

"I don't know. The doors were all locked. I checked."

We stare at each other, puzzled, until I remember that we have never *had* a CD player. When I point this out to Barry, he says, "But there's a big empty hole in the dash."

"That's always been there," I say carefully.

A long, silent minute later, he says, "I don't know. It just seemed like something was missing."

■ ■ ■

We are, all of us, daily more exhausted and more distressed, battered not just by the constant grief and the new difficulties of daily life, but by the stories spreading through the city like a virus. In another context we might dismiss these as urban legends. Now there's no way of knowing whether they're true or false, unbearable fact or manifestation of what we most dread. They spread at the river shore, at the dog park, at dinner parties and hospitals, delineating the circles of damage and trauma: the friend who finds out, after days of ignorance, that an acquaintance was on one of the fatal planes. The young relative whose first day in New York includes a meeting with a friend who retrieved his car from Battery Park City and found the windshield spattered with blood and body parts. The fellow dog owner whose journalist friend, walking through the rubble near Ground Zero, saw a gun and holster on the ground and—thoughtfully, kindly, wanting no one else to be damaged—bent to pick it up and so, inadvertently, held for a second the fragment of torso it still enclosed. The medical students who, another acquaintance says, have volunteered at the morgue to help sort through and label the heaps of remains and whose lives are being reshaped by this experience.

Everyone has a story, or knows a story; they spread like shards of shrapnel, hacking parts off the people who hear them. Yet we can't, despite that, keep from repeating them; only repetition seems to make the wounds bearable. At a lunch delayed, and then finally held, all any of us can talk about are the events of the past weeks. Where we were when it happened and what we first knew; who knows the person to whom this or that happened; who lived, who died, who saw what unspeakable thing: the stories, the stories, the stories. On the table, which is in a lovely room filled with congenial people, in a nice restaurant on a pretty day, a long wooden tray filled with rows of green apples sits glowing, demanding to be recognized as beautiful and worthy. All of us look at it, all of us are for a moment consoled and refreshed. A minute later, all of us are bent close to each other again, urgently telling more stories. This is home now, I realize once more. This is where I live. This is not going to get easier.

In the Hollow That Remains

. . . .

by
BARBARA HURD

> Go inside a stone.
> That would be my way.
> CHARLES SIMIC

On a recent December day I found myself squeezed into a cleft in 350-million-year-old limestone, trying to remember the final lines of Charles Simic's poem. Just an inch from my nose, a small circle of wet rock glowed in the light of my headlamp. Above me, the fissure narrowed into darkness. I felt as if I were inside a gash whose skin at the top had healed over, sealing me in at the bottom. I could swing my light up, watch its small beam skim over ancient walls, wrinkled and creased, like ocher-brown muscle turned to stone. Here at the bottom, I kept my body turned sideways in the cleft, shoulder blades pressed against the back wall. To move, I had to inch one foot slowly to the left, shift my weight to it, bring the other foot along, resist the urge to turn ninety degrees and stride ahead, an urge that, if heeded, could get me seriously wedged in stone sixty feet under the earth, two thousand feet away from the cave entrance. I took a deep breath, felt my upper body expand against the walls in front of and behind me, remembering that I love Simic's poem because it asks me to imagine space inside an object I'd thought of as only solid, impenetrable.

I'm clumsy in a cave. And nervous. My first attempt at caving ten years ago began in inspiration and ended in terror. I'd been teaching creative writing at an environmental camp for middle-school students who were scheduled to take a field trip to a nearby cave. For two days before the trip, I primed them with stories about Mohammed in the cave, Plato's cave, why caves so often symbolize rebirth. It's a hidden space, I told them, an unexpected, inscrutable space. Shy things live in there, eyeless salamanders, albino fish, a prophet's epiphanies. I decided not to suggest to them that going into a cave might be like going inside one's own mind, crawling around in the pitch-black, nook-crannied labyrinth of the human psyche. Nor did I anticipate trouble. I didn't mention claustrophobia or the guide's warning that we'd need to belly-squirm down the initial tight passage. We were all outdoors lovers, and on the day of the expedition, we fastened the chin straps of our helmets in anticipation and lowered ourselves into the muddy mouth of the cave. One by one, the kids dropped to their knees, lay down on their bellies, and disappeared headfirst down a dark chute. Of the two guides, three instructors, and dozen students, I was the only one who couldn't do it.

I tried. But lying on my belly just inside the two-foot-high chute, pushing with my toes, I felt something moving toward me. Not just stone, but something else: the Mack truck that barreled into my cousin's car moments before his death, as if I'd been in that silent car with him, windows rolled up, both of us speechless as an impossibly large pair of headlights, steel bumper, and grille loomed into the side-view mirror, bore down on our watery bodies of burnable flesh, only I wasn't there, I was here in a dark tunnel and couldn't see what I felt, knew only that I was about to be flattened by the thing that moves inside stone, the thing that was hurtling down that tiny tunnel toward me, who was by now scratching and clawing my way backward, out of the mouth, into sunshine and fresh air.

Claustrophobia? Maybe, though as a child, I'd loved hiding in closets, under beds, under attic eaves, inside the three-by-three-foot toy box my father had made out of plywood and painted red. Hallucinations? Maybe. For years, I had no explanation of my cave terror and still don't.

But slowly I tried again. Something drew me, some curiosity about that unexpected terror and a lifelong love of stones. As a child, I'd created endless small-stone dramas in the woods behind our house, built hospitals for injured stones, performed surgery on them, nursed them back to health. In college, I signed up for two semesters of geology, mostly because I'd heard that in the labs you got credit for rubbing and licking stones. I love geodes and the rock exposed when road-building crews dynamite away the side of a mountain—anything that lets me look at what's been concealed for thousands of years. How could I let one afternoon of terror keep me from the ultimate intimacy with stone: to go inside it? I wanted to try caving again, and so I started in commercial places like Howe Caverns, their interiors sidewalked and brightly lit, spangled with dripping stalactites so fabulous you can almost forget you're inside a mountain. And later in an easy "wild" cave in nearby West Virginia, and then, on that recent December day, in a winding, deep, undeveloped cave under Laurel Mountain in southwest Pennsylvania.

Like Simic, I'm drawn to both stones and hidden places, the not-so-obvious rifts, the unexpected gaps and niches, especially the ones created by some force, physical or emotional, that has moved through and removed the insides, hollowed out the interior matter, left a space behind. Not just caves, but excavated city lots, littered and graffitied; woodpeckered trees; the lowland after the beaver dam breaks; the self after loss. There's a Tibetan word *shul,* meaning the hollow that remains after something has moved through. Buddhist monks use the word to refer to the path of emptiness, the way that opens up when one stops clinging to dogma. In Yiddish, *shul* means temple, a place to pray and to learn.

On the day I was squirming around under Laurel Mountain, I wasn't, of course, thinking about Yiddish or Tibetan words. I was exploring caves, not out of any spiritual seeking, but out of my wish to not be afraid of what I love. Mostly I was curious. And then tired. Two hours into those limestone fissures, I asked the rest of the small group to go on without me. I knew from the map that they would have to retrace their steps, that I could rejoin them on the return trek. Not only did I need to rest, but I also needed the stillness of just sitting and not fretting over where to place my foot, my fingers, how to clamber up and over a boulder I could see only in fragmented light as I swung my headlamp over it. The group disappeared down a passageway and I sat down, leaned against a stone wall, took a deep breath, and turned off my lamp.

Deep inside a cave, there's absolutely no light. You squint, hold your hands up to your face, wait for your pupils to dilate. Nothing happens. No glimmer, no pale outlines, no softening of a darkness so palpable you feel as if you ought to be able to wring it, wrest from it a beam or two of light. Total blackness. You wave your hand in nothingness, sure your fingers are setting off ripples of darkness, that your hands are leaving behind them a V-shaped wake of the less-dark. Without landmarks or skymarks, you begin to lose your bearings. You pick up a rock, consider hurling it toward the last wall you saw, consider how you'll feel if it doesn't thunk, but instead sails noiselessly and forever through the silence of an abyss at whose edge your backpack teeters, how it could be you're not halfway be-

. . . .

tween Millstream Passage and Sleepy Rock at all, but somewhere else equally immense, sunless, moonless. You put down the rock.

I wish I could say that silent darkness moved me to some instant insight. That I suddenly understood why Buddhists prize emptiness. But what mattered was that nothing dramatic happened. The memory of my previous terror, the visions of my cousin's death, brushed faintly through me and triggered an almost imperceptible moment of anxiety. I flipped my light on, looked around, turned it off again. Stillness. It was as if those events had happened to another me. It became, in fact, oddly peaceful in that niche two thousand feet inside a limestone mountain. I became very conscious of invisible space. The limestone cracks gouged out by acidic water so many millions of years ago, the cavern walls inching back, the stone hollowed out. And some space in me opening up—what happens, perhaps, when fear unclenches its fist, uncurls its fingers, opens the palm wide. Room. An underground recess full of nothing.

Until footsteps and a small light approached and a voice in the dark said he, too, needed to rest and did I mind? Although he was apparently one of the group, and, like me, too tired to continue, I couldn't picture which man this was. The one in khaki overalls? The guy with wire-rimmed glasses? I saw his tiny beam go off, heard him drop his pack, settle himself on the cave floor. For a few minutes neither of us said a thing. And then, with no introduction, he told me he'd once been frozen to the deck of a navy ship in the early sixties, that they'd had to chip the Arctic ice from around his body, that he'd permanently lost all feeling in his right nostril. From there to his various jobs, the vagaries of his long marriage, the indulgences and difficulties, gestures of courage or supplication.

"I'm with my son on this trip," he told me. "We used to cave together often. Maybe this'll be good for us." His voice was soft, with none of the guilt of confession, nor the neediness of bravado. It didn't feel so much as if he were unburdening himself, hauling secrets out of deep hiding, sharing them, trembly voiced, with a stranger he knew he'd never see. It was more as if I were sitting inside his secrets. And then he inside mine, my small moments of bravery and shame, romances and job disappointments, the time when I, disillusioned by college, lied to my parents and left campus to ride a bus for ten days with only clean underwear and a few dollars in my pocket. It was more than the ease of talking to a stranger in the dark. It was as if the fissures and folds of our minds had slipped outside, become a part of the cave's cool interior, a place where we both could talk and listen carefully. Something about all that invisible space elicited an interaction that lacked agenda or charge, until finally even the very personal became, oddly, neither his nor mine, became simply the acknowledgment of human foibles and the occasional thought: *Ah, that too.*

In spite of the weight of some things we said, there was nothing weighty about anything we said, nothing intense about our conversation. The drama of our lives grew lighter, became no big deal. Picture a watercolorist diluting an intense indigo sky, adding water, more water. The sky lightens, fades from deep blue to pale blue, gets larger and more open, less threatening. Our words floated out into the dark and disappeared. On and on we went, the tedium of trivia and fatigue, of fear, his despair the day they diagnosed Parkinson's disease, the pain of my habitual reserve.

I surprised myself. I'm usually fairly private, certainly vigilant about solitude, famous (or infamous) among my friends for protecting my time alone. Selfish even. And yet there I was sixty feet below the earth's surface, my intention to settle into the great stillness of a cave broken by an invisible stranger with whom I sat, cross-legged and contented. The minutes, the half hours, slipped by. We kept talking. He said he could see my aura. Imagine it? I asked. No, *see* it, he said. It was pitch black in there. In other circumstances, I might have grown skeptical, bored, irritated at his intrusion, chagrined by my own admissions. But inside the stone fissure, those usual, easy reactions seemed to evaporate, dissolve in the darkness. It wasn't apathy or indifference I felt, but, curiously, a *dis*passionate interest in what we were saying. There seemed to be plenty of time, an eternity, in fact. And a growing awareness of tremendous room. This was the irony which, in retrospect, interested me first: it was spaciousness, not claustrophobia, that I felt inside that stone cave. And the spaciousness was not just physical but psychic as well. Was there something about that ancient, mostly undisturbed space, that *shul,* that made such largesse, such generous attentiveness, possible? The man and I were anonymous, invisible to each other, almost disembodied. The only sense we had of the other's place in the world—what position, status, what class we usually occupied—was rudimentary. We knew only that we happened to be in that cave at the same time. Everything else seemed interesting but mildly irrelevant, as if such a space unnamed us, made us any two humans paused within the normal pleasures and troubles of their lives.

A few weeks earlier I'd attended the annual conference of the National Speleological Society, wandered around a huge parking lot full of vehicles with bat bumper stickers, had coffee with some cavers. I'd asked a group

. . . .

of them what the draw was. Why crawl into such dark places? It's the great equalizer, they told me. Only one thing matters in there, and it's not your job, nor your looks which nobody can see anyway, not your degrees nor the speed of your Internet access. Everybody enters a cave dressed in rough overalls and hard hats, boots with good tread and gloves. You can study the others, try to get a sense of body shape and maybe age by limberness or lack of it. But that's about it. You could be inching on your behind down a scrabbly slope in the mostly dark next to the Queen of England and you'd never know it. The only thing that matters in a cave, they told me, is your ability to stay calm in dark spaces.

Later, that afternoon, standing in the convention's art gallery, I studied a drawing titled *Cave beneath Mt. Virgin*. It's dark in that cave, too, except for a section of interior wall, which the artist had stippled platinum and pearl, a band of luminosity above a woman who stretches, naked, on the cave floor. The edge of her body glows orange. A woman stood next to me, both of us admiring the work. "Are you a caver?" I asked. "Yes," she answered. I asked her why and she told me a story about her addictions to drugs and alcohol, and about a friend who'd been killed in a cave. She'd felt such despair and such anger—why would anyone risk his life rappelling into the utter blackness of a sixty-foot well in old rock? His death compelled her to make her first trip into a cave in England. It turned her life around, she said. Instantly. I looked at her. Something about going into all that darkness, she struggled to explain. I'd heard cavers insist that anyone who's not comfortable in a cave is afraid of her own mind, that without the trappings and markers of our above-ground lives, the only thing left is the mind, and most of us aren't easy there. I told her about my own first cave terror. Perhaps it hadn't been claustrophobia or hallucinations at all, but a fear of empty space, the potential that absence holds, some inkling that those are inner spaces too. Robert Frost knew it: "I have it in me so much nearer home / To scare myself with my own desert places." The woman tried again to explain, but soon fell silent. Coffee was brewing on a table behind us; somebody was making change at the cash register. The question I really wanted to ask her was one I couldn't quite articulate, and even if I could, I knew she wouldn't be able to answer. I bought the artwork and left the gallery.

The ineffable is, by definition, what words can't quite say. It's what silence is for. When we could hear the rest of the cavers returning, the man and I grew quiet. I heard him stand up, heard the rustle of nylon as he shouldered his pack. By the time the others' lights bounced off the walls and ceiling and their boots mingled with ours, he'd melted back into the group. I didn't look for him afterward, all of us out in the gray December day, unfastening our helmets and wiping the mud from our pants. It would have been wrong, a violation, as if the intimacy we'd had couldn't immediately be transported above ground. Suddenly shy, I pulled the hood of my sweatshirt up and headed for my car.

Hearing this story later, a friend wondered if the man's coming back to sit with me had been motivated by something other than fatigue. A subtle flirtation? That hadn't even occurred to me. I'd had no sense of intent, felt none of the teasing or testing of seduction. Had I been too trusting? When all those markers that usually help determine our behaviors with another are absent, how do we gauge one another? What remains to guide us? At first, maybe nothing. Or fear of nothing. Maybe too much innocence. That last time, under Laurel Mountain, I wasn't afraid. Instead, it was as if that dark invisible cave-space invited the man and me to relax our boundaries, to expand.

I think now of the troglobites, permanent cave dwellers, which have no need for color protection deep inside the earth and are, therefore, often albino, almost transparent. Like the eyes of many cave creatures, those of the Kentucky cave fish have degenerated; the fish is blind. But its pale body is studded with vibration receptors, tiny sensors that can detect even a slow human hand dipping into the water. Ghostlike, the fish darts away. Cave crickets and beetles, a whole community of pale, blind creatures relying on extra-long feelers, their sensitivity to one another's vibrations.

No, I told my friend, the man wasn't flirting. I may have been unable to see, may have been literally blind to his intentions, but my other senses were highly tuned and we were, for that brief time, not the parrying, sexual selves we so often bring to human interactions. Perhaps such space, hollowed out and dark, a kind of rarefied air, allows for presences more limpid, diaphanous, magnanimous, out of which emerge a lot of attentiveness, empathy, quiet voices, and highly tuned ears in a vast underground space.

What happened in there? I wondered later. Nothing, really. No terror, no startling revelations, no new friendship. A momentary connection with someone I'll never see again. And an unexpected sense of spaciousness. "Nothing happens?" the Spanish poet Juan Ramón Jiménez asks. "Or has everything happened, / and are we standing now, quietly, in the new life?"

■ ■ ■

Though for me it was an actual cave, a fissure in ancient stone, that precipitated that sense of spaciousness, that's not the only way to become aware of it. Loss can do it too, hollow you out, leave you, like an old stone, riddled with invisible caverns. The only ghost I've ever seen came in the shape of a dog. A week earlier, a good friend had died, unexpectedly. There were things we'd needed to say to each other and hadn't. It was Christmastime, the streets and stores decked out, everywhere the flush of plenty, abundance, and inside me this stunned silence, a saber-shaped absence I felt in my body as danger, grief like a weapon I could wound myself with if I moved too fast in any direction. The atmosphere thins in sorrow time. Things that had seemed centrally important a week earlier floated toward my peripheral vision, disappeared. Everything seemed suddenly fragile, less solid. Among his friends, his children, his wife, a sudden intimacy, our boundaries collapsing as we hung onto each other.

A week after his funeral I woke in the middle of the night to hear chains rattling outside. From the window, I saw an alabaster blur circling the lilac tree at the corner of the field. I pulled on boots and went outside. The moon was full, the night sky bright with stars, the ground frozen under a foot of snow. A still night of silver and shadows and a pure white dog, his chain wrapped and wrapped around the base of the lilac.

I live in the woods, miles from town, and I know the two dogs who occasionally stop by on their treks along this ridge. I'd never seen this one before. He stood, neck trussed tight to the tree, and wagged his tail. I let him smell my palm and then I took his collar and we walked slowly around and around the tree, unwinding the chain. I was half asleep, not thinking about anything. I held onto him and walked in circles, each one a little wider than the last. Three times around, four. And then I wanted to keep going, to keep unwrapping his by-now-unwrapped chain, let him keep expanding the circle, making the orbit larger and wider, tracing an invisible, elliptical path through the woods, across the cornfields, down into the valley, back up through the woods, each orbit more far-flying than the last, the moon circling overhead, a dog at the end of a tether that grew longer and longer until he'd take off, some kind of airborne ghost-dog that would keep tugging the circumference of grief outward.

My boots crunched in the moonlit snow as I removed the chain. Untangled, the dog hesitated. And then he turned and loped across the yard, into the woods, and was gone.

I've never seen him since. How to explain all this? It was an actual dog. I went out in the morning and looked at his paw prints. In the spring, I watched the bark on the lilac close over the gashes. I have no idea to what world, if any, my friend had gone, whether he'd sent the dog to me, whether the dog was somehow his spirit. What I do know is that the dog and I acted out some silent drama that night. Neither of us said a thing. We moved together around a tree, and at the end of his tether the world billowed outward and somehow I felt I was untangling my own grief, knew that this silent, spiral-out ritual in the middle of a wide December night did more to help me let him go than did the funeral mass, the poems of tribute we wrote, the nights of reminiscing. The dog appeared on a night when I'd felt emptied by grief, and our movements, mundane as they were, took on the feel of ritual, became ecstatic, not in the joyful sense, but in the original sense of the word: taken out of one's place, taken to a different place. A larger place, a *shul*, in which a dog appeared.

You wait in the dark, in the blank absence, the void, and sooner or later, something appears, begins to take shape, something that could not have come into anything other than absence. Something, in fact, that needs absence first in order to have form later. In *The Dream and the Underworld,* James Hillman says that "dimension sensed as loss is actually the presence of the void. . . . Here in depth there is space enough to take in the same physical world but in another way." A voice in the cave. A white dog.

■ ■ ■

Or stalactites. At Luray Caverns in Virginia, I entered underground rooms bejewelled in cave pearls and cave orchids, the exquisite white lace of aragonite, rooms lit up like palaces and hung with millions of stalactites. The process begins in a limestone mountain reamed out by water. It begins with blank walls, bare ceilings, a newly opened space in the dark. If it's a wet cave then, for thousands of years, water drips into the emptiness. Millions of drops, each one seeping through the cave roof and dangling from its ceiling. If it hangs there long enough, it releases its carbon dioxide, which causes calcite to be deposited in a tiny ring at the very point where the drop touches the ceiling. Then another drop of water seeps through, drips through to the bottom of the ring, pauses, deposits another tiny calcite ring. What grows, then—all those fantastic shapes, all that dripping festoonery of stalactites and flowstone, thousands of burnished soda straws—requires, first, the cave's hollowing-out, and then centuries of dripping, the tiny bits of mineral left behind. In the midst of Luray's lit-up fantasia, it's hard to remember that beginning. But if you step off the path,

. . . .

peer into a side chasm where formations haven't grown, you won't forget you're underground in an ancient hole. You'll see only rough stone, un-interrupted blankness. Back on the main walkway, you'll see how all the now-decorated main caverns were, once, just slits in stone, how the walls inched back and back, how for thousands of years there was only an empty cave, full of dank air, the slow dripping of water.

Not even the splendor of the forms can obscure the original hollow. I want to remember this, to pay attention to the lull between emptiness and form. I want to watch the mind leaning across a blank space, reaching for a story, artifice, something, anything, to complete the metaphor. I wonder if it's possible to pause that leap, to imagine that inscrutable space the mind leaps *over*. What kind of training or discipline would it take to linger for a few moments in that blank space, image-absent and unfilled? Could I see in slow motion how a drop of water dangles? or how grief can change shape, lighten a little?

■ ■ ■

How hurt can too. A couple of years ago, I sat in a chair at the edge of the Thar Desert in India, not far from the Pakistani border. I'd been traveling with a lover who had just disclosed something that made me want to walk away, far away, out into the desert, to just keep walking, across that flat, dry expanse. It was twilight. Someone brought us cups of chai, wanted to know if we wanted music. No, I said. I wanted nothing but the nothing-ness of the desert. I got up out of my chair, headed away from the small vil-lage, the dancers, the decorated camels, walked in the soft sand, the small grains working their way into my shoes. The desert drew me as surely as if it were a magnet and my body a collapsing stack of iron shavings. I kicked at anything, spat out a searing attack to the empty dunes. I wanted to pound something—his head, perhaps. The desert that evening stretched everywhere, its sands of gritty buff strangely lit beneath a high ceiling of lusterless dusk. I clomped one foot after another after another into the sand, which shifted just slightly. But nothing else happened. The wind didn't gust, the Pakistanis didn't come roaring over the border, I didn't feel fortified by the satisfaction of being the one so clearly wronged, and no one from the village came to bring me back. Nothing happened. When I turned around, I couldn't even see my tracks. Everything seemed swal-lowed up in the vastness, the endlessness of sand, that ancient Indian sky. And finally the need to lash out in revenge lessened. I didn't have to yell or

sulk or grab the first flight home. It wasn't that the hurt lifted but that
there was, out there in the desert, more room for hurt, and so it didn't
press so hard. That familiar sense of needing to explode with emotion
eased and it had to do, I think now, with not feeling so confined, so
squeezed by, so dense with hurt. Plenty of room in a desert to feel what
you feel, and plenty of time to decide what to do.

The next year I was back, farther north, where three friends and I traveled up the Ganges River, almost to its source, to find a Hindu holy man.
At a ceremony the night before, a priest had pressed sandalwood into our
foreheads, chanted, thrown sacred leaves into the river in the names of our
children. Drums pounded, bells clanged, the village chanted. We took off
our shoes, offered rupees and scarves, spent the night huddled in bed
under blankets, listening to the Ganges and went groggily the next morning to the holy man's hut. I confess that I have forgotten or didn't understand most of what he said. I do remember the light-headedness at 11,000
feet, the craggy Himalayas rising even higher around us, the cold, the
noise of the river, glacial white, the tidiness of his tiny hut, his lively, piercing eyes, and a single image he offered in the midst of a rambling two-hour
talk: the heart, he said softly, is the only real temple. Worship there. Everything else is distraction.

And, weeks later, Sunithi, an elderly Indian woman to whom I'd told
the desert story, said to me, "The heart, you know, is the widest secret
space. That's where the spirit is free." She wrote *Guhaiya* in my notebook, the Sanskrit word for secret space. *Guhaiya,* which sounds like *Go
here.* Everything else is distraction? I love India for its cow-jangling, horn-
honking, sari-swaying excess, its lavish moon palaces and plumed ele-
phants, the elaborate, erotic carvings on its temples. "Yes," Sunithi said,
showing me a Hindu temple's exterior, its evocative stone figures. But the
farther into the temple you go, the less elaborate the carvings. The inner-
most sanctum is always dark and unadorned. Like the human spirit, she
explained. *Guhaiya.* The heart is a *shul?*

■ ■ ■

I don't wish to imply that a fleeting and delicate awareness of spaciousness is a gift of the cave, death, the Indian deserts or Himalayas. We stum-
ble into our own hollowed-out interiors just by getting up and going to
work every day, just by trying to stay reasonably alive. There are plenty of
caverns inside our psyches, places that have been emptied by grief and

losses we're not even aware of, plenty of stony pockets where water drips slowly and all the flashlight batteries are dead. Places, probably, where nothing happens, empty pathways, uninhabited tunnels. Here, too, are concealed worlds, the secret passageways, the dead-end chutes. Uninhabited space. Not just in caves, temples, our own secret interiors, but all around us too. It's the place that Rilke describes so beautifully:

> some evening take a step
> out of your house, which you know so well.
> Enormous space is near.

In that enormous space, it's possible, he says, with the eye of imagination, to lift one tree, to raise it, to hold it up against the backdrop of sky and "With that you have made the world." You crawl into a cavern, stand up in unexpected space, peer through a broken stalactite, imagine you can see the desert dunes. You walk outside into a winter night and there's a dog who will help unwind the tightness of grief. Is it possible that the wide winter night, that enormous space, is everywhere around us? In the middle of Times Square, in a roomful of people? And in us? In all of us, somewhere, even in the cacophony of emotional confusion?

Guhaiya, Sunithi tells me. Secret space. *Go here,* she says, pointing to her chest. Wrapped in a brilliant orange sari, her wrists bangled with silver, a woman beautifully adorned, she's no ascetic. She isn't advocating renunciation; she's trying to tell me that space is ether, the element that's greater than all other elements, greater than earth, fire, water, wind; that it is space which permeates all other matter. It's *here,* where the small circumference of our lives moves outward and what's possible has nothing to do with solace or salvation or redemption, but something more important: the possibility of opening to an intimacy with a larger world.

Go inside a stone, Simic says. Who knows what's in there? The fantasia of myriad dripping stones, cave orchids, rimstone pools. A voice. An unexpected open-heartedness, generosity. A white dog. Maybe a moon, Simic muses, some reflected light, strange writings and maps: *Starcharts on the inner walls*

First emptiness, then form. Probably emptiness again. It's the sequence I want to keep in mind, the undulating wave of something rising out of nothing, dissolving again, the practice of paying attention to the lull. I want the openness of a cave's darkness, an openness that can scare, force my back against boulders, the walls to bear close. Or to move backwards, the crevice expand, become the space between planets. The viscera of absence calls us to grope where we can't see, where the normal constraints, habits, identities, and the definitions by which we live might lift, dissolve momentarily, leave us in enormous space. Here the imagination twists and searches, fumbles, gets ready to say what we can't quite see. We stand in the absence, in the clearing, the hollowed-out place and discover, not wisdom or enlightenment, but spaciousness. Room. A *shul.*

The Color of Drought

. . . .

by

TERRY TEMPEST WILLIAMS

The moss in Owl Canyon was so dry it could not even accept the water we poured over it. Instead, the small beads simply rolled off its cushioned body like tears in the desert. I had no idea of the depth of drought in our country.

My friend and I were walking up the serpentine canyon on the edge of the Colorado River in Utah. I bent down and placed my hand on the river's bank. Cracked, dried mud looking like a snakeskin shed crumbled between my fingers. Tadpoles were desperately trying to become frogs before the last pothole of water evaporated. Airborne swifts pulled down by the heat drank drops of water from a once trustworthy spring. Purple penstemens, barely able to send shoots of green to compete with last fall's plant skeleton, shook in the wind like rattles. Everywhere we turned, we witnessed a world parched.

The air barely stirred. We said few words, feeling all around us the necessity of energy conserved. Not even the ravens, tricksters extraordinare, chose to break the silence. Instead, all life crouched low in the throbbing heat of summer.

Up ahead, we noticed a peculiar maroon ring had formed around one of the dried pools. My friend who is a biologist said simply, "algae." We knelt down and rubbed it with our fingertips. Miraculously, the maroon algae turned orange. I rubbed it again, gently, only to discover that the greater the agitation, the more vibrant the color. It was an orange I couldn't place within my own spectrum of experience. The color was more radiance than pigment. It was, in fact, carotene alive on my index finger.

The art of transformation is the art of participation in place. Is this

39

what early Desert Dwellers knew as they painted their histories on red-rock walls? There is an unknown palette of wisdom before us and it is available to us right here on the surface of the Earth.

We couldn't help ourselves. We painted spirals on the palms of our hands. Laura placed dragonfly crosses on the tops of her feet. I marked my forehead, throat, between my breasts, and the back of my neck with one orange dot, moved down my body and circled my navel, knees, and drew a thin line down my shins. I cannot explain our actions. I can only tell you something much older than our rational minds seized us and we responded. The algae exposed now rubbed on our bodies became our faith. We painted the soles of our feet and continued walking up the canyon.

Susan Griffin writes, "What at one time one refuses to see never vanishes but returns, again and again, in many forms."

Drought. Life without water. Life without life. I wonder what other forms of drought are manifesting themselves right now around the planet, even as the historic, beloved city of Prague floods. Are these the natural cycles of a dynamic Earth or are these the drastic circumstances specific to our times? Is this evidence of global warming or simply, the result of global awareness? When one stands in the presence of the extreme, it hardly matters.

Just yesterday, a friend who is living on the atoll of Palmyra, located in the heart of the Pacific Ocean, wrote to say that the stomachs of the Ahi they are catching are empty. The biologists are puzzled. El Niño? The depletion of the seas? Where do we go for answers to the questions that haunt us, the problems of pain in this world that are so clearly stressing other species, as well as our own? How to live with an awareness of both beauty and terror?

I turn to the poets.

They say such things are stored
in the genetic code—

half-chances, unresolved
possibilities, the life

passed on because unlived—
a mystic biology?

—Adrienne Rich

. . . .

I turn to the Earth.

Lizards drew near to us as we sat on an outcropping of sandstone, the fork in the canyon where we couldn't decide which path to take. The heat had melted our minds. We had little water left. We could go left or right, forward or backward. Or for now, we could just sit and contemplate the subtle beauty around us.

The lizards, turquoise blue with orange beads on their backs, began pumping themselves up and down, up and down in the dry wash, creating their own cooling system. We laughed at their sudden bursts of energy wondering if it would inspire our own. Animated life begets animated life infusing the air with joy.

It was time to move, to gather our energies and take what we had seen home.

As our pace quickened downcanyon, Laura and I still carried the orange spirals on our palms from the algae that had brought forth its essence, first through awareness and then through engagement.

We found ourselves opening our painted hands to the sage, registering the shock of orange against its pale silver-blue. Suddenly, the sage seemed to awaken. In concert with orange, the sage appeared strengthened. We tried our orange palms against saltbrush, and like sage, the green thirsty leaves seemed to quiver. Our palms became a backdrop for everything alive: rabbitbrush, paintbrush, even the old juniper trees so sturdy in their reach. We sauntered through the desert with beginners' eyes, this time wide open, where before, it had been easier to squint, even closing our eyes to the grief around us. Our hands dropped down and framed the moss so tired in this heat. If nothing else, we offered shade.

And then turning the corner, we found a mirror of our penultimate orange reflected in the petaled cups of globe mallow, a meadow of distilled light in the desert against an open sky of blue—this was the orange we were wearing on our bodies—exactly. It had been here all along, the secret hue of Earth we can draw on in times of drought.

■ ■ ■

My husband, Brooke, and I awoke to thunder. Our bedroom flashed white with lightning. Eyes open. Dense clouds were the blue of pinyon jays traversing the sky.

It began to rain.

We ran outside not believing what we heard to be true. Rain. Rain. And more rain. We had not had rain in our country for months. The Colorado River was so low in parts, you could walk across it. The red clay floors of desert washes where no water had flowed were not only cracked, but peeling back like burned skin.

Thunder. Lightning. We watched a fire start at the base of Round Mountain. Flames. Flames quickly subdued by rain. Blessed rain. We danced until we were drenched, throwing our heads back to drink and then we ran back inside to gather every pitcher we could find to fill with rainwater as it cascaded wildly off the corners of our roof. We had forgotten that even in drought, there are moments of abundance.

Not a drop to be wasted.

Famous Builder

. . . .

by
PAUL LISICKY

The early American Village has achieved enthusiastic acclaim for quality, dignity, and colonial charm by the 400 families now living here.
BOB SCARBOROUGH, Barclay Farm brochure, 1962

1.

In a deep socket of an empty acre lot in South Jersey, a wiry boy with dark eyebrows, burnished blond hair, and thick lenses in his glasses clears pathways through the milkweeds, trying to preserve as many of the leafy, muscular stalks as he can. He works harder than he's worked in weeks, so hard that he doesn't even hear his father's car engine in the distance, or his mother ringing the cowbell for him to come inside for dinner. This is Telegraph Hill: the first community he's built that he's genuinely proud of, from the curving of the cul-de-sacs as they wind through the woods, to the discrete street names he's penned in meticulous, Early American script on scraps of faux-antique pine he's pilfered from his father's workshop: Saybrook Road, Weston Drive, Lavenham Court, Henfield Road. No wonder his fingers are cracked and cut, his toes sore from using the front end of his sneaker as a tool.

The wind rustles the weeds. He's about to back up the slope, to look out over his first fully wooded community, his belief so deep that he can practically see the lanterns trembling on, the hushed couples stepping up the sidewalks toward the Northfield, the most recent two-story model (vertical, rough-hewn siding, copper-hooded bay window). Then Tommy Lennox, his neighbor, walks toward him with a football tucked beneath his arm, the faintest suggestion of a smirk around the corners of his lips. "What's that?" Tommy says.

A ripple, a blush to his skin. The boy's pleasure has been so private, so intimate, that he might as well have been making love to the land. He can't even raise his eyes. "A development," he says finally.

He swelters inside his shirt. The boy imagines Tommy stepping through the community casually, knocking street signs aside, crushing the tall can that stands for the silo at the entrance. Sweat drips down the center of his back. But when the boy finally lifts his head, he's surprised to see the animation in Tommy's face, the quizzical expression that suggests he's waiting to be shown around.

In no time at all, Tommy's building his own development, Willow Wood, in the open land beside the single pine along the back of the lot. He's out there every day, just as the boy is, digging with his mother's garden shovel, replanting tablets of moss until the knees of his pants are soaked through. But why doesn't this feel right? The boy doesn't have the heart to tell Tommy that straight streets intersecting at right angles went out with 1949. And what to make of the names Tommy's assigned to them: Motapiss Road, Vergent Court. They practically carry an aroma, suggesting all sorts of things no one likes to talk about: flesh, death, the mysteries of the body. At least Tommy's sister has the good sense to know that she should pay attention to what's attractive. Although Cathy Lennox's Green Baye is entirely misnamed (what bay? what water?), the boy cannot help but be impressed with the added *e,* and with the skillful way her streets meander down the slope.

Still, neither of their projects can stand beside the elegance and understated good taste of Telegraph Hill.

Today all the neighborhood children roam the field, some down on their knees, others carving out streets, all squinting, foreheads tightened in concentration.

The boy looks up at the houses across Circle Lane, where he and his friends spend their time when they're not in school or out here. Of course, it would be their misfortune not to live in a real development, but in a neighborhood in which all the houses are decidedly different from one another, with no consistent theme. Although his mother tries to invoke the word "custom" as often as she can, he's not having it. Most of his fifth-grade classmates live in the newest developments, places where the wood-plank siding's coordinated with the trim (sage green with aqua, barn red with butter), always that pleasing sense of order and rhythm. Truth be told, he frets about living in a place with no name. Just to say "Timber-wyck" or "Fox Hollow East" or "Wexford Leas" and be entirely under-stood! His dilemma even seems to bewilder that substitute teacher with the kind face and the gray, washed-out hair in whom he confides one day.

"You don't live in a development?" she says. "How could you not live in a development?"

Flushed, he turns away.

"Have you talked to your parents?"

He shakes his head. He steps back from himself, watchful, distant. Silent boy, ghost, so weightless and emptied he barely has a body.

What would she say to the story the *Philadelphia Bulletin*'s just written on him: "BOY, 12, LONGS TO BE FAMOUS BUILDER"? He imagines her unfolding the newspaper at her kitchen table, spreading orange mar-malade on a burnt piece of English muffin as her teakettle whistles on the stove. Would he be real to her now? Though it tells of the 600 brochures he's collected from developments all over the country, and of the fan let-ters he's written to Bob Scarborough, whom he wants to work for some-day, it frustrates him, if only because it's written in that cheerful yet patronizing tone that suggests his work is mere play, that he'll come to his senses in a few years. Hard not to wince when he sees it tacked to his prin-cipal's green bulletin board. How he hates being on display like that, lying on his stomach in the photograph, marveling at that brochure in his hands (is it Charter Oak?) as if he'd never seen one before. He'd like to tell the substitute it's an ineptly written piece, a foolish piece, but he's as guilty of the lies as anyone. Why did he simplify himself when he talked to that re-porter? Why did he allow her to think there was something less than pro-found about the binders of street names he'd collected? Here he was, hiding the ferocious depths of his passion inside something harmless and benign, when all he really wanted was to move her, to show her he was in love.

When he looks up from his reverie, Tommy and Cathy and all the oth-ers have wandered back toward their houses, the sky charcoal above the rooftops, the trees.

He gets down on his knees. He shivers inside his jacket, which he zips, chucking the skin of his throat, but he'll work long after the streetlamps have blinked on, defying his mother's cowbell, ignoring his long-division assignment, the piano scales—all those dull, grinding duties that suggest his life has nothing to do with pleasure, the warmth of this soil in his hands.

2.

> "It didn't matter who you were or where you came from but how you
> lived your life. Mr. Levitt enabled us to have the good life."
>   DAPHNE RUS, Levittown, New York, resident
>   *Levittown Tribune*, February 4, 1994

> "You're so crazy about Levitt, let me ask you something. Where is
> Levitt now?"
>   "The Man Who Loved Levittown," W.D. WETHERELL

And there he is, pacing the terminal of the airport in Brookhaven, Long Island, in a marine blue sport coat, light slacks, and fawn-colored oxfords.
He taps out another cigarette before he's finished the one already in his
mouth, its smoke curling up into his face. He pats down his lapels, smooth-
ing back his gelled, wavy hair, but the truth is, he's a wreck. He looks as if
he's lived into every one of his seventy-six years. The San Juan casinos, the
Scotch, the sparring with his brother Alfred, the lenders, the wives—all of
it has marked his face like a plat map of his nearby Strathmore at Stony
Brook development. Even his oxfords, once impeccably buffed and shined,
now look like they could have been bought off the rack at the Huntington
Goodwill.

So there's no reason that the boy, his ardent admirer, should be hiding
behind a column, five feet from his idol, so burdened with intense feeling
that he thinks he might need to be rushed to Dr. Boguslaw. That's the least
of his problems. Why does he still have the body of a twelve-year-old
when the calendar above the rent-a-car desk says 1986? How did he get
here from there? And why is he still wearing that same awful pair of dungarees from E.J. Korvette that scratch in the crotch, that ride too high in
the waist? It occurs to him that he might be dead, struck by a car on one
of his determined bike rides to Point of Woods or Cambridge Park, developments five or six miles from his house. Once he shakes out his arm,
though, he can tell he's as alive as the rest of the people fidgeting about the
tiny airport. Certainly his mother must be in the car outside the terminal,
where she waits for him to walk out the door with maps and brochures,
the beautiful news of how streets get their names.

But enough dawdling. He sniffs, stiffens his neck and walks forward,
extending his hand to Bill Levitt. Instantly the famous builder claims every
inch of his six-foot frame.

"If it was for a penny less than $92 million, I'd walk out right now."
The boy is too scared to blush, whimper, or hyperventilate.

. . . .

"One more stunt like this," Bill Levitt says, "and I won't do business with you again."

The boy steps backward. He thinks of running out to his mother—of course this was a mistake; of course he should have stayed safely back in 1972. But as he's about to give up, he tells Bill Levitt that he was the one who wrote the fan letter, the boy who saw his first model homes at nine and hasn't stopped talking about them ever since.

"Ah," he says. "I thought you were a little young to be in S&L." He sits down with a sigh, patting the seat on the bench next to him. "Cigarette?"

The boy shakes his head no.

He squints, draws in some smoke until the tip flares orange. "Paul Lipstick?"

"Lisicky."

Gratitude and awe flash through the boy's cheeks. Bill Levitt *remembered*. In the distance, a bulldozer pushes a bank of torn-up potato vines into an enormous mound. Beyond that, workmen hammer up two pre-fab walls.

"So what makes you want to be a builder, honey?" Bill Levitt says.

He shifts back and forth on the bench. His eyes burn and tear from the smoke. *Honey?* Impossible to answer such a thing. Could Bill Levitt? Even if the boy said, "I want to build the kinds of developments that make people happy to be alive," he wouldn't exactly be telling the whole truth. His feelings run deeper and colder than Long Island Sound. They mean more than any single component: an imaginative street name, the pleasure of redesigning a Colonial as a Contemporary, the swirl of feeder roads, color codes, and cul-de-sacs on a master plan.

"I want to do what you do," he says finally.

Bill Levitt's smile is tinged with remorse. His eyelids look heavy. "Here's my only advice." He leans in close until his mouth brushes the boy's ear. "Beg, borrow, or steal the money, then build, build, build."

And then he spills every drama from the start of the year. The sums borrowed from family charities, the down payments spent from Florida's Poinciana Park development—how was he to know that a single stake hadn't yet been driven into the sand? Or that his third wife would have such expensive tastes, expecting a present every month on the date of their anniversary? All the failed ventures—Nigeria, Venezuela, Iran (Levittshar!)—all the money lost, and now he can't even afford to pay for treatment at North Shore Hospital, the hospital he paid millions of dollars to build decades ago. He's sold his château in Mill Neck, the Rolls Royce, the 237-foot yacht once docked beneath the Brooklyn Bridge. He doesn't even have a dime to call a cab. And if those bastards from Old Court Savings and Loan don't show up in five minutes—he taps the face of his Cartier with an elegant forefinger—there's going to be hell to pay.

"Miniature Lane," the boy says, his eyes welling. "I hope you're going to have a Miniature Lane in Poinciana Park."

Bill Levitt stubs out a half-smoked cigarette in an ashtray. His eyes fix on the carpenters in the potato field.

"Tardy Lane, Italic Pass," the boy says. "You took the time to be inventive, original."

"Those workers?" he says, pointing in the distance. "They're Union. But we couldn't have built Levittown with Union. Those assholes tried to shut us down."

"The altered setbacks," the boy continues. "The see-through fireplaces, the village greens."

"We kept our profit margin low. 17,447 houses in 5 years. Our own lumberyard, our own roofers. And that's how we slaughtered the competition."

"You gave style to the masses, things only rich people could have afforded before."

"And blacks," Bill Levitt says. "The minute you let the blacks in, the property values dive. I mean I have nothing at all against the blacks; some of my best workers have been blacks, but look what's happened to Willingboro. Or Belair at Bowie or Winslow Crossing. I had every right to keep the blacks out, but you couldn't do that after 1964. And look who suffers but the homebuyer."

A calm in the terminal. The air tastes grittier, more troubling on the boy's tongue—is that sawdust blowing through the open doors? No, something else: he feels it in his eyes, tastes it high in his throat. He knows things he'd rather not about Levitt. Not just that he restricted Jews from the high-end Strathmore-Vanderbilt or black people from the three Levittowns, but sins of lesser sorts. Flooded conversation pits in Monmouth Heights' Contempra; "streamfront" lots in Cambridge Park that bordered a concrete culvert. And, then, of course, his ties to Joe McCarthy or any corrupt individual he thought could be of use to him. "How can I be racist," he replied years later, "if I'm Jewish?" The boy can't begin to understand such things. Nor why Bill Levitt is not the least bit interested in the poetry of building rather than the making of money, which doesn't matter to the boy at all. Here they are, seated side by side on a bench, a

. . . .

cornucopia of detail to be exchanged between them, but right now he feels vague and unsatisfied: Massasoit trying to hold a conversation with Miles Standish.

"The masses are asses," Bill Levitt murmurs to himself.

The boy gazes out at the development burgeoning in the potato field. Hammers swing, nails pierce. Piece by piece the neighborhood comes into being. Nothing that Bill Levitt says is going to sour his morning. He thinks about what's sure to come a few months in the future: the signs in refined script posted outside the exhibit homes, the copper beeches leafing out along the strip of grass between sidewalk and street. Inside "The Ardsley," the Luganos stand in the foyer, looking up the staircase at the light fixture overhead, before Richard, Lori, and Kate rush forward, imagining themselves into the next ten years. There they are with their cousins, tangling their arms and legs together on the Twister mat on the dining-room carpet. There they are, just the five of them, trimming the arbutus, planting pink geraniums around the patio in grateful, pained silence, taking in the news that Mrs. Lugano's treatment has been successful, her illness in remission. And yet as much as the boy tries to hold onto his vision of a kind, perfected future, in which no one is hurt or stunted and all longings are satisfied, he can't stop seeing an overlay. 1996, and the children have moved away, resentful, bored, though not quite knowing why. Mr. and Mrs. Lugano stay put, wary of strangeness, difference, suspicious of the two black men who come to deliver the new sofa one day. A tree hasn't been planted in years. Unclipped limbs rub and shadow the bay window, and no one on Hornblende Lane gestures when Mr. Radwin, a neighbor, walks past. The traffic crawls. The sprawl takes over Middle Country Road, and . . .

"Look what I've done." Bill Levitt's voice is full of forced authority, as if he's talking to an S&L guy again. He pulls out at least a dozen clippings from his pocket, all taped at the seams, and presents them with quivering hands to the boy.

Nothing new here: the 1950 *Time* magazine cover story; later articles announcing ventures in Paris, Puerto Rico, Madrid, Frankfurt. The boy pores over the stories and pretends he hasn't memorized them in a carrel of the Cherry Hill Library. And for some reason he knows that Poinciana Park will essentially remain a tree farm during his lifetime. Although he hasn't nearly fallen out of love yet—that takes longer to acknowledge than a fizzy, unsettled feeling inside the body—he can already sense that his own future will be more complicated and alive than he ever could have imagined.

How to live without the dream of making, building?

"My mom's in the car," the boy says, in distress. He stands up, and pats the shoulder of Bill Levitt's marine blue sport coat.

"Listen," Bill says, tapping out another cigarette. "One thing you'll promise me."

"Yes, sir?"

"Don't call your first Lisickytown."

The boy is silent. Not that he ever had such an idea, but didn't Bill Levitt get to rename his first huge development in honor of his family? Would Island Trees have ever gotten the publicity of Levittown?

"That kind of thing's out of style. Why do you think the schmucks from my New Jersey project changed it back to Willingboro?"

"What do you suggest?"

"I don't know. Green Park?"

The boy feels the corners of his mouth pull. "Whatever happened to your imagination?"

"Ahh," he says, waving smoke away. "That was Alfred's department. Give me eighty bucks at the craps table and I'll turn it into two thousand." Bill Levitt steals a glance to his left, waiting to berate the lender he's convinced is still coming to meet him.

The boy steps backward. With a nod, he turns around and heads for the door.

"Paul?"

He stops midstep. "Yes?"

"Get yourself some decent pants, for Christ's sake."

The boy looks down at his dungarees from E. J. Korvette. A blush fires up from the soles of his feet, scorching his scalp until his hair feels damp.

"Don't be hurt. Here's some money," he says, and offers a bill. "Here, take it."

"I thought you were broke."

"Try Brooks Brothers. Get yourself a decent suit."

The boy takes the fifty that's extended to him and inadvertently shakes Bill Levitt's hand. His palm is dry and vaguely cold, as if he's already thinking about the life to come, the grander developments he'll build in the next world.

"And one other thing. Don't judge me, all right? And don't feel sorry for me. I've lived."

The boy slides the bill in his back pocket. "Would you like my mom to give you a ride somewhere?"

. . . .

But before Bill Levitt can respond, the boy has vanished, back to the tyranny of the linear, the parameters of time that have been dealt to him.

3.

I was glad when they said to me,
"Let us go to the house of the Lord."
    PSALM 122: 1

The man and his friend Denise drive down Route 73, groaning at all the trophy homes behind the big-box stores. He's not entirely surprised that the 32-foot globe at the New World entrance is gone. So much of what they remember has been torn down, refurbished, paved and planted over: the Holly Ravine Farm and its petting zoo, the Clover supermarket, the broad green entrance lawns of Wexford Leas with its brick tollhouse. Still, he sighs. A wince, a film falls over his eye, and it's 1972: the boy and his mother stand in a field to watch a pinpoint above the South Jersey farmland. Blades beat, crowds mill. Drivers pull onto the shoulder of the road to see what all the fuss is about. And then the big, bald revelation, just as the Friday *Courier-Post* predicted: REPLICA OF UNISPHERE TO BE TRANSPORTED BY HELICOPTER TO ROSSMOOR DEVELOP-MENT. The boy and his mother gaze skyward, a little skeptical, yet certain that change is on the way. They clap, giving themselves over to the collective shock and thrill (wasn't a statue of Jesus transported like this in a Fellini movie?) when the great globe falls from thirty feet above. The ground rumbles. The helicopter blades go *trk-trk-trk-trk-trk*. The boy and his mother feel more than they have a right to—weren't they just making vague fun of the developer's appeal to the good life, even as the boy clutched the brochure to his chest? The crowd scatters. The sky darkens with the passage of the cold front. And yet mother and son keep watch until their backs are tired, as the banged-up world's lifted onto its pedestal.

Denise looks out at the serviceable two-story Colonials that have taken New World's place. "Whatever happened to it?"

"The world?"

"The development. These aren't the models I remembered."

The man tells his friend—have they really known each other for eighteen years?—about the sewer moratorium that stopped the project. (Among all that fills his head, he can't believe he's cataloged this lowly fact.) Only a few dozen homes—Tudors, Haciendas, and Contemporaries—out of a proposed thousand were built before a local firm later took over the project and renamed it Willow Ridge.

"This is just"—she gestures at the boxy, bland houses beside the road—"isolating, *grim*. Do you remember what New World meant?"

He nods vigorously. And then they both roll their eyes, smiling at the gap between who they were then and who they've become.

"I mean, those homes were like"—Denise takes a breath. "I don't know, wrapped Venetian candies."

"Hollywood soundstages," the man offers.

"They *fizzed*. And it wasn't like they flexed their muscles. Not like the trophy homes these days."

"A little populist glamour."

A few miles later they pull into Sturbridge Estates, the model homes they've decided to check out. Something about what they're doing feels deliciously subversive, a little dangerous. After all, neither would ever choose to live in a new suburban house. But that doesn't stop them from wanting to revisit every now and then what captivated their childhood imaginations. How many hundreds of houses did they explore with their parents every Sunday afternoon after church? Impossible to name and number them all, but the ritual is part of who they are. It dyes their blood, indelible as the ink of all those hymns, responsorial psalms, Eucharistic prayers. If it wasn't its own religion, then it was a coda to the Mass, an extra occasion to exalt. How they walked from room to furnished room, hushed and holy, as if they were already passing into the next world, the better one to come.

But time has worked its changes on them in ways that are deeper than they can articulate. Today they're trying on who they might have become had sex, art, books, and years of school not complicated things.

"This is it?" says the man. "Whatever happened to five furnished model homes?"

They stare out at a 5,000-square-foot château with a stucco veneer and plastic punch-in window dividers.

"I guess this is the one we get to see," says Denise.

They get out of the car and stare at the impeccably sodded lawn, shadowed at this hour by the stretched pattern of a weeping willow. The yews glitter in the sprinkler water. There's only one other car parked in front of Denise's.

"I don't know about this," the man says.

"We'll just breeze through. We don't have to stay very long."

"It looks mean," says the man. "I think it's glaring at us."

. . . .

"Oh, stop."

They nudge open the front door. They feel smaller than they're used to: the foyer is the size of a small ballroom, and the second floor soars thirty, thirty-five feet, bordered by a staircase with a railing of bleached wood. The ceiling above sparkles with granulated spray. Everything smells adhesive. A circular window on the landing overlooks the treetops in the backyard.

The man steadies himself. "Whoa."

They step lightly in their shoes. Music tinkles through the sound system. The living room, the dining room, the family room: all are so enormous that the furniture looks lost in them. A violet orchid glowers on the coffee table. A boxy sofa hunkers beside the gray wall, trying as hard as it can to command. But it seems to feel as they do. It clears its throat, pats down its sleeves, and wishes it were inside a warmer, more congenial space.

"This is a house for the family who doesn't want to spend any time together," the man says.

"This is a house that wants to bully you the minute you step into its mouth," says Denise.

"But it's cheaply built," the man says. "Look." And he runs his palm over the woodwork, as something catches. He shows his hand to Denise, who scowls at the blond splinter piercing his thumb.

Carefully, they ascend the staircase. No other visitors this afternoon. No salesperson coming forth to welcome them, to shake their hands and pass out a price list. Denise is entirely immersed in the finer facets of the interior (is that because her ex-husband lives in an earlier section of the same development a few streets away?), while the man's attention has scattered like the flock of sparrows he watches through the circular window. All he wants is a brochure. All he wants are names, maps, renderings: the lyrical essence made concrete. Perhaps that's all he ever cared about, really, all those years he wanted to be a builder. Names, maps, renderings: loving the particulars of a world inside and out, upside and down, until it made the brain glow.

"Oh, my God," Denise says. "Look at this bedroom."

They stand, dazed, inside a chilly white room with clerestory windows. Like the sofa downstairs, the king-sized bed's dwarfed by the room. The orchids this time are a deep violent yellow with crimson threads. But the enormity of the space strikes him as more severe here: the man feels as if they're caught inside a chilled glass cathedral, without pews or a congregation, which doesn't permit anything resembling spontaneity or laughter or a casual human touch.

"Can you imagine someone fucking in here?" the man says.

"Sweetheart," Denise says, "this house isn't meant for someone who fucks."

And when they look up, a colossal salesman with a green golfing cardigan is standing in the doorway.

He doesn't say hello. Or turn up the corners of his mouth. He holds them entirely in his gaze, making it plain he's heard everything they've said. He knows exactly who they are, not the husband and wife they were sure they'd resembled, but something stranger, impossible to categorize: excommunicants who've wandered into the realm of a particularly righteous church.

"Beautiful home," the man says.

"Thank you so very much for your time," Denise says.

They squeak past him. And they walk down the stairs, first slowly, then a little faster, nearly tripping over their laces before they run, run, run to the car.

CODA:

Perennial Lane	Pennant Lane
Botany Lane	Alembic Court
Slender Place	Artesian Place
Radium Lane	Pennypacker Drive
Manikin Lane	Birdseye Court
Hepburn Lane	Quarum Place
Galaxy Lane	Quasar Court
Unique Court	Quiverbrook Court
Merry Turn	Conifer Lane
Wisp Lane	Chelmont Lane
Wafer Lane	Viewpoint Lane
Ballad Lane	Waxberry Lane
Exhibit Lane	Margin Turn
Panorama Lane	Superior Lane
Bendix Lane	Swirl Lane
Wisdom Lane	Mackle Lane
Wicket Gate	Magnetic Place
Marvel Lane	Privacy Lane
Ovalstone Lane	Tardy Lane

Just What Is It That Makes Today's Homes So Different, So Appealing?

. . . .

by
BERNARD COOPER

My induction into the world of avant-garde art began in my junior-high school library. Polished tabletops, hushed voices, sunlight falling through Venetian blinds—the details rush back readily because, in a lifetime of generally sluggish and imperceptible change, this was a moment of such abrupt friction between who I was and who I would become, it's a wonder I didn't erupt with sparks. Instead of looking up the major exports of Alaska for my geography report, I slouched in a chair and leafed through an issue of *Life* magazine. A boldface headline caught my attention: "You Bought It, Now Live with It." The article profiled the handful of New York art collectors who were among the first to buy the work of Pop artists. Although Pop artists were routinely savaged by critics for exalting the banal—billboards, supermarkets, Hollywood movies—this "new breed of collector" didn't care.

"All that other stuff," grumbled collector Leon Kraushar, referring to the sum total of art history before Pop, "it's old, it's antique. Renoir? I hate him. Cézanne? Bedroom pictures. They'll never kill Pop, they'll just be caught with their pants down." *They*, Kraushar seemed to imply, were stuffed shirts, scoffers and doubters, the enemies of fun. Kraushar was shown in his Long Island house, lounging on the couch next to a stack of Andy Warhol's Brillo boxes. Behind him stood a life-size plaster jazz combo by sculptor George Segal, the three musicians frozen into a white glacier of improvisation.

Another collector, Harry Abrams, was shown watching the real television set in Tom Wesselmann's painting *Still Life with TV.* "Whether it's on or off," marveled Abrams from his recliner, "the painting is different every time I look at it." Cleo Johnson, the Abramses' maid, appeared undaunted by modern art; she took an amused, sidelong glance at the clock in a huge, messy painting by Robert Rauschenberg. According to the caption, the clock worked. So did Cleo, who wore a starched uniform and carried a plate of cornbread.

Robert and Ethel Scull were perhaps the most avid collectors mentioned in the article. Pictured in their immense Manhattan apartment, Mr. Scull, a taxicab magnate, watched his wife dust the plump enameled ham that sat atop Claes Oldenburg's *Stove with Meats*. "Ethel thought I was crazy when the stove arrived," Scull said, "but now she calls it 'my emerald' and won't let anyone else touch it." On the next page, clearly a convert to Pop, Mrs. Scull beamed while standing in front of the portrait she'd commissioned from Andy Warhol—innumerable, mugging, multicolored Ethels.

As I turned the pages and stared at the photographs, it was difficult to tell the difference between a kitchen and a painting of a kitchen, or a man opening a door and a sculpture of a man opening a door. Reality was up for grabs, and my sudden unknowing made me giddy. I'd always thought that art sat mutely in a museum, but if televisions and clocks were part of these paintings, then art blared commercials, told the time, and had to be plugged into an electrical socket like an ordinary appliance. And yet the word *ordinary* didn't apply; a soup can, a panel from a comic strip, an American flag were more mesmerizing than I ever thought possible. Even the advertisements in the magazine that featured, in full color, a Sealy Golden Sleep mattress, a Swanson's Fried Chicken Dinner, and a Phillips 66 gas pump, seemed suddenly vivid, lit from within.

Up until that day in the library, I hadn't known or cared much about fine art. What little I knew, I gleaned from the art in my parents' house. I liked the Parisian street scene in our hallway; the pedestrians, with a few deft strokes, were reflected in the rain-soaked pavement. In our tropical-theme den, a reproduction of a painting by Diego Rivera hung above a bamboo bar. It showed a man strapping to a woman's back a basket so huge and laden with flowers, she bent beneath it like an animal. This reversed the roles of labor that obtained in our home, and suggested that abundance could be a burden. My father had bought it as a gift for my mother, the two of them calling it "wonderful," "exotic," seemingly unaware of its grim implications.

But the most unsettling painting in my parent's "collection" was a portrait by my older brother, Ron, of our eldest brother, Bob. The portrait had been hanging in the living room since Bob's death from Hodgkin's disease four years earlier. Ron had been an amateur painter, the bedroom he shared with Bob redolent of turpentine and linseed oil. A rickety easel was stationed by Ron's bed, ready, I used to think, should he jump up inspired in the middle of the night. Despite Ron's limited skills, his portrait perfectly, if inadvertently, captured the physical essence of Bob's illness; something in the thinness of the pigment, as grim as watery soup, never failed to remind me how chemotherapy had turned Bob's skin translucent, as if he were stripped of all protection, layer by layer, his ailing insides harder to ignore. My parents had hung the portrait in a gold baroque frame, and even back then I understood that this was their way of forever containing Bob's memory, of paying him elaborate homage. In that sense, the frame was like a headstone, strangely funereal for a portrait in which a twenty-one-year-old boy with a flattop is dressed in a dapper shirt and tie, his eyes conveying the hope that he's handsome. But none of these qualities in themselves accounted for what turned out to be the painting's revelation.

One afternoon I was sprawled on the living-room couch, steeped in the idleness which, at the age of nine, I regarded as a calling. Light poured through the bay window and struck the portrait at an odd angle, and I noticed that the dots running vertically down the center of Bob's tie were more than decorative daubs of paint. I rose and walked closer, and as I did, the dots clarified into tiny letters. *"Oh Bob,"* Ron had written on the tie. *"Poor Bob."*

Ron had moved away from home to attend law school at USC shortly after Bob's death, leaving me, the late child, to grow up alone. Now he had his own car and apartment and part-time job—triumphs that exempted most young men, or so I believed, from unhappiness. Yet there it was in the afternoon light: the keening of one brother for another, a grief so precise, so carefully encoded, you had to look long and hard before you noticed. I stood inches from the surface and couldn't move. The power of art to startle and compel had come into focus like the writing on the tie.

A reclusive boy, especially now that my older brother had left home, I began to spend hours drawing with the pastels Ron had given me as a birthday gift, fascinated by the greasy lines, the hues blended by smudging the page. The nature of the medium—sticks of pigment as dense as clay—lent itself to landscape. John Nagey, an exuberant, goateed bohemian on Channel 5, set up his easel every Saturday morning and gave me lessons on how to render "majestic" mountains, "fleecy" clouds, and "babbling" brooks. While drawing, I seemed to hover above the paper, disembodied, losing track of time. The successful replication of a tree or a barn filled me with the thrill of omniscience. But for all the satisfaction in making those landscapes, they were, in the end, someone else's idea of beauty, little more than quaint imitations.

Not until I came upon the article in *Life* magazine did I see that art's subject matter could be gleaned from the city, from my very own home. Even better, paintings by Pop artists presented a point of view entirely different from Ron's mournful portrait of Bob; Pop was enamoured of a world in which all that's lost or obsolete is simply replaced by a newer model; Pop was based on unjudgmental wonder, without a trace of the suffering I was too young to know we all must bear, an abundance strapped to our backs.

Once I was sure the librarian was distracted in the aisles, I quietly tore out the article in *Life* and folded it into my shirt pocket. I kept it in a drawer next to my bed and spent hours gazing at the juxtaposition of a Coke bottle, a Goodyear tire, and a pair of bare legs in *Silver Skies,* an enormous painting by James Rosenquist that took up an entire wall in Robert and Ethel Scull's dining room. Amazingly, Mr. Scull was photographed sitting at the table and calmly reading the morning paper, oblivious to the images colliding behind him.

One day, eager for more to read, I searched through the art section of a bookstore on Hollywood Boulevard and found *Pop Art* by John Rublowsky. Printed in 1965, it was one of the first American publications to document the phenomenon of Pop.

The photograph on the first page showed Claes Oldenburg, Tom Wesselmann, Roy Lichtenstein, James Rosenquist, and Andy Warhol posed at a group exhibition of their work. The wan fashion model, Jean Shrimpton, stands among them, mascara'd and miniskirted, her hair molded into the stiff, symmetrical curls of a flip. In another photo of the show, art patrons wander among a roomful of Warhol's Brillo boxes, looking for the most part glum and bewildered, as if they'd accidentally stumbled into an industrial warehouse. One elderly art lover in a turban and high heels glances around in consternation, while the woman beside her wears a dress in the spirit of the occasion, the fabric a pattern of labels reading, Fragile, Handle with Care.

Rublowsky's book was prescient in that it treated these five artists as the celebrities they were to become, capturing for posterity their every brush stroke and contemplative pause. Each of them was given his own chapter and shown mixing paint or hefting rolls of canvas, hard at work in their

·   ·   ·   ·   ·   ·   ·   ·   ·

cavernous studios. Each of them, that is, except for Andy Warhol; he
sprawled on a couch, relaxing like a sultan while two handsome assistants
in T-shirts and tight jeans dragged a squeegee across a silkscreen of Elizabeth Taylor. In the background, dozens of other paintings by Warhol leaned
against a wall: one-dollar bills, the electric chair, and Jackie Kennedy in a
black veil, each image repeated over and over. The text claimed that the
detractors of Pop found Warhol's multiple images numbing, but they
dazzled me, like the stutter of TV channels when I twisted the dial, or the
brand names and logos and slogans that bombarded me every day like
the sun's ultraviolet rays—Duz, Malt-O-Meal, Dippity-do. As far as I was
concerned, the glut of words and images was all a fine, intoxicating non-
sense. Andy's art was fun. I got it, with a wallop.

Though I believed that Warhol made, or had his assistants make, great
paintings, I was mystified by the man himself. In every photograph he
lacked expression, the skin of his face as tight and shiny as a marionette's.
He claimed that his fondest wish was to be a machine, and he referred to
his studio in Chelsea, whose interior had been painted silver, as the Factory. The place looked as echoey and reflective as the inside of a tin can.
One photograph showed Warhol dressed in a suit and sitting atop the Factory's silver toilet. Though there was hardly a glimmer of natural light in
the room, he wore a pair of sunglasses, the flashbulb reflected in his lenses
like two glaring, empty eyes.

The chapter on Warhol told how the Factory attracted a gaggle of misfits on whom Warhol lavished his blank gaze. These were the "superstars"
who slept, smoked, or rambled aimlessly in his movies. At that point, I
hadn't actually seen a Warhol film, but they sounded like an avant-garde
version of one of my favorite television shows, Candid Camera, where the
host, Allen Funt, "caught people in the act of being themselves." I thought
of the Factory as the home of an eccentric family for whom Andy Warhol,
with his ghostly pallor and silver hair, was a kindly, albino uncle.

High art and low, the significant and the trivial—Uncle Andy made no
such distinctions. Though I couldn't have put it into words back then, there
was something appealing in this neutral viewpoint. I liked his painting of
Chicken Noodle Soup better than his painting of Navy Bean Soup because
I thought it was a better flavor, though not necessarily a better painting.
For what other reason could I have preferred one over the other? They
were virtually the same painting with different labels. The absurdity of this
judgment, or lack of judgment, was not lost on me, nor was its shock value.
When I brought Rublowsky's book to my mother and showed her the

paintings of Campbell's soup, she looked at me askance and patted the spongy rollers in her hair. My mother was a woman who shopped avidly and often, maneuvering her cart down grocery-store aisles with the instinct of a tigress hunting for prey; she seemed to sense ridicule, rather than celebration, in Warhol's oeuvre. "Da Vinci," she said, "he isn't."

In some ways, it's surprising that my mother couldn't appreciate the abundance and commercial subject matter that typified a work by Warhol. Both of my parents were second-generation Jews whose families had immigrated to the United States from Eastern Europe. Growing up in Chicago tenements, they'd heard their parents bemoan in Yiddish all the comforts and conveniences they lacked. Now that my parents had moved to the Golden State and my father was solvent in his law practice, they were thrilled to be able to buy for our home a five-speed blender, a portable TV, an electric blanket with dual controls. They opened these purchases with great ceremony, intoned the instructions like Talmudic texts—"Make sure switch is in *off* position!"—and unfailingly mailed in the warranties. It was a point of pride that they stocked our Spanish house in Hollywood with brand-name rather than discount products. "Why buy crap," my father would ask, "when you get something good for a few pennies extra?" "We'll save in the long run," mother would add, turning around to beam at the Westinghouse or Zenith box propped beside me on the backseat of my father's new Cadillac.

Yet those ancient days of scarcity had bred in them the habit of hoarding. They'd stash away even the smallest objects, stray odds and ends that others might have discarded without a second thought. My mother reused sheets of tinfoil, kept a sizeable brown bird's nest of rubber bands in a kitchen drawer, saved matchbooks and bottle caps and even pieces of broken crockery she vowed to glue back together some day. Claiming she needed them when she cleaned, she stuffed a fire hazard of rags into the utility closet along with shreds of the clothes and bedsheets she couldn't bear to part with. She'd stock our pantry with, say, two dozen cans of Del Monte pitted cherries if they happened to be on sale, never stopping to ask herself if we liked or wanted or needed cherries, that flaccid, pale, syrupy fruit garnishing our plates for weeks on end. So crammed were our cupboards that, during the Cuban missile crisis, I remember being certain that we'd duck and cover when the bomb was dropped, then sit in the rubble and feast like kings.

My father also hoarded the flotsam of our prosperous life. On the shelves of his workbench in the garage, rows of used jelly jars (mother had

．　　．　　．　　．　　．　　．　　．　　．　　．

rinsed them with scalding water) held screws, washers, eye-hooks, nails of all sizes and degrees of straightness, fuses, thumbtacks, and stray springs whose origins were a mystery. Should the need for one of these odds and ends arise, he'd pluck it from a jar and go about his chores, as if it were a small but crucial detail he'd recalled while telling a story. "It's meshugge," he'd always say, "but you never know what'll come in handy."

Cash in hand, my parents assimilated into American life, but with the persistent suspicion that their prosperity would someday come to an end. No matter how much money my father earned, no matter how often my mother shopped, no matter what they crammed into cupboards or kept in glass jars, their belongings were borrowed, meager things, the privations of the tenement only a reminiscence away. We lived, I was given to understand, in a house full of fine but tenuous possessions.

Pop was a movement tailor made for the son of first-generation Americans, a boy who'd been weaned on the promise of plenty. Pop wanted me to have art that was push button, wide screen, charcoal filtered, ready to eat, disposable, and one size fits all. Pop wanted me to enjoy things while they lasted and didn't sneer at the world just because it was fleeting and gaudy. "Pop art represents our particular moment," I read again and again in the foreword to Rublowsky's book, "reflecting this particular civilization in its acceptance of the mechanized and mass-produced. These artists face the now, the today. Tomorrow they leave to the future." I loved the martial tone of those lines and had never thought of "today" as a noun, a thing I might possess as well as live through.

One of my favorite chapters in *Pop Art* contained photographs from the Supermarket, a 1964 exhibit at the Bianchini Gallery in New York City. The gallery was divided into aisles featuring canned goods, produce, and meat. Chrome apples by Robert Watts could be purchased individually or by the dozen. A plaster ice cream bar by Claes Oldenburg sold for $369.99. Andy Warhol signed real Campbell's soup cans that were stacked into a pyramid and labeled *Today's Special.*

Inspired, I insisted on accompanying my mother on her visits to the Safeway. She interpreted this as helpfulness on my part, a healthy interest in domestic chores, but I'd often wander the aisles alone, dazed by the orange vortex of a Tide detergent box or the green, unearthly cellophane grass that grew beneath the avocados. Every package and label and display was designed to wrest my attention and fill me with longing, which is exactly what happened. The overhead lights flickered at the perfect frequency for a trance, reflections of the neon tubes shimmering in the polished floor. Muzak, which seemed to seep from the very air, homogenized popular songs into an endless, buoyant melody. I was too contented to care if I looked foolish gawking at a vacu-formed Butterball turkey, or a fat, inflatable Dole pineapple that hung from the ceiling on a string and bobbed on the gusts from an air vent. What a thrill when I realized that, apart from permanent fixtures such as meat cases and cash registers, the supermarket was sent promotional items that were always changing. I could visit the Safeway every week and never see the same things twice!

On one of our visits, my mother finally noticed my fascination with packaging. We were standing together in the checkout line. While she browsed through the magazine rack, I became transfixed by a pack of Wrigley's gum. In the Wrigley's ads that adorned bus benches all over Hollywood, working people chewed a stick and, according to their thought balloons, water skied, danced at a ball, or imagined some other antidote to drudgery. Life is like a dream, I thought. Sound had stopped. A white foil rectangle gleamed in my palm, emblazoned with slender letters. The cashier's fingers were poised above the keys as she patiently waited for my reverie to end. "Are you all right?" my mother asked. She must have looked up from *Good Housekeeping* to catch me staring at a pack of gum as if it were an ingot of some rare ore.

If it sounds as if I were a budding consumer instead of a junior aesthete, let me add that it was of no consequence whether my mother actually bought the things I admired. Purchases were beside the point. I wanted only the luxury of looking, a total saturation of the senses. Not buying may, in fact, have been part of the pleasure, making the objects of my contemplation less like products and more like art.

Supermarkets weren't my only source of inspiration. I went into raptures over used-car lots, coffee shops, telephone booths, gas stations, freeways, and especially downtown intersections. Whiffs of bitter exhaust, vendors hawking stuffed animals and hot pretzels, store-window mannequins whose limbs were flung into ludicrous poses—whenever I stepped off the bus to visit my father's office on Spring Street, the city stretched before me like a vast, man-made wilderness. A native Angeleno, I'd never seen snow or autumn leaves firsthand, but I'd seen, on the billboard facing my father's office, a pat of butter melting into an Everest of steaming peas.

Every Saturday on Channel 5, John Nagey continued to churn out a seemingly inexhaustible array of majestic, fleecy, and babbling subject matter, and yet I began to view his art through the lens of irony. He made bad art that was good because it was bad. Posing before his spindly easel, hamming inspiration for the camera, he played the role of eccentric-artist-as-celebrity. Nagey, in short, was an unwitting Warhol.

By the time I was fourteen, the few assumptions I had about beauty were turning inside out. Art didn't have to be somber and lofty; it could be as laughable and blunt as a pratfall. All the "serious" art I'd seen in reproduction—*Mona Lisa, Blue Boy,* the *Thinker*—rankled with its piety and made me impatient. Sure, these might have been masterpieces in their time, but to honor them and ignore the world around us seemed a kind of hopeless nostalgia. The glorious light of Renaissance landscapes, the jewels and robes of nobility, the still life's cascade of flawless grapes—such antiquated themes barely roused my interest. Besides, printed on T-shirts and placemats and posters, masterpieces were as common as weeds. Eschewing all claims to greatness, turning its back on posterity, Pop won me over by being unpretentious. Pop was the hick cousin who shows up at a black-tie affair in a checkered suit: loud yet guileless, a breath of fresh air. Trash Can School, The New Vulgarians—when epithets were hurled at Pop, I grew more brash and unwavering in my adolescent love.

If the city streets were a huge museum, then was every sneeze and car horn music, every shrug and yawn a dance? No sight or sensation could be taken for granted.

Some nights, contemplating the democracy of Pop left me too agitated to sleep, and I would throw off the covers and compose rambling manifestos, a word I'd learned from Rublowsky's book. In one manifesto, dated 1966, I scrawled in the loopy cursive of my teens: "Taking something that means nothing and making it art just by CALLING it art is something we have taken too long to do! It is glorifing [sic] the ordinary—producing excitement from dull purpose from purposeless [sic]—IT IS ART! IT IS MORE THAN ART!!!" I'd caught the spirit of hyperbole, which resulted in the royal "we," underlined words, and rampant exclamation points.

If I decided to read in bed before I fell asleep, it was usually a book or magazine article about Pop art. One work in particular haunted me: a 1956 collage by the British artist Richard Hamilton. Because the collage was seminal in the history of Pop, I came across it again and again. In a newly furnished, shag-carpeted interior, a bodybuilder lifts a gigantic Tootsie Pop (according to some art historians, this was how the movement got its name), his thighs and biceps bulging. On the couch across from him sits a woman who wears nothing but a lampshade on her head and pasties over her nipples. A large canned ham sits on the coffee table between them. *Just What Is It,* asked Hamilton's title, *That Makes Today's Homes So Different, So Appealing?*

The answer, as far as I was concerned, was the man's physique. He looked a little like Mr. Rippey, my thick-necked, swaggering gym teacher. Throughout junior high, I'd tried to picture the muscular body beneath his clinging, regulation shirt. "Today's topic is homos," he'd once bellowed at the beginning of a health class, stunning the assembled boys into silence. "Any questions? No? Good."

Pop art, it seems to me in retrospect, was the perfect guise for my nascent homosexuality. Pop scoffed at convention. Pop defied the prevailing aesthetic by not only tolerating, but reveling in, the "unnatural." Pop found a place in art for everything that society discarded, devalued, ignored. If there existed a precocious, self-congratulatory aspect of my devotion to Pop art, a willfulness to set myself apart and cultivate my youthful iconoclasm, that devotion also felt helpless, inexplicable, and driven.

In any case, the bodybuilder appealed to me more than the woman on the couch, no matter how hard I tried to make myself believe otherwise. Weighing and evaluating my response to those different forms of flesh, my eyes darted back and forth, back and forth, pausing at that can of meat in the middle—*Just open, heat, and serve!*

My artistic apprenticeship continued throughout junior-high school. One Saturday I bought a small primed and prestretched canvas at the local art-supply store and set out to paint, in the hard-edged manner of Roy Lichtenstein, something mundane. I looked around the house for a suitable subject and chose one my father's razor blades. The blade was blunt on one side, with the brand name, Gem, embossed along the edge. In some vague way, I was intrigued by the incongruity between the name and the object, but mostly I figured that, being a simple rectangle, a razor blade would be easy to paint. I used a ruler and a wide felt-tipped marker to draw the blade, then painted the background with orange acrylic. Woozy from fumes, swept away by the glee of completion, I ran downstairs and showed the painting to my parents, holding the canvas from behind by its stretcher bars and waiting for murmurs of appreciation. That my parents might react with a kind of mute incredulity to their teenage son having painted a huge razor blade didn't so much as cross my mind, and when I lowered the canvas from in front of my face, I saw that they were wearing suspiciously wide smiles, like mouths that had been cut from toothpaste ads and stuck to their otherwise troubled faces.

·   ·   ·   ·   ·   ·   ·   ·   ·   ·   ·

"What's it called?" my mother asked, ever diplomatic.

"Gem," I said.

My father grunted, "Hmm."

"And you plan to hang it where?" asked my mother.

"I guess in my room."

They looked at each other and exhaled with relief.

I dismissed their lack of enthusiasm as precisely the kind of misunderstanding my artist-heroes must endure every day. In fact, my parents' bemusement turned out to be far more gratifying than their approval ever could have been: I found it more refreshing than an ice-cold Coke.

Soon I was scavenging trash cans for material with which to make mock Rauschenbergs. Junkyards provided the small, twisted scraps of metal I epoxied into a tortured jumble, just as John Chamberlain had welded together the shrapnel of crashed cars. I bolted an actual terrycloth towel to a painted rack, homage to the bathroom interiors of Tom Wesselmann. My room became a gallery in which I showed derivative work and brooded on what it meant to be modern.

With each passing month it seemed that the chasm between my parents and me opened wider. Mystified by my passion for art, they never asked a question or ventured a comment, afraid to betray any sign of ignorance about the culture they strived to blend into. My immersion in the avant-garde must have reminded them that the country in which they'd worked so hard to find a stable place was rapidly changing: color TV, area codes, strip-o-grams, passenger jets. Even their son was becoming a stranger. Still, their parenting had been based not only on the liberal wisdom of Dr. Spock but on a Jewish ethos that honors intellectual investigation of all kinds; as a result, they left me pretty much to my own devices, wearily tolerating the disappearance of household objects that would sooner or later resurface in my artwork. I considered myself in touch with, if not ahead of, the times. My parents remained on the shores of the Old World, with its bland cooking and Yiddishisms, while I departed for the new.

By the eleventh grade, I refused to let trivialities like homework and what my mother called "a boy's basic need for fresh air and exercise" get in the way of making art. My grades in liberal arts courses were fair, while those in math and science plummeted. This, combined with my propensity to stare at a bottle cap or dish rack and ruminate over its physical properties, was especially alarming to my mother, who'd begun to wonder about my eligibility for college, not to mention my mental health. It wasn't unusual for my mother to find me fishing an empty box of Kraft macaroni out of the trash can, or collecting lint from the dryer because I had a hunch I could "use it for something." My drive to hoard useless things was no more odd or inexplicable than hers, and yet, all these years later, when I picture my mother dressed in her housecoat, looking at me wistfully, I understand at last how perplexed she must have been.

In the presence of her friends, my mother minimized her worry by dubbing art my "nutty hobby," which made it seem like an eccentric aside to her son's otherwise normal preoccupations. By 1968, however, "normal" was considered an insult not only by me, but also by most of the kids I knew. "Freak" was the term for anyone scruffy and unconventional enough to merit the admiration of his peers. I first heard the term while smoking pot in the back of Eloise Blau's van during lunch period. Draped in the shawl she'd knitted herself, Eloise took a drag and rasped, "My lover, Jasper, is such a freak. The guy sleeps naked and grows his own dope."

The walls of Eloise's van were covered with handbills for bands like Jefferson Airplane and The Strawberry Alarm Clock, the illegible text dripping onto paisley or rainbow backgrounds. With my shoulder-length hair and wire-rimmed glasses, I fit the hippie image to a T, allied with the times in most respects—except for aesthetics; psychedelia repelled me with its florid distortions, its airless excess. Psychedelic art borrowed heavily from Art Nouveau and stressed the undulations of nature, the decorative tendril and flowering bud, whereas I was excited by the repetitions of mass production, the bold graphics of advertising. My circle of friends found Pop art as shallow and corrupt as modern American society itself, and my obsession with it baffled them almost as much as it did my mother. "Pop is so plastic," one friend remarked. She meant, it took me a moment to realize, "plastic" in the pejorative.

Lovers of psychedelia, my high-school friends possessed an endless tolerance for hallucinogens. I'd dropped acid a couple of times, but found the experience overwrought and ugly. One Saturday morning, right as we were peaking, Eloise and I went to eat at a restaurant next to the La Brea tar pits. The patrons (I realized later they were senior citizens who'd swarmed the place to take advantage of a cheap breakfast buffet) looked stiff and mineral, like fossils dredged from the ooze and resurrected, and this, along with the grains of salt breathing in the shaker and the faces staring back from wood grain of the table, caused me to lose what little appetite I had. We spent the drive back to Eloise's house, which seemed to

.   .   .   .

take several days and required unexpected detours through foreign countries, trying to remember if we'd left the waitress a tip, paid the check, or
gone inside the restaurant at all. Eloise found our confusion profound—
she made some declaration about memory that evaporated the second it
was said—while I regarded the entire morning as a kind of voluntary mental wreckage. My consciousness felt expunged rather than expanded, and
it became clear that, if I disliked the psychedelic aesthetic, I'd dislike the
drug from which it sprang.

In the twentieth century, the museum and gallery have assumed an almost
religious authority when it comes to vanguard art; renegade and here-
tofore unacceptable objects are sanctified within those walls. Marcel
Duchamp understood this earlier than any modern artist. By mounting exhibitions of his work that included a bottle rack, a snow shovel, and, in the
most notorious instance, a urinal, he not only gave these objects the impri-
matur of art, but suggested that choosing an object is tantamount to creating one. Duchamp called these found objects "Ready-mades," and they
embody his aesthetic every bit as pointedly as the art he made by hand.

   Although I may have possessed a precocious sympathy for such ideas
when I first read about them in high school, they were inarticulate inklings
at best, dim apprehensions. A thrilling paralysis, a churning in my solar
plexus; these were (and to a large extent have remained) my sole criteria of
judgment.

   In any case, my longest exposure to the transformative white environment of high art came when I was in the eleventh grade. At this point, a
one-man show seemed the only way to prove to my parents, and myself,
that a life in art was the right aspiration. And so I spent a summer afternoon tromping into galleries and asking dealers to take a look at the Polaroid Instamatic snapshots I had taken of my paintings of towel racks and
razor blades. In lieu of a portfolio, I'd pasted the Polaroids into the pages
of an empty family album I'd found in the basement. "Family Album," in
fact, was written across the cover in fancy gold script, befitting the fierce,
one might say biological, pride I felt about my paintings.

   In those days, the north end of La Cienega Boulevard was almost entirely taken up by small, thriving galleries. Everything from moonlit seascapes to the glossy, monochromatic plastic slabs by Los Angeles artist
John McCracken filled the display windows facing the street. Because the
galleries were located in West Hollywood, antiques shops also flaunted
their stock of French provincial chairs, Federal breakfronts, and brocade

drapery. Elegantly ghettoized, the north end of the boulevard was redolent of a somewhat pampered, old-fashioned homosexuality, an ambience that both made me feel at home and threatened me with a self-knowledge I wasn't ready to accept.

Despite the boulevard's bustling outward appearance, I was consistently surprised to find the galleries silent and empty except for the dealers, mostly well-dressed, middle-aged men who sat behind enormous desks. Not one of them was charmed by an overeager high-school kid thrusting in front of their faces his family album, and since they seemed to be doing nothing more than stewing in a vacuum, they couldn't, with much conviction anyway, blame their lack of interest on an urgent phone call or a demanding customer. They dismissed me with a flick of the hand, a condescending smile. Could the commerce of art be as impenetrable and lonely as it seemed? I'd imagined an enterprise as frenzied as the stock market, but in gallery after gallery, I found dust motes swirling in shafts of track lighting, the sound of traffic a distant whisper.

By the time I entered the Barbara DeVeers Gallery, I'd pretty much given up on the idea of a one-man show and was wondering how I could earn extra cash for art supplies. I didn't bother to show her my portfolio, which I'd tucked under one arm, nor did I look at the prints on her walls. Instead, in a last stab at audacity, I marched up and asked if she needed an assistant. After sizing me up and asking a few questions, she hired me on the spot.

And so, three days a week, I unlocked the gallery at noon, dusted the desk, vacuumed the architectural carpeting, Windexed the enormous plate-glass windows, and watered the potted palms. I became—you'll forgive the Duchampian pun—a ready-maid, keeping clean the context of art.

My employer arrived at work with the tailored, coiffed, and moisturized look of a woman of means. Barbara remained unfailingly buoyant during the long hours in which there was little to do except sip coffee, open mail, and straighten the Chagalls and Picassos in the print cabinet. She performed these tasks with attentiveness and pleasure. More art arrived at the place than ever left it, and because the realm of personal finance was still a mystery to me, I spent a great many of those idle hours wondering how she made money. Though always kind, Barbara wasn't a particularly forthcoming woman, at least with me, and it was largely by eavesdropping on her private telephone conversations that I gleaned the story of her divorce from a corporate executive who'd left her for a younger woman and, in a pang of guilt, agreed to support her gallery until it got off the ground. "It just may take me the next ten years," I once heard her boasting to a friend on the phone, "to show so much as an itty-bitty profit."

During her lengthy lunches (from which she returned flushed and humming), I sat in the swivel chair behind the desk, alphabetizing files and signing for deliveries. In the rare instances when someone asked to see a print, I wanted him or her to think I was an art-world prodigy. Before sliding a lithograph from its drawer, I had to don a pair of white cotton gloves that made me feel as formidable as a surgeon. I wasn't especially interested in the artists whose work we sold, but I soon discovered that, when showing art, a noncommittal attitude was the most aggressive sales tactic of all. Should I sense that someone was intimidated by having to stand there and stare, I might, after a good long while, break the tension by saying something like, "He's very free," in the case of Picasso, or "Those floating lovers," in the case of Chagall. I quickly learned that the most obvious tidbit of commentary could sound so knowledgeable, so cleverly epigrammatic, in the velvet setting of another's silence.

In those days I was only partially aware of how badly I wanted to belong to something—a movement, a style, posterity itself. As deeply as I believed in the challenging spirit of the avant-garde, and especially in the playful effrontery of Pop art, I still craved some form of normalcy and acceptance; all the more so since I feared that my sexuality might lead to ostracism.

More often than not, Manhattan was the geographical focus of my yearning to belong to an artistic elite. Apart from the fact that I could visit its museums and see art I'd only known in reproduction, I imagined the city as that most romantic of paradoxes: a community of misfits. Here was a place where one's eccentricities, chronic alienation, and skewed perceptions of the world were looked upon as badges of distinction rather than flaws to be overcome; they comprised, if one was lucky, the elements of sensibility. Never having set foot in the city allowed my fantasies to run wild. The recurring theme involved addressing famous Pop artists by their first names: *You're looking a little pale, Andy! Nice turtleneck, Roy! Oh, Claes, you nut, sit down already!* The presumption of it quickened my pulse.

The notion that artistic (and personal) redemption was not only possible but probable in New York City had been planted long ago by Rublowsky's book. An entire section juxtaposed Pop imagery with artistically cropped street scenes, making a clear connection between the cityscape and the art that flourished there. Other photos showed Warhol walking

. . . .

though wind-blown litter; Oldenburg gazing into an appliance-store window. Shot from the cautious distance at which one might observe a tiger or an elk, these photographs suggested the caption *Artist in Natural Habitat.*

Manhattan's status as an artistic Mecca was also reinforced by the art magazines that arrived at Barbara's gallery—*Artforum, Art News, Art in America*—the bulk of text and advertising devoted to the East Coast. Reviewers covering the galleries in Chicago or San Francisco or Los Angeles seemed like ambassadors reporting from outlying colonies. Picture, if you will, the pastels of every other state blanched from the map; I mistook Manhattan for America and vowed to get there however I could.

I'd recently sent away for applications to a couple of art schools in Manhattan—the School of Visual Arts and Cooper Union—and toward the end of summer, I filled out the various forms. Each school required a lengthy essay in which the applicant explained why he'd chosen to study fine art. In an effort to drum up ideas, I dug from the bottom of a bureau drawer the yellowing art manifestos I'd written when I was thirteen. What a shock it was to read them again! By then I'd gained enough distance on my past to cringe at the capitalizations and exclamation points. No doubt I'd been convinced of my sophistication when I'd scrawled them in a fever of inspiration, but now lines like "Take the common egg which we eat every day but ignore even though it means BIRTH and CHICKENS and EVERYTHING!!!" made me weak with embarrassment. How easily my zeal had boiled over. Were my present convictions equally absurd? I couldn't help but suspect that several things I'd said that very day were lying in wait to shame me in the future.

Each of the art schools' cover letters stated that the admissions committee placed special emphasis on one's portfolio rather than on grades. This suited me fine, since my grade-point average was modest at best. Nor was acceptance based on SAT scores, a big relief considering I'd received the lowest SAT score for math in my entire graduating class. A counselor had called me into his office to break the news and inform me that, according to the *Scholastic Aptitude Handbook,* my number (around three hundred) was the probable score one would get if they had simply guessed at every answer. He'd intended, I think, to humiliate me into studying harder, but I was awed that the statistics, in a kind of numerical clairvoyance, had revealed my method of taking the test: darkening all the ovals in a pleasant but random pattern.

■ ■ ■

The night before I left Los Angeles to attend the School of Visual Arts in New York City, my parents made an uncharacteristic attempt to offer guidance. Up until that point, they'd never interfered with my decisions, remaining steadfast in the belief that my destiny would take its own course. Besides, they had their own problem to contend with: a mutual estrangement that had all but nullified their marriage. For years I'd been aware that an icy silence had descended on our house, but it wasn't until the months before I left home that my mother voiced her suspicions about my father's infidelities. She told me about the bills from local motels and florists that she'd been intercepting. So desperately did she want a witness to her betrayal that she went so far as to pluck a pair of his lipstick-stained boxer shorts from the laundry hamper and wave them between us like a white flag. I tried to play both sides, sympathizing with my mother's rage while at the same time offering possible explanations on my father's behalf. Thinking up excuses strained my imagination, especially when it came to the lipstick stains on his underwear, and by echoing my every guess— "Strawberry jam?"—my mother made them all seem foolish. Perhaps my parents' visits to my room that night were an attempt to stake independent claims on my affection, or to compensate for the steady wayward drift—one son dead, one busy with a law practice, the last about to move across the country—of our family.

My mother was the first to knock on my door. She perched beside me on the edge of my bed, warning me that drugs were easily available on college campuses and urging me not to get "hooked" on marijuana. She wanted to touch me, I could tell, but both of us had relegated displays of familial affection to the past, and our differences—sullen housewife and artistic hippie—made us shy with each other. Still, her timid voice broke my heart, as did the fact that, unbeknownst to her, pot had motivated my late-night forays to the kitchen where I devoured enormous portions of canned fruit cocktail—chunks of wet confetti!—and laughed, for a change, at my father's corny jokes. She'd beam at these inexplicable moments of family bliss and chalk them up, I suppose, to the fleeting possibility that things hadn't gone so wrong after all.

My father took her place on the edge of the bed a little while later, asking whether I was sure, absolutely sure I wouldn't be better off in a more lucrative profession. Lucrative was what my father would have called, without irony, "a two-dollar word," and he reserved it for only the most serious occasions. I'd always suspected that my father's resistance to art stemmed from his belief that, since art didn't guarantee a monetary return, it was, occupation-wise, a decorative flourish dwarfed by more important matters, like one of those frilly paper ruffs they stick on a lamb chop. Now and then I'd considered professions other than fine art—furniture designer and actor among them—but none promised a substantially better shot at financial security. Besides, every summer job, household chore, and hour spent in school seemed like a distraction; I was always aware of my restless hands and an inexplicable surfeit of feeling that only making art could ease. Heart-to-heart talks were as foreign to my relationship with my father as the geography of Mars; although he once instructed me on how to write a check, in every other respect my father expected me to learn about the world through osmosis or trial and error. And so his proximity on the edge of the bed, his grave patience, and the fact that he actually searched my eyes, were cause for alarm as well as warmth. Don't misunderstand: I long ago stopped blaming the loneliness of my youth on my parents; benign neglect was the very medium in which my artistic ambition thrived, and I appreciate, to this day, the advantages of solitude. Still, my father's sudden regard left me, if not speechless, then too startled to defend, at any length, the gamble of a creative life.

"Art is all I think about," I said.

My father rose, wished me luck, and switched off the light.

In the dark I pictured a huge white room somewhere in Manhattan, its emptiness so enticing I could barely fall sleep.

My Des Moines

. . . .

by

ELIZABETH MCCRACKEN

Wilkes-Barre, Pennsylvania

Before Des Moines, there was Wilkes-Barre, Pennsylvania, where my great-grandfather, Samuel McCracken, was president of the bank. I don't remember ever seeing a picture of him, but my grandparents owned the silver platter etched with signatures that he had received upon his retirement. An important man: he must have met everyone who came through town. This is what my grandmother Jacobson liked to believe: her grandfather, Rabbi Louis Sharasefsky—gentle and charcoal colored in the photo she hung over the TV—briefly held a pulpit in Wilkes-Barre. Surely he met his future unmet in-law. The actual math makes it unlikely. Still, I've always liked to think of them together, my great-great-grandfather the rabbi a smudgy gray, shaking the hand of my great-grandfather, the bank president, whose silver coat flashes with etched signatures. They are exchanging prayer books: they are exchanging passbooks, any number of leather-bound volumes filled with a code I cannot make sense of. They are happy to make each other's acquaintance. "A pleasure," says the rabbi; "An honor," says the bank president, and then, together, "What is your name?"

The rabbi did not hang around the Wyoming Valley very long. He went west, married, had children. The bank president stayed home but otherwise did the same. Years later, as a matter of pure coincidence, their descendants ended up in Iowa. Drake University hired the bank president's son to teach Latin and Greek—to be, in other words, the entire Classics Department. The rabbi's granddaughter fell in love with a shopkeeper. And her daughter went to Drake University, and so did the classics professor's son, and while taking a class on Shakespeare, the children met. And fell in love, and left Des Moines. And *they* married. And *they* had children.

And so it came to pass that my brother and I spent our childhood vacations in Des Moines, Iowa.

The Middle of the Midwest

Iowa has culture, my grandmother Jacobson liked to inform people, culture and hills. She might be in New York, or Seoul, or Jerusalem, or Reykjavik, explaining this to people who, if they'd given it any thought at all, imagined Iowa as a Grant Wood painting, with a little *Music Man* thrown in. She paired the two things so that the culture would seem as irrefutable as the rolling hills of eastern Iowa, but it came out sounding as though it was as unlikely. We have an art museum, my grandmother would say. And the art museum has a Goya. How about *that*. Hills, a Goya. Jews. Skyscrapers, even.

Whether something is contradictory or complementary depends on your disposition. My childhood begins in Des Moines, Iowa, though I never lived there: I grew up partly in Boston and partly in Portland, Oregon. My father is a tall Wasp, my mother is a short Jew, and it only makes sense that they met in central Iowa, the middle of the Middle West. I get corrected if I say that either of my parents is from Des Moines. My mother is from Valley Junction; my father moved to Des Moines from Virginia when he was eleven. But Des Moines is where all my living grandparents made their homes when I was growing up, the place we spent several weeks every year, in the summertime or at Christmas or both. Des Moines is an old member of the family: I don't remember the first time I met her; when I go back (I manage it at least once a year to see friends, though all of my Des Moines relatives have died or moved), I cannot quite remember what she looked thirty years ago, or twenty, or ten. I just plain recognize her, from George the Chili King's to the Merle Hay Mall, from the Greenwood Lounge to Waterworks Park. The Iowa Statehouse—a glorious building—means more to me than the similarly golden-domed state capitol three miles away from my apartment near Boston.

My oxymoronic imagination has its root in these things: Iowa Skyscraper. Des Moines Goya.

1232 Thirty-ninth Street

My grandparents McCracken lived in an enormous yellow house that had once belonged to the editor of *Better Homes and Gardens*. The whole house had a museum feel to it: silent, clean though suggesting millennial dust, dark. My grandfather was a code breaker: Greek and Latin for his studies, classically based ciphers for the government during World War II. After his retirement, he devoted himself to genealogy. An utter owl of a man, quiet unless he was telling a story, and then he could talk a good long time.

His wife, Emily Elizabeth Swettman McCracken, was the daughter of German immigrants who settled in in Hazelton, Pennsylvania. As a young woman, she had the lean, cool look of a European movie star. It's nearly a requirement to report that female relatives were beauties as young women, but I can say that nearly everyone else in my family was interesting, pretty, exotic, decidedly good looking, or merely pleasant: Emily Swettman, on the other hand, was a knockout. I cannot recognize my no-nonsense grandmother in those shots of the backlit blond young woman. By the time I knew her, she'd permed her hair in tiny, easy-to-care-for curls; she wore durable polyester clothes; her little-boy's eyeglasses were too small for her face. Her nose was as Roman as the Statue of Liberty's. Still, no bushel was big enough to hide all of that light. We brown-eyed people are liable to envy the most ordinary of blue eyes; my grandmother's were enormous and lovely and always, as I remember them, a little damp.

Their house was filled with objects. *Fascinating* objects, I was about to write, but in fact they were prosaic, and fascinated only me. Beneath the kitchen table (formica topped, trimmed in ribbed chrome) was a giant ball of twine, and though it was probably only two feet in diameter it suggested to me a picture I'd seen in *Ripley's Believe It or Not* of a man leaning casually against a ball of string as tall as a house. Somehow I got it into my head that my grandmother was gunning for the record. She'd never have done any such thing: the twine was for use, not frivolity. With it she bound stacks of the magazine my grandfather edited, the *American Genealogist*. In the basement was an avocado green exercise bike that was clearly a toy—by which I mean, an instrument of make-believe—despite grown-up assurances to the contrary. I liked the odometer clipped to the handlebars, which counted off the imaginary miles, black numbers on white wheels. It didn't take much peddling, standing up in the stirrups (the seat was too high), to turn over a tenth of a mile.

Upstairs, in the enormous bathroom, was a scale; I weighed myself often, though I don't know if I ever bothered to look at the actual numbers. The hallway walls were covered with my grandfather's many, many diplomas and certificates, including one from the American Academy in

Rome, illustrated with an engraving of Romulus and Remus and their adoptive mother, the she-wolf. Because of this document, I first learned the meaning of the word "suckle," though I can't remember who told me. Sometimes I stayed overnight in the room at the end of the hall on the cold vinyl daybed. Summer nights I listened to a spring-loaded electric whirring sound that I assumed came from the Iowa power lines strung outside my window; not for years did I realize that what I heard were cicadas, and even then I didn't believe it. Nothing living could explain that noise.

My grandfather's study was next to the guest room, a model lair for an absentminded professor: shelves and shelves of books, sheaves of paper, the bakery scent of dime-store pipe tobacco. In the center of the room stood his typewriter, a giant IBM Selectric. The steel case was black and slightly pebbled, like the cover of a leatherette diary. Back home, my mother's electric typewriter was basically a manual that you didn't have to bang so hard: the letters lived on the ends of metal levers, arranged like the audience in an amphitheater. The Selectric, however, had an efficient little ball like the one that dropped in Times Square on New Year's Eve, but paved with the alphabet. This, my grandfather once explained to me, was an *element*. You could snap it out and snap in another: one with italic letters, or Greek. My grandfather the classicist owned both.

I can still feel the wool of the oriental carpet beneath my cheek as I stared up at the reproduction Holbein in the living room (a large-print *Reader's Digest* open and unread beneath my forearm), or over at the pillow shaped like the head of the Exxon tiger on the loveseat. This wasn't a toy, either. My grandfather was a Princeton man. Sometimes he'd call me up from my indolence to blow out one of his matches after it had made the slow trembling journey from matchbook to pipe bowl and away again.

They owned two long-haired, slow-moving cats, known as the Mother Cat (she was a calico) and the Yellow Cat (her son). The vet had forced my grandmother to name them for their medical records, and so on paper they were Kitty I and Kitty II. I'm afraid that makes my grandmother sound as though she had no imagination or sense of humor, but she did. She wrote poetry and short stories and was kind in a way that only the truly imaginative can be: she believed the best of everyone. My grandparents hired ex-convicts from the halfway house affiliated with their church and did not care what crimes they'd committed. One elderly man who pulled weeds was a famous murderer. The others could have done anything. They loved my commonsensical grandparents.

I did, too, no mistake. Even now I can imagine the wry expression my grandmother must have had when the vet's receptionist said, "You have to call them *something*. They have to have *names*." When she heard something that amused her, she'd make a profoundly mischievous face, her blue, blue, very German eyes fixed with a look that might have been damning if her mouth hadn't been working so hard not to smile. It was better than anyone else's belly laugh. It is the thing I miss most about her, one of the last remnants of her old self left when, in 1986, she fell in the bathtub and sustained—what an odd word!—a serious head injury. She sustained it for three years: the first one in a series of facilities in Des Moines and the next two in a head injury center on Cape Cod, closer to her children. My grandfather had dinner with his children, my father and his sister, the night of the terrible fall. He thanked them for flying from the East Coast so immediately. Within two weeks, he died of a heart attack, which seemed a remarkable, thoughtful, lucky thing: my grandfather could not have lived alone for a day. He probably couldn't have done so at age forty, never mind age eighty-two. Once my grandmother came out of her coma, her wry expression was damped down, less extravagant, as though the fall had dulled her sense of humor—and I really mean dull; I really mean sense, as surely as hearing or taste or touch are senses—along with the ability to speak clearly, and walk. Really, I can't imagine she ever found anything particularly funny again.

It goes without saying that I didn't know any of this was to come as I hopped up the wide stairs to look at the scale or tried to read the etched signatures on the silver tray. Even more than most kids, I lived in the present, and the present was composed of the oriental rug and the indolent cats and my grandparents themselves. My grandmother introduced me to *butterfly kisses,* lowering her eyelids right next to my face so that her lashes brushed my skin, a kind of kiss that can never be taken by force. My grandfather invented *grandpa kisses,* which was a sudden raspberry applied to the cheek that left me giggling and shrieking and ecstatic. All *grandpa kisses* were stolen, even the ones I demanded.

In the summertime, my grandmother would mix up bubble solution made from Octagon dish soap and pour it into a tinfoil pie pan, which she would carry out to the back porch. At Christmastime, we made cookies, including *leibkuchen,* her German mother's recipe. We did everything quietly, though now I'm not sure whether that was so we wouldn't disturb my grandfather, the scholar, or because both my grandparents were losing their hearing and their caution and quiet were catching.

My older brother and I were allowed to roam the house so long as we did not run. We were allowed to read any book we wanted to, or to hunt through the vast backyard, which included a sundial in the center and a gazebo in the far corner. Back in its day—when it was a Better Garden in back of a Better Home—it had been a showplace; now it, like the editor and my grandparents, was in retirement. Mostly I entertained myself inside with the exercycle and the scale, or read a book of poetry called *The Janitor's Boy,* written by a child prodigy from the 1930s named Natalia Crane. "Oh, I'm in love with the Janitor's Boy/And he's in love with me . . ."

4225 Grand Avenue, Apartment 4

My grandmother Jacobson's world, on the other hand, was one of action. Oh, she owned things, possibly more things than my grandparents McCracken: she loved to shop and she loved to travel, and her two-bedroom apartment was filled with souvenir Buddhas and relatively modest fertility gods (she must have shopped carefully) and lacquer boxes and bamboo carvings. She had books, too, but she also had a color television set and a candy dish—at home we had neither—and those are the only two objects I really remember obsessing about.

My grandmother Jacobson was a small, glamorous, fretful woman. We called her Grandmother. She vetoed *Grandma* and *Bubbe* and *Nana,* anything that smacked of a cookie-scented, gingham-flocked old lady. She was a businesswoman; she accepted a job title. We called the McCrackens Grandma and Grandpa. Grandmother Jacobson wasn't kicky or childish, but she liked to Stay Young—indeed, even her children could only guess at her real age. Until 1977, she ran the women's clothing store she'd inherited from her husband fifteen years before, Jacobson's Apparel of West Des Moines. Later she became a small-business consultant and eventually was appointed executive director of the Senior Corps of Retired Executives, which necessitated her living in Washington for three years. She did not like sitting still and letting her numerous worries collect. We'd jump in whatever small, white, American car she owned at the time and drive to her country club to swim or her dinner club for their famous popovers. We'd head for the Merle Hay Mall—my brother and I loved the magic store—or to the miniature golf course, where we'd putt between the legs of a plastic cow. That was as agricultural as my time in Iowa ever got: a plastic cow on plastic turf, under the midget shadow of a midget windmill.

Then we'd come back to the apartment, whose front entrance was half space-age carport, half drive-in root-beer stand. The lobby smelled wonderful and waxy. I always thought it was coming from the giant half-burned candle on the front table, but some years later I realized it was the artificial perfume of twist-up room freshener.

Temple B'nai Jeshurun

I don't know what I made of religion when I was a kid, other than it seemed to exist only in Des Moines. Friday nights, we went to services at B'Nai Jeshurun, which had, in the hallway to the sanctuary, the distraction of photographs of confirmation classes through the ages. I liked finding my mother and her twin sister in their white robes and late-forties glossy hairdos. Sundays we went to the Cottage Grove Presbyterian Church, which had communion with little trays of grape juice. Mostly I remember flipping through prayer books and trying to figure out how much longer the service would go on.

Life in Des Moines felt a little more Jewish than Christian—we had more relatives on my mother's side, for one thing, and my grandmother Jacobson had lots of friends, all Jewish. "There's a cousin," my grandmother would say at Temple, pointing to some woman who'd married a man who was a distant cousin of a cousin. *Mishpocheh*: part of the extended family. I remember them, their fruity 1970s perfume and gold-toned costume jewelry, their beautiful, alliterative, *Yiddishe* names: Sylvia Siegel, Gertrude Greenhill, Rita Latween. They played cards and served on volunteer boards. "Honey, you're a Jewess," one told me fondly, an old-fashioned word that made me feel both cozy and dubious.

Most of the Jews I knew lived in Des Moines. My grade school in Massachusetts was almost entirely Catholic, though the city itself was not. Not till I got to junior high did I have Jewish friends, and by then we were all smart alecks, and I could groan about the Temple's Jewish Food Fair (fifty elderly women eating sweet-and-sour meatballs and muttering, "Mine are better"), or my grandmother's pain at my clothing (she did not think tie-dyed painter's pants were acceptable dinner-table wear), or—this is my favorite—the bar mitzvah we crashed, catered by my grandmother's friend Rose, who was the sort of industrious woman with a reputation for doing things well largely because she insisted she could. A lovely woman. A terrible cook. She'd baked giant off-centered bread-dough Stars of David, absolutely inedible: I remember chewing one point for about an hour, feeling half pagan, half hound dog, since the stars had a sort of rawhide appeal. Her husband had made for dessert his famous mints, which looked and tasted like guest soaps.

Maybe I felt more *Yiddishe* because I knew more relatives from that side of the family, but probably the material was just better. "There are Jews in Iowa?" people would ask, and later, "I can't help but notice: your last name. It's McCracken." No one would ever smile to me in that you-said-the-secret-password way if I revealed suddenly that I was Protestant. Jewish, but Des Moines Jewish: an even more exclusive club with even funnier punch lines.

My Jewish relatives were educated and sophisticated, but still I'm not sure how much they understood Christianity. My grandmother Jacobson said it gave her "the willies." What part? I asked. *"Everything,"* she said, shivering. My cousin Elizabeth, who was around my grandmother's age, once convinced me to crash a Catholic wedding (she was invited, I wasn't). Afterward, she remarked upon "the gruesome puppet" hanging over the altar. She meant the crucifix. No matter how much I explained it, she could not believe that it hadn't been given by some big donor whom the church couldn't afford to offend.

But everyone got along very well. They might not have understood each other, but we had dinner parties together, at the house or the apartment or a restaurant. My grandmother had her dinner club, but the McCrackens would take us to Bishop's Cafeteria, where you could pick the slice of chocolate cream pie you liked best. That was my idea of class.

I have a photograph of a party celebrating my sixth birthday at the McCrackens'. My serious grandfather is wearing a pointy hat and smoking a cigar; my occasionally frivolous grandmother Jacobson has foregone the paper chapeau because it would muss her hair. You can date the photo as early 1970s by her and her alone: she is wearing octagonal glasses and the kind of very tall, layered, lacquered hairdo that disappeared forever—even on women of a certain age in Des Moines—in about 1976. Her skirt is no doubt short, though it's hidden under the tablecloth. No one else in the room cares enough about styles to change from year to year, or even decade to decade.

I think my grandparents McCracken would have been confused by the concept of staying young in the face of growing old. My grandfather, after all, devoted a great deal of time to family trees, to charting birth dates and death dates and generations, to first cousins dozens of times removed. Unclear statistics were aggravating: on the one hand a fella seemed to have died of diptheria at age five and on the other to have married at age forty-two. Same person? Cousins? Coincidence? If you claimed on official documents to be younger than your youngest sister, you were a pain in the neck. You'd probably been one in real life. Facts were facts. You were how old you were.

He understood the concept of *mishpocheh*: he dealt in its taxonomy. But I'm sure he would have been stymied at my grandmother's lax attitude toward cousinhood if he'd gone with her to Temple. (I don't think he ever did. My parents were married by a rabbi at the Hotel Fort Des Moines.)

There's a cousin, my grandmother would inform him, pointing.

But how? Mr. McCracken might ask.

Oh, Mrs. Jacobson would say, *someone married someone.*

Mr. McCracken: *Yes, dear lady, someone always does, but the question is who?*

For goodness sake. You might as well claim the cat as family.

A Borrowed Toyota Corolla

The last day of my childhood, in some fundamental way, was 13 August 1986, a month before I turned twenty. Three friends and I took a trip across country together, from Boston to Texas to California; by the time we headed back, three of us had come to hate the fourth. He wasn't a bad guy, but the car was small and we were young, and then he almost drove over the heads of two people in sleeping bags at a campgrounds in Salt Lake City, and it was time to get home already.

So on August 12th, we stopped in Des Moines.

"Oh my god!" said my friend Margi. "I can't believe how great it is to be in a city where *someone* knows the street names!"

Because we'd been driving as fast as we could, we got to Des Moines too early to do anything but eat breakfast out, and so we went to the Happy Chef, a chain restaurant that my brother and I had always loved: there was a giant statue of the eponymous chef outside with a button you could push to hear him speak. He sang "Mairzy Doats," I remember. That morning, we pushed his button like toddlers, laughing and laughing, until an employee came out and suggested it was time to come in already.

Later, we visited my cousin Elizabeth; we had dinner with my grandparents McCracken; we stayed overnight with my grandmother Jacobson, all of us in her two-bedroom apartment: Marguerite and Maureen on the pullout bed in the den; Mike, our black cloud, on the sofa. I shared my grandmother's bed. Her doctor had told her sleeping with your head elevated was good for the circulation, so she'd jacked up the headboard with old phone books. She was used to it; I kept sliding down to the bottom.

We got up in the morning, all of us stiff and groggy, and vowed it was time to get the hell home. No sight-seeing: we hit Interstate 80 and drove, made 1,300 miles in 24 straight hours. I went to my house and found the door uncharacteristically locked, and in a grump walked to the pay phone at the end of the street and called my mother at work.

"I got home!" I said, aggrieved. "All I want to do is sleep, and I can't even get in!"

"Shhhh," she said, "listen."

I was in Boston; my father was in Des Moines. His mother had fallen in the bathtub.

Margi is still one of my dearest friends, and I am bound to her in a now irreproducible way: she met all my grandparents, and my cousin Elizabeth. Oh, I love to tell family stories; I am compulsive. But the friends of my adulthood can only meet one generation of my family. There are days when this doesn't seem near enough.

The Iowa Jewish Senior Life Center, formerly the Iowa Home for the Aged

Don't kid yourself: even the nicest nursing home in the world is a kind of nightmare. The hallways are designed so that wanderers will keep wandering in a circle; the doors are guarded so lucky wanderers who crack the child's puzzle of the architecture can't just keep going: across the front drive, and the lawn, and the parking lot, and the river. Because they want to: they want to go *home*. They've forgotten everything else.

Take me home. I want to go home. What is this place?

Even those who have—what do we want to call it? their wits? their minds? their bearings? their souls still in mint condition?—want to go home. They just know better than to ask.

I knew both the addled and the lucid at the Iowa Jewish Home. Eventually it seemed like the place where all the scattered pieces of my Des Moines childhood came to rest. Every time I went for a visit, I could look at the list of residents and find another name I recognized. Old friends of the family, distant cousins, *mishpocheh*.

I'd never been to the Jewish Home until my great-aunt Blanche came to live in Des Moines in the spring of 1989. My grandmother, her older sister, had flown to Florida and asked Blanche—muddled, soup-stained Blanche—if she wanted to go to Iowa. The day Blanche finally said yes,

. . . .

my grandmother drove them to the airport and bought tickets for the next flight. She'd already packed their bags.

I was going to graduate school in Iowa City and came to Des Moines often to help my grandmother, but soon enough it was clear: Blanche was so Alzheimer's addled—the disease had killed two of their sisters—that she could not possibly live alone. She had a sense of humor still, but also a raging temper. After a summer of agony, we moved her into a facility some miles away while she waited for a space in the Iowa Jewish Home to open up. For someone to die, in other words, and we would have felt guilty wishing for the death of a stranger if we hadn't been so aware that their own families might have been praying ardently for the same thing. Finally, Blanche's name came up on the waiting list, and we moved her in.

At first Blanche was one of those residents who adds to the nightmare of a nursing home. A screamer. A rover. Men from moving companies had to be daily turned away by the front desk; Blanche had called, wanting an estimate. She packed her bags. People were stealing her things, she told us. She hated them. She hated us. The nice women she was supposed to eat with in the dining hall tried to soothe her. *Give up*, they meant. *You'll be happier when you surrender.*

And eventually she did, and she was. My grandmother was dead by then, felled by a heart attack in her own home at the probable age of ninety. She had her wits, her bearings, a very black sense of humor, the last acquired in her later years. There was a young man named Jim who worked at the home—it really *was* the best nursing home I've ever seen, full of kindness and patience—and he said to me once, "Blanche wasn't a happy person when she moved here, but now she's a happy person." And she was. She'd forgotten her rage. I adored Jim; once I'd found a Valentine's card to Blanche signed, "Love from your friend and housekeeper, Jim." Never-married Blanche thrived on attention from men, even if by that Valentine's Day she was long past recognizing it. She got worse and worse. Just when you think a person with Alzheimer's can't make any less sense— insisting that crowds of women have been keeping her up all night by dancing across her bed, for instance—she does. Her sentences line up, sort of—"The machine, the machine there, it's no good for you." Then they don't. Eventually they turn to a patois of English and Mumblish: subjects lose their objects, then their verbs.

That's what happened to Blanche. I got to Des Moines a couple of times a year to visit what was left of my family, as well as a dear friend I'd made in graduate school, and I'd visit my great-aunt, whom I'd met only once, briefly, before she'd come to this strange Midwestern city. Once upon a time she'd recognized me, though she never bothered to learn who I was, other than that Nice Young Woman. Sometimes she'd hold my hand and mumble. Well, she'd hold anyone's hand. They must have pitied her at the home; so many other residents were visited by generations of family. "Bye, Blanchie," I'd say. It got sadder to leave once she no longer puckered up at the sight of someone else's kiss-ready, puckered lips.

Then I'd go off to visit someone less depressing: my cousin Irene, my distant cousin Yetta, my grandmother's wonderful friend Estyre. I got to really love several women I'd scarcely known outside of the home, because they could still talk to me, offer me boxed cookies, act like the Jewish grandmother I was missing. I had to keep adding to my route, because, of course, some of those women got worse, then as bad as Blanche. But life kept sending my grandmother's friends to the Jewish home. I'd sit with these women and chat, then go back for a few last moments of Mumblish with my great-aunt.

Except one visit: suddenly she made sense. Oh, not really *sense,* but somehow she'd gotten ahold of language again. "Are you going to the party, honey-honey?" she asked me. "Aunt Blanche!" I said, amazed.

Just then Jim, her friend and housekeeper, walked by. "She's much better, don't you think?" he said. "They adjusted her medication, and really, she's *much* better." He was dressed in rose-colored scrubs and holding a mop; he wasn't paid to notice the residents or care about minute changes in their ability to communicate. He was only paid to disinfect.

"I was just thinking that," I told him, still astounded. He smiled and continued down the hall. Blanche would outlive him, too: six months later my friend Wendy, remembering how fondly I'd spoken of a blond guy named Jim who worked at the home, would send me his obituary. And when I called the Life Center to ask about his family so that I could send a letter explaining what an extraordinary man their son had been, I was given the name of a female roommate: Jim's family had disowned him, because he was gay. *Ah,* I thought, full of rage. Well, Blanche had been disowned, too. Her family was lost to her because she could not recognize them, and she—like little old ladies in rooms all the way down the hall— begged for one thing: *home.* "My mother will be worried about me!" I once heard a woman say in anguish, and then Jim's quiet voice: "It's OK, Molly, your mother knows where you are. Your mother always knows exactly where you are."

. . . .

Greenwood Cemetery

My family has never been much for cemeteries. I grew up in Boston and thought of graveyards like I thought of forts and replica schooners: depositories of colonial history. So though I had relatives buried in Des Moines, I never saw their graves.

Then when I was in graduate school, my grandmother Jacobson decided she'd like to stop in Greenwood Cemetery. We came through the back way and walked straight up the hill to the Jewish section. And there they were: the Husbands.

Of course I knew that all those ladies, family and friends, were widows. Their husbands appeared in stories. Here in granite were their names: Benjamin Sideman, Frank Perowsky, Moses Swartz. My grandfather, Harry Jacobson. And others, too—my ancestor M. L. Jacobson. My cousin Elizabeth's mother, Anna Werblowsky. It was as though I had come across the graves of fictional characters, ones I'd loved and cried over, only to realize I hadn't loved them enough, cried enough—only to realize, in other words, that I'd loved and grieved my own ability to love and grieve.

They'd been real people, the Husbands. My grandmother and her friends had been brides and mothers before they were widows. My grandmother put three stones on Harry Jacobson's grave, but there weren't enough loose pebbles for her to mark everyone she'd known.

I am realizing as I write this: nearly all of my beloved dead died in Des Moines. Some of them are buried there and some in their old hometowns, and some have had their ashes scattered. It isn't fair to poor old Des Moines for me to think of it as haunted, but I do. No, that's wrong, not haunted: the opposite. Empty. Renovated. New wallpaper, new carpet, new names on the mailboxes. I do not want to climb onto the back porch of 1232 Thirty-ninth Street and see what's become of my grandmother McCracken's kitchen. I can't bear to even drive by the house.

My grandmother Jacobson is buried there too, now, next to her husband. I had to bawl out the stonecutters: the one thing she'd asked for was a stone identical to his, and the one they'd installed did match but was much bigger.

I saw the stone when Blanche died in 1998, on Valentine's Day. She'd given up talking entirely at least a year before. I was living in Michigan and came out to plan the funeral, just a small graveside ceremony. It seemed awful that she'd died in this strange city, that no one would read her obituary and remember her as a younger person and show up. Single, childless Blanche, dead on Saint Valentine's day. I wanted mourners. After calling around, I managed to scrape up seven: six human beings and one golden retriever puppy. The friends I was staying with had just acquired him, and Blanche had loved dogs the way she loved everything—way past the point of eccentricity. She would have been delighted at the very idea of a dog at a funeral.

"I don't understand," said the rabbi when I informed him of the puppy, "was she close to this dog?"

"No," I said, and eventually he shrugged and said OK.

The puppy was well behaved. When the crank that lowered the casket turned and squealed, the keen-eared dog began to cry, just a little.

It had not occurred to me to do likewise until that moment.

The Cottage Grove Presbyterian Church

Years before this. May 1989. My grandmother Jacobson is alive. Blanche has just moved to Des Moines, is sleeping on the sofa in the den and sneaking out at night to walk back to New York City, which she imagines is just over the hill. She is confused but still funny. My grandfather McCracken is three years dead. I have been living in Iowa City—and so, I have just found out, has my grandmother McCracken. That is, I knew that she'd died the autumn before in a head injury center on Cape Cod, but I hadn't known that she willed her body to the University of Iowa Medical School for dissection. (My grandfather hadn't been thrilled by this, but that was my grandmother: if she could do a favor for someone, she would. I imagine she thought of it as not so different from saving the fat off bacon to make soap: don't throw away what could still be made useful.) At any rate, while I was on one side of the river, being educated, she was on the other, educating. In the spring, her church held a memorial service for her. Because so many of the parishioners were elderly, they waited until May, when the ice had melted.

I think of this ceremony as one of the most entertaining moments of one side of my family colliding with the other. My father had come to town, but I drove over with my grandmother in her white Pontiac, a car I would inherit 4 years later—13 years old, 3,000 miles on it. Blanche rode in the passenger's seat. We went to pick up Elizabeth Dubbleya, who came out of the house in what she surely thought was fine funeral wear: the kind of black Reebok walking sneakers that plenty of women convinced themselves in the eighties looked just like regular shoes; a purple running suit;

the giant oriental 1930s clay pin shaped like a mask that she always wore; and a mink cape. She was in her early nineties then.

"Oh," said my grandmother in a voice of doom, "I hate that cape."

Though the cape was possibly *de trop,* the sneakers and the running suit blended in with the clothes on the women of the Cottage Grove Presbyterian Church: other nice running suits, or twenty-year-old polyester knit dresses worn with beige orthopedic shoes. For my stylish grandmother Jacobson, this was just another thing she didn't understand about the Protestants.

The service itself was lovely. The minister spoke lovingly about my grandmother McCracken and read several of her poems. Afterward, we went to the basement for a reception, and congregant after congregant told me what wonderful people my grandparents had been. There wasn't a moment's sadness: we all knew that in some fundamental way, Emily McCracken had no longer been Emily McCracken from the moment she fell in the bathtub.

My uncle Morris Matulef—he was a Polish immigrant and my *mishpocheh*: my mother's sister's husband's father—had come, too, and he sat with me, my grandmother, Blanche, and Elizabeth at one folding table. He opened the foil-wrapped hot sandwich he'd been given: ham and cheese. Morris kept kosher.

"What a wonderful service!" Blanche said. "The rabbi was beautiful."

"Yes," my grandmother Jacobson said absentmindedly, eyeing Morris's sandwich. "You know, they really *should* have thought that someone might be keeping kosher—" Then she looked around and realized she was in a church basement and probably no one should be blamed for serving a hot ham-and-cheese sandwich to someone who had come to services.

"I'm going to tell him," said Blanche.

"What dear?" Cousin Elizabeth asked.

"I'm going to tell the rabbi what a beautiful service it was." Blanche gestured toward the minister.

"No, Blanche," said my grandmother. In those days, she could not bear the idea of strangers knowing that Blanche was senile.

"Why not?" Blanche jumped to her feet. She was in her eighties, but lithe and light footed. My grandmother grabbed her forearm. Blanche broke away.

"Follow her," my grandmother mouthed. Meanwhile, Morris—such a lovely man, and how I miss him, too, and everyone seated at that table—was eating his ham-and-cheese sandwich and smiling at me.

So I followed Blanche, who approached the minister and took his hand. "Oh, Rabbi," she said, "that was so, so lovely. So lovely. I especially liked the story about the lamb."

And the fact is, if you were a little senile, or just not paying attention, the differences between this service at the Cottage Grove Presbyterian Church and one at Temple B'Nai Jesherun might escape your notice: the lack of iconography (no gruesome puppets here!), the plain dome in the sanctuary, the aging congregation, the offers of food and handshakes, the prayers all in English, led by a nice young man wearing a prayer shawl, a lovely young man with a beard and great stores of patience, who is saying to you now, only slightly confused, "Yes. Yes, thank you. Thank you for coming. It's a pleasure. What is your name?"

A Poet in Hollywood

. . . .

by
CAROL MUSKE-DUKES

Not long after I moved to Los Angeles from New York City, I attended a cocktail party with my actor-husband. At the party, which was full of film and TV-industry representatives, a man asked me what I did for a living. I told him that I was a writer. "Right," he said. "Half hour or hour?" I smiled indulgently. "Neither," I said, fixing him with what I like to think of as an Oversoul gaze. "Lifetime." He smiled back. "Oh, you work for cable," he said.

I originally told this story in the pages of the *New York Times Book Review*, minus the guy's rejoinder about cable. I knew that readers east of the San Gabriels would get the TV-program time allocations (they're actually something like twenty-three and forty-eight minutes) but the Lifetime cable network was new at the time and seemed a less accessible reference. I was wrong. One or two serious-minded readers of the serious-minded book review wrote to me, reminding me that I'd missed a punch-line opportunity. We do not lack punch lines about Hollywood, and my interest was not, after all, in dissing my new hometown. My interest lay (and continues to lie) in considering the influence of the manufacture of powerful images on the idea of the subversive. And what art form, historically, in all its avatars, has been more subversive than poetry?

When I first came to L.A., I thought of it as exile, and for some time I remained indifferent to the desert, the verdancy coaxed from desert sands, the strange architecture, the existential freeways. I have gotten more writing done in Los Angeles than I ever accomplished in my many years in New York, because the sense of isolation one feels here as a writer is profound. (It is possible to put together a crowd of friends on a given night, as long as people are willing to drive. Or it's possible to hide out for weeks.) Writers before me have felt this isolation. Some welcome it, some don't; but always, despite the peculiar literary-advocacy groups and boosterish faux bonhomie of "community" in a town that requires a minimum of twenty minutes of speeding solitude to be anywhere, it remains the central fact of daily existence. The ongoing relationship of the writer to reality has been the subject of endless discussion, but a poet's existence in a city whose main industry is the serious production of illusion has not often been explored.

Alienation is the real home of poets and other writers; they work well in adversity, in conflict, in the drafty mansions of displacement. Blake chafed at newly industrialized London ("O Rose, thou art Sick"), and Shelley rejected it as philistine and soul dead. In the same spirit, a century later, Bertolt Brecht, in wartime exile in Los Angeles, wrote these lines:

> On thinking about Hell, I gather
> My brother Shelley found it was a place
> Much like the city of London. I
> Who live in Los Angeles and not in London
> Find, on thinking about Hell, that it must be
> Still more like Los Angeles.

Brecht was wrong. L.A. is not Hell, maybe not even Poet's Hell. It is famous for both beauty and ugliness, but not for its sense of proportion, the key element in creating a poem and a real city. A real city might inspire a tough-minded *terza rima,* even city planning. The question is inevitable for a poet: is L.A. *serious* enough to be Hell, with its Dr. Seussish palm trees and its earth as shaky as liposuction landfill, making it (if it is Hell at all) Hell Lite? O chardonnay and brimstone! O twelve-step Satan!*

---

* To be fair, the argument made historically by writers against L. A. outweighs my lite fancy dramatically. Malcolm Lowry (who lived in Los Angeles off and on throughout the thirties) offered his own view of the city through the eyes of one of the characters in an early novel. The character considers the "barren deathscape of Los Angeles" and "all he could think was that it was a hell, the sort of hell his spirit would have wandered to had he killed himself." William Faulkner, whose famous collision with Hollywood set a critical standard for L.A. distaste, points out to a friend, in *City of Nets,* by Otto Friedrich, "They worship death here. They don't worship money, they worship death." Nathanael West, Pope of his own disinherited, sleazy Vatican, is pictured in Lionel Rolfe's *Literary L.A.* lying abed in sweltering Hollywood summer heat, feeling as if "the whole of Los Angeles were an inferno." He expands this image in *The Day of the Locust.* In the novel's background, an artist paints, prophetically, *The Burning of Los Angeles,* and West comments: "He was going to show the city burning at high noon, so that the flames would have to compete with the desert sun."

. . . .

I can see the Hollywood sign above in the hills (if it's not too smoggy) by walking a block west and glancing north, but other signs, markers of the strange fellowship of poetry and Hollywood are harder to read. Since one would assume a more or less natural antagonism on the part of poetry toward the industry and vice versa, it's startling to find a distinct lack of allergic reaction toward the (*X-File*-ish?) implantation of Hollywood values in the circulatory systems of its poets. As a matter of fact, the ratio of poets to actors in Hollywood would be hard to determine, given the propensity of poets here to identify themselves with Hollywood, and with the Hollywoodization of "venue," i.e., the pumped-up presentation of the once froglike humble poetry reading. ("I'm nobody! Who are you?" asks Emily Dickinson, trusting that her interrogatee will not be "somebody." "How public—like a Frog—/ To tell one's name—the livelong June—/ To an admiring Bog!")

Poets, too, long to be touched by Goddess Fame—which is, after all, the essence of Hollywood's promise. But the seduction of that promise lies not in imitation of empty deities with capped smiles and cue-card conversations. In fact, Hollywood (materializing like Zeus in his most provocative and protean form) is both screen god and ordinary mortal, linked simultaneously to both populist and elitist longings. Nothing that happens in Hollywood is only local. Its power to influence the world is a vast yet intimate power. And poetry (powerless but universal) operates similarly. Poets are servants of the commonplace and arcane force which is the imagination. They know it is possible to *be* anyone or anything.

Certainly, Hollywood's own brand of seduction has already enthralled academia. Witness Camille Paglia, that cultural demagogue, cracking her whip on the covers of her best-selling books; witness the Film Studies overload in colleges and universities across the nation. The curricula of local and national colleges and universities—even before the advent of Cultural Studies—bristled with Film and Lit, Film and Popular Culture, Film and the Fetish, Film and How You Feel About It as literature courses, often wholly supplanting (like Theory) the study of literature itself: the image that ate Beowulf. Professors of contemporary literary ideology (the stylists of literature) might feel a little frisson of importance if a local celebrity asked to sit in on a class (a fairly regular occurrence here), but a larger thrill would involve a crossover book, one that can *celebrify* a typically nerdy academic type, airbrush away the nose hairs and bald spots of predictable academic discourse, provide a jacket photo that argues for an alarming rereading of what we've termed, in the past, *erotic presence.*

"Hollywood" and "commodification" turn up almost interchangeably as terms, and the two often cohabit (marketing implicit now in almost all media productions). But Hollywoodization as a process goes further into the contradictory longings of the pop psyche. To buy into Hollywood is to be seduced but never quite abandoned: pursuit is endless, once through the gates. The transformation from undiscovered to discovered is not just a mythical, miraculous transaction but also homely reassurance about one's personal worth, one's sexual appeal. The Hollywood poet exists, in a way, to dramatize our capacity for paradox, our temptations to be both sought after and iconoclastic, famous and private.

Now poets routinely rise up in spotlights to "perform" their poems, as opposed to reading them. In stand-up poetry, a reading is called a set, as in jazz. The inclination to perform does not derive from a desire to honor the poem's history as oral expression, but to express the self, much the way acting class determines performance value by evocation of emotive content. What is *felt* becomes vastly more important than what has been taught about the art itself, what poetry is. ("I was visibly moved," a Hollywood star remarked recently, staring into the camera.) Just as the study of film (a medium that is two dimensional, existing wholly within time) replaces the study of an art that is multidimensional, as re-created in all the senses, outside of the conventional borders of time, in the limitless chambers of the imagination.

That many poets drift out of these limitless chambers toward the glittering cogs of the image-making machine (or what Budd Schulberg, in his famous 1959 essay, called "the insistent hum of the dream factories") is in no way surprising. Film is immediate; film seems (compared to an art that counts syllables) instantly gratifying. Although in Hollywood's past, Faulkner, Graham Greene, and even Brecht were seduced by the idea of writing *for* Hollywood, certain contemporary poets may be the first examples of individuals writing to *be* Hollywood, writing as actors. (When Wallace Stevens said that poems were actors and books, theaters, he was thinking of the "poem of the act of the mind," the voice—the same voice one uses to read aloud when one is alone—inside the head.)

Frankly, what is less understandable is the way Hollywood has slouched toward poetry of late, pursuing poetry as an acquirable taste, like a Cohiba cigar. (A hot gift among producer types now is a rare book, bound in vellum, a trophy made of pages.)

A very successful and insinuative Hollywood film agent once asked me if Helen Vendler (the distinguished literary critic) had ever reviewed my poems. (This agent had been calling me nonstop, asking me to lunch and

. . . .

drinks at tony restaurants, passionately listing his qualifications to represent me: *me*—an internationally unknown author of poems and two midlist novels, the second of which he thought was "real literature" and wanted to represent on its way to becoming a film.) The Vendler question came some weeks into his pursuit, when my appeal had somewhat dissipated, and after he'd successfully stalked (as he might have put it) some gamier literary prey.

In a way, his question offers a heartening view of the extent to which, in the last two decades, American poetry has assumed a new and accessible public role. Yet it also dramatizes the degree to which this new public role has done nothing to threaten a set of drearily familiar assumptions about the marketing of influence in America. It is obvious that the question not only seeks to determine value through endorsement, it reveals precisely what my one-time admirer wished to reveal about himself as a negotiating tactic: that he was, and is, in the privileged position of buyer, that he is an informed consumer, savvy. That he believes he can see into and judge a world that has traditionally resisted the scrutiny of noniniti-ates (that is to say those unwilling to read or love poetry on its own terms, rather than those who call poetry obscure or elitist) based on a transfusion of what he thinks is buzz. And which is, after all, *buzz*.

If a Hollywood agent can Vendlerize without Cliff's Notes, perhaps we've reached Shelley's ideal *backward*—poets are not the "unacknowl-edged legislators of the world," they are, in fact, its unacknowledged lob-byists. *We may not be popular, but we have a rate of exchange, a currency; we can buy into the legislation of public taste.*

That Helen Vendler has never campaigned to be the belles-lettres Black-well has not saved her finely tuned criticism from being reduced and quoted as a kind of Best and Worst Dressed status-izing device. Still, the appearance of her name in the mouth of a Hollywood agent demonstrates not only how literary Hollywoodish poetry has become, but how literary Hollywood is striving to be. Audiences watch the credits scroll, note that they will be viewing "Jane Austen's *Pride and Prejudice*," "Henry James's *The Wings of the Dove,* Bram Stoker's *Dracula.*" (If they begin filming poems, will we see Anonymous's *Twa Corbies?*). In *Four Weddings and a Funeral,* an Auden poem is given a cameo role and *Il Postino* is a hymn to the great Chilean poet Pablo Neruda. Guess ads routinely use facsimile poems.

Martin Amis's darkly hilarious short story "Career Move" imagines a

parallel universe in which poems are given the cachet and box-office potential of screenplays:

> He had taken his sonnet to Rodge at Red Giant and turned it into an ode.
> When that didn't work out he went to Mal at Monad, where they'd gone for
> the villanelle. The villanelle had become a triolet, briefly, with Tim at TCT,
> before Bob at Binary had him rethink it as a rondeau. When the rondeau
> didn't take, Luke lyricized it and got Mike to send it to Joe. Everyone, in-
> cluding Jake Endo, thought that now was surely the time to turn it back
> into a sonnet.

The monolithic gaze has at last (it would seem) window-peeped into
a once-hermetic world, turning outward with a Polaroid shot of poetry,
with a pricetag on its ass—indistinguishable, finally, from any other object
of development potential. Is that it?

Or is it that we see poetry stepping out of its elfin grot, smiling for the
cameras? Poets themselves are unsure what is happening. They have witnessed cometlike trajectories of names made overnight (defying the comforting tradition that assures all poets that their reputations will be
established years after their deaths). A poetry student asks about the
"market value" of a book of poems based on "personal confession"; a student asks about the "contacts" necessary to build a "career." "Of course
we were ambitious in our youth," a poet friend said to me recently, "but
poetry was what you loved, not what you built a 'career' on. Yes, there
were kingmakers and poison tasters and empire builders, but their world
was a tornado in a teacup."

One has only to pick up a copy of the recently made-over *Poets &*
Writers Magazine (once a meek and mild insider newsletter) and read a
few of its through-the-grinder puff pieces, its writer profiles, slavishly imi-
tative of celebrity interviews; its horoscope columns, providing advice
from the same heavens once apostrophized by Dickinson and Whitman
and Tu Fu on how to score big publication-wise to grasp that the teacup is
now the size of a chamber pot at *Vanity Fair.*

> Just remember in November when you're working harder than anyone else
> (whether you're climbing the corporate ladder or the Matterhorn or simply
> writing a novel that gets longer and longer): Keep working. Mars is in your
> sign. . . .

After all, if one is "simply writing a novel" (versus climbing that all-
challenging corporate ladder), it is imperative that one get a head's-up
from the zodiac.

. . . .

This rhetoric is not unique—writers' conferences lure paying poet-students by offering sessions with agents (*agents* for poets?), publication panels, tips on how to make contacts, acquire networking skills. *(We can sell your sestinas!)*

Do literary wannabees appear to be a dismissible market? They are not. *Any* market is a market, I suppose, but the consumer potential of all those who want to write (versus say, those who want to *read*) seems limitless. For all the recent racket about how well poetry is selling, university and small press editors offer instructive anecdotes about poetry contests that attract thousands of applicants but sell only a few hundred copies of the book chosen for publication. Everyone wants to write; far fewer want to *read*.

There are further ironies in the war of Real Literature versus Everybody. There is the dueling duality of the academic versus the performance poet, a battle promoted by "community-minded" poets who feel that those who teach in an academic setting are privileged, status-quo minded, well connected in terms of contacts, and not of the people. The irony here is that academics, in turn, tend to look on writers as interlopers and "primary text" producers, therefore not classifiable in their own self-referential jargon. Academics often do not want to acknowledge the poet-critic. In a recent essay in the *Writer's Chronicle* entitled "Of the Living Dead: The Poet-Critic in an Age of Theory," Sandra Gilbert asks, "What has happened to the poet-critic—traditionally our foremost theorist of literature—in the age of . . . hegemonic theory? . . . From Sidney to Wordsworth and Arnold and Wilde, there were no such entities as 'English Departments.'. . . While in the last third of the century, the body of specialized writing traditionally known as 'literature' has continued to expand with no more than the usual changes in mode and mannner, the social and cultural roles of literary thinkers have been notably transformed by their institutional affiliations." Poets are not considered, by this group, to be literary thinkers. "Gradually the writers in [creative writing] programs began to seem more and more like *idiot savants* or 'wild children,' savages on display for the edification and education of the sophisticated professionals who produce true 'theory.'" And though the author is considered to be dead by many of these sophisticated professionals, Gilbert believes (as one believes in the existence of fairies) that there are "poet-critics still among us: 'literary thinkers' who can and must interpret the deeds of the imagination. . . ." A further complicating factor is that some academics wish to be "performative" themselves—a sobering thought.

Thus, the poet who happens to teach college students is doubly jeopardized, subject to misrepresentation, and caught in a binary squeeze of misapprehension.*

At the same time as writers are lionized, they are unwelcome presences at the banquet. Self-perpetuating "arts" societies, agencies, and clubs have given themselves face-lifts and set new fund-raising goals, offering whatever's hot as topics for their panels and round tables and conferences: how to sell one's words *and* market diversity. But don't overemphasize reading, the life of solitude, the writer's necessary apprenticeship to a craft.

Recently there's been an appropriation by poetry itself of billboards at strategic points around my town. (Educating the commuter about poetry here in L.A. is a different process than it might be in, say, Chicago or other cities, where enthusiasts can slap poems up next to subway and bus hemorrhoid ads. We are not a mass-transit city and never will be. Drivers must be confronted where they live.) The billboards are emblazoned with short poems or lines from poems by Emily Dickinson, T. S. Eliot, Wallace Stevens, Mark Strand, Charles Bukowski, and others. At twelve thousand a pop for billboard rental, it seems likely that Poets Anonymous (the group taking credit for the displays) is more likely Producers Anonymous (those literary lions!) or Wealthy Would-Be Poets Anonymous (read rich actors), since it is a sad fact that most poets' expendable liquid income rarely exceeds the high two figures. (The myth of poetry's incorruptibility is built on this famed lack of reward by the material world, but this too is changing as huge foundation grants and "genius" fellowships and substantial reading fees grow commonplace for poets.)

It was mildly instructive to observe how Hollywood absorbed these twenty-foot-high linguistic fragments. Almost immediately a local religious group put up an imitation with a stirring bit from Scripture, attributed to "God" rather than, say, Charles Bukowski. I conducted an

---

* My own school, the University of Southern California, provides a case in point. Of five hundred English Department undergraduate majors who are declared, over half are in creative writing. Although this kind of huge majority clearly adds up, making our English Department in cold reality (though no one would dare whisper it) a Creative Writing Department with an English emphasis. And although creative writing brings in the tuition dollars, providing the departmental income, there are only five full-time creative writing faculty members versus thirty-some English faculty. There are always obstacles to hires in Creative Writing. As in a Thurberesque cartoon of a frightened Mom and Pop, who sit in their parlor, refusing to look at the enormous pink elephant seated across the room from them, creative writing is the thing that cannnot be recognized.

. . . .

informal poll at a gas station and discovered that many motorists glancing up at the poem fragments thought that they were reading ads—and indeed, the Calvin Klein underwear and Comme des Garcons come-ons on adjacent billboards whispered non sequitors, posed rhetorical questions, or flung out erotic challenges and appeared (given our postmodern crush on disruption) somehow as close kin to the poetry excerpts in drive-by consciousness. I repeated the Dickinson billboard lines to a gentleman at the pump next to mine:

Opinion is a flitting thing—
But Truth, outlasts the Sun—
If then we cannot own them both
Possess the oldest one—

—1455

He cocked his head, then ventured, "United Colors of Benetton, right?" This was an astute guess from a man living in a milieu rife with cryptic selling texts. What clues might he have intercepted to tell him that this was art, and beyond that, not runway art or Hollywood idea repo? What clues might be available to a population now largely tone deaf to heightened language, blind to thematic imagery, and uniquely positioned to accept marketing's messages onscreen, online, or on big signs? (After all, the Marlboro Man had presided over Sunset Strip on his venerable billboard for years.) Need-generating fragments had stolen what looked like poetry's fire, and poetry's fire was not burning that brightly.

The noble intent of those who plastered poems twenty feet high for all to read, is, in itself, the argument for originality based on the most primitive and egalitarian of symbols—the big sign with messages on it. Certainly an ambience is created, but one not entirely connected to anything. Poetry on billboards offers yet another chance for interpretation without meaning. But the possibilities of meaning, when and if they come, come hand in hand with the politics of meaning. If one said Emily Dickinson's poem was superior to a Calvin Klein meditation, for instance, one might be accused of elitism. (One can live like a Brahman here and still be "of the people"—the irony is that being accused of elitism would precipitate a quick loss of status.) "Yikes," said my gas-station interviewee when he heard the words confronting him were a poem. "I didn't know they could use billboards for grammar."

Poetry's new visibility comes not from any grassroots coffee-house movement or from a billboard, stand-up sensibility, or writers'-conference

.   .   .   .

renaissance, it comes from a new idea of acquisition. Performative acqui-sition: *I can have that, I can act that.* Here is the *sheen* of poetry, here is its patina, its silver screen.

Here is the evolving definition before our eyes—twenty feet high—unreadable by most souls, yet still available to us, by which I mean *see-able,* purchasable, even as those figures of mystery, film stars, on their towering screens, are seeable and purchasable—perhaps exactly to that degree.

Leaving Rwanda

. . . .

by
DERICK BURLESON

1.

"Let us go then, you and I, when the evening is spread out against the sky like a patient etherized upon a table," I say.

"Margaret are you grieving over goldengrove unleaving? Leaves, like the things of man, you with your fresh thoughts care for, can you?" Anita says.

"Snow falling and night falling fast, oh, fast in a field I looked into going past," Thadée says.

We huddle together around the gearshift knob of a Mitsubishi bus as if it's a campfire, shivering against the damp chill. Outside a light rain is falling. Behind us fifty of our friends, neighbors, students, and colleagues sleep or whisper in groups of two or three. Our bus is the last in a line of ten buses. The windows fog over with our breath, and the students who couldn't find a place, or who have chosen not to find a place, pace the night away in long circles from the barricade at one end of town to the barricade at the other and back again. When they pass the fogged windows, their blurred outlines look like ghosts.

This is Vunga, a small town in northern Rwanda, just past midnight and into the early morning of February 7, 1993. Only one road leads through the narrow valley. Shops and houses are lined up along the road in the shadows of crowding hills. One water hydrant. No telephone. Hills lean in, their broad shoulders letting in a little light from the full moon glinting silver through the low clouds of mist and light rain.

We are refugees. Ten kilometers behind us the battle for Ruhengeri rages on, and we can still hear the rumble of mortar shells and heavy machine-gun fire. We figure they've taken the campus by now. We are refugees being held hostage by a group of our own students. So far today, I've been shaken awake by explosions after an hour of sleep, I've listened to mortar shells falling a few hundred yards away, had a gun pointed at me, and have had a confrontation with the leaders of the thousand students holding the rest of us hostage, the same guys I played basketball with two days ago. I'm cold, I'm wet from being ordered at gunpoint out of the bus into a driving rainstorm, and I'm dying for a cigarette since I ran out hours ago and the shop owners have closed their shops and refuse to sell any of us anything. There aren't enough buses to carry all of the students, and the students who won't fit on the buses refuse to let those of us who are in the buses leave them behind in Vunga, where, at any moment, all of us might be massacred, killed by the people who live here and who consider us to be outsiders. Or we might be killed in the crossfire if the battle drifts our way. Nobody is coming to rescue us.

In the back of the bus, our friends Roger and Fulgence huddle with their girlfriends, whispering under blankets. Eugene is driving his own bus, so he's there, like me, behind the wheel, in case we need to make another run for it. My bus has about one-sixteenth of a tank of gas. This is also true for the other buses. We won't be running far.

Thadée Ntihinuzgwa, our friend and fellow teacher from the English department, leans forward from his seat behind us and says, "I can't sleep. Do you feel like talking?" So Anita and Thadée and I lean together and talk for a while. Then we begin to quote all the poems and parts of poems we can remember.

2.

"Stasis in darkness. Then the substanceless blue pour of tor and distances," Anita says.

"April is the cruelest month, breeding lilacs out of the dead land, mixing memory and desire, stirring dull roots with spring rain." Thadée says.

"O chestnut tree, great-rooted blossomer, are you the leaf, the blossom or the bole?" I say.

Anita and I, newly married before we left Kansas, had lived in Rwanda for a year and eight months, Peace Corps volunteers teaching at both campuses of the National University of Rwanda—one in Butare in the south, the other in Ruhengeri in the north. A little more than a year after we and the other twenty-four Peace Corps volunteers were evacuated from Rwanda in 1993, a small, highly organized group launched a plan that had been devised and meticulously implemented all around us during the previous two years. Lists had been made. Secret meetings in the middle of the night. On April 6, 1994 President Juvenal Habyarimana, returning from signing power-sharing accords in Arusha, was assassinated, his jet shot down as he returned to Kigali. Within an hour of the president's death, extremist militia manned blockades across Kigali, and the attacks on Tutsi and politically moderate Hutu began. Death squads roamed the streets, armed with lists of the names of those to be killed.

In the next hundred days, one million people were murdered. This was not a war. Most of those who died were unarmed. Most were hacked to death with machetes. No one knows the exact death toll. No one ever will. I say one million since that's what Rwandans say. The Western media usually say 500,000 to 800,000. Among the dead were our colleagues, our students, our friends.

3.

"Suddenly I realize that if I stepped out of my body I would break into blossom," I say.

"I saw the best minds of my generation destroyed by madness, starving hysterical naked," Thadée says.

"We real cool. We left school. We lurk late. We strike straight," Anita says.

We met Roger Kalisa Rusangwa Remera in Bukavu, Zaire (now the Democratic Republic of Congo), just across Lake Kivu from Rwanda. Even though Roger was Rwandan, he was finishing high school in Zaire because it cost less. *Petit Séminaire,* Roger's school, also housed the Peace Corps training center where we had been studying French seven hours a day, six days a week. The first thing he said to me was, "Whew. Your French is really bad."

Roger graduated and we finished our training at the same time, so when we moved across the border to our new house, Roger appointed himself our personal guide in all things Rwandan. And, after a short visit to his home in Kigali, he moved in with us to begin the huge task of setting up our household and of teaching us all of the million things that we needed to know and that the Peace Corps hadn't taught us: where to buy a bed, how much to pay for mangoes, how to dance the intricate dance of Rwandan body language and social customs.

Visiting is at the core of Rwandan culture, and a real visit can last for weeks. Roger had been staying with us for about a month, and we were beginning to wonder if he would ever leave when we mentioned that our first wedding anniversary was coming up in a few days. "I was going to leave tomorrow," he said. "But now I must stay to help you celebrate. I couldn't think of leaving you alone for such a big occasion." We set the timer on the camera and still have a picture of us all having our anniversary dinner together. The worst thing that can happen to a person in Rwanda is to be left alone.

As I write this, our tenth wedding anniversary is a couple of weeks away. Roger is moving from Houston, where he's been living with us for four years, to Philadelphia to take a job as an administrator for the American Friends Service Committee, Africa Program. I mention, feeling sad about his moving, that he's going to miss our tenth anniversary. "I'll send you a card," he says. In many ways, Roger has become an American. Roger has been granted, after an epic battle with the American Embassy in Rwanda and with the Immigration and Naturalization Service here, political asylum in the United States.

He never has to go back to Rwanda unless he chooses to. From what he's said, he doesn't want to. Not yet, anyway. "It's still too tough for me to go back to that place," he says. "To see all those places again, it would make me have bad memories."

The last time we saw Roger before we met him again on the other side of customs at the Houston Intercontinental Airport in late June 1997, he was with Fulgence and Eugene, waving good-bye as we and all the other Peace Corps volunteers were evacuated from Rwanda. A few minutes before that, Roger and I had run a race for a couple of hundred yards down the asphalt runway. We'd always said we'd see one day who could run faster, and this was our last chance. As Eugene and Anita cheered and Fulgence marked the finish line, we clumped down the runway as hard as we could go. I won. To this day Roger claims that he let me win. And then Anita and I and the twenty-four other Americans climbed the stairs onto the plane. We took off and looked down on the tiny figures of our waving friends and the green thousand hills of Rwanda for what was, for most of us, the last time.

. . . .

4.

"Things fall apart; the center cannot hold; mere anarchy is loosed upon the world, the blood-dimmed tide is loosed, and everywhere the ceremony of innocence is drowned," I say.

"I heard a fly buzz—when I died—The stillness in the room was like the stillness in the air—between the heaves of storm," Anita says.

"In a dark time, the eye begins to see, I meet my shadow in the deepening shade; I hear my echo in the echoing wood," Thadée says.

There's a kind of waking up when you've been dreaming and you don't know if you're really awake or if you're still in the dream, dreaming that you're awake. In front of our house across the street from campus I come back to myself this way. It's 3 A.M., February 6, 1993, the morning before we'll be held hostage. Roger and I have been asleep for maybe an hour after finally getting back home from the volleyball tournament in Kigali at 2 A.M., far past the 11 P.M. curfew. The government soldiers had passed our bus through each checkpoint only when the students begged and showed them the trophy our team won. When we arrived in Ruhengeri, the town seemed deserted, the checkpoints abandoned. As we turned toward campus, a squad of soldiers stopped us. They boarded the bus, grim, guns pointing, and checked everyone's identity cards before finally letting us go on. We should have known then that something was going to happen soon.

When I finally wake up in the chilly predawn air, I think it's a joke. "What are we all doing standing here," I ask. *"La musique de guerre,"* Fulgence says. Then we stand there and listen—Anita, Fulgence, Roger, all the neighbors—machine guns, mortar rounds. I'm still waking up. I don't remember getting out of bed and walking down the hall through the living room and out the front door. When we speak, we speak in whispers.

From where we were, a mile or so away from the battle, we could see the bright streaks of tracers zipping back and forth between armies, hear the heavy rhythm of .50-caliber machine guns, the chatter of small-arms fire, the thumps of mortar rounds and artillery.

When you have to run for your life, you take what seems most important to you at the time. I saw a man carrying only an iron, the hollow kind you put burning charcoal in and then iron your clothes quickly before you burn a hole. Another man had a pig in a burlap sack slung over his shoulder.

Then, standing there with our fellow academics, listening to them discuss in rapid-fire French mixed with Kinyarwandan what exactly must be done, we see a government soldier, weaponless, hopeless, limping by, leaning on a flimsy stick he has snatched somewhere in his panic, limping south as fast as he can with a bloodstained bandage around his calf. When someone asks him about the situation, he shouts "They're coming!" and keeps on limping south as fast as he can.

So we shoulder our bags, turn our backs on the Virunga volcanoes, and join an infinite column of the other refugees stumbling south. Soon we pass the wounded soldier. His bandage is soaked through and the blood's trickling down his ankle, filling his boot. As we walk south the machine-gun fire fades at our backs. We can still hear mortar rounds, but even those explosions seem quieter now, muffled and somehow safe, like the distant thunder of a storm that's already passed. We're four people among the steady stream of a hundred thousand refugees taking up the entire road, everybody loaded with as much they can carry: clothes, water jugs, pots and pans, sacks of beans and maize. Some drive the family cows and goats ahead of them. A tailor carries his sewing machine.

5.

"So much depends upon a red wheel barrow glazed with rain water beside the white chickens," Thadée says.

"About suffering they were never wrong, the old masters," I say.

"Until everything was rainbow, rainbow, rainbow and I let the fish go," Anita says.

When the genocide began, Roger, Fulgence, Eugene, Thadée, their families, and all of our friends and colleagues were caught in the middle. Rwanda quickly became the worst Hell anyone could imagine. While most were killed with machetes, sometimes the militia would give you the option of paying them all of your money to shoot you rather than killing you with a machete, to save them the trouble of looking for your money after you were dead. People were told to gather at churches for safe haven. But then, having gathered all the victims conveniently in one place, soldiers and militia, the Inharamgwe (those who strike together) as they were called, would throw grenades through the windows. One million killed in one hundred days, four hundred and seventeen an hour, the highest rate of murder the planet has ever witnessed. Bodies clogged rivers, clogged the streets, filled churches, covered the floors of schoolrooms. There's a church in Rwanda where they left the bodies as they found them, a memorial, the bodies still sprawled, only bones now, in the postures of their deaths.

While Anita and I, safe at home on the sofa, watched these events transpire on television, Roger lived them. Here's some of what Roger wrote on his application for political asylum in the United States.

> After four long days of walking, we were finally stopped by soldiers at a checkpoint in Butare on April 21, 1994, and the soldiers decided to kill us. It was 5:15 P.M. when the soldier marched my brother and I into the forest. Behind me my brother was pleading with the soldier when he was shot. At the same moment, I turned to see what was happening to my brother, and the same soldier shot me too with his Kalashnikov. I fell down and lost consciousness because I was shot in the arm, the finger, and in my side as I turned to see my brother. Later, I woke up and called my brother, "Remy, Remy," but he didn't reply because he was already dead.
>
> With difficulty I got up and went out of the forest because I wanted to be on the road where someone would find my dead body. The night had already fallen, so no one found me. Minute after minute I waited for my turn to die because I was losing a lot of blood. I couldn't move anymore and I spent all night on the road.

6.

"I wake to sleep, and take my waking slow. I feel my fate in what I cannot fear," I say.

"The soul selects her own society—then—shuts the door," Anita says.

"All changed, changed utterly: a terrible beauty is born," Thadée says.

"Where is that stupid Emmanuel? Where is that stupid van?" Thadée and I wonder several times together. The machine-gun fire and mortar rounds seem quite a bit louder now than they were at 3 A.M. We speculate that the battle's moving in this direction. I can't hear the .50 caliber anymore. Out of ammo maybe.

Most of the students and teachers, including Anita, wait at a church compound a few miles south. We have driven the truck back at the vice rector's request, and now it's off somewhere loading up all the stuff the administrators have deemed worth saving. We were supposed to be picked up a half an hour later by Emmanuel and the van. That was three hours' worth of artillery and mortar bombardment ago.

The day heats up, the sun pricking holes through my scalp. Thadée and

I pick up our bags and go find a spot under a tree. We watch one of the detachments of campus employees build a barricade of rocks at the north gate. The few refugees still moving south down the road keep looking back over their shoulders toward Ruhengeri. The mortar rounds sound like they're falling just over the hill. I keep searching the horizon for dust from the explosions but can't see any.

Thadée tells me he came back to his house to fetch a contest application from the U.S. Embassy's Information Services that he'd forgotten. If he wins, he tells me, he gets to travel to the United States for a conference on American literature and the birthplaces of American writers. The group reads *Huckleberry Finn* and then goes to Hannibal, Missouri, to see where Mark Twain grew up along the mighty Mississippi. We speculate on whether or not the embassy will still give out the prize now that the war's back on again. Thadée hopes so. "Any place is better than here right now," he says, pitching his voice beneath the blast of another mortar shell.

Then a really big one falls. I feel the explosion resonate in my chest and travel out through my legs. I realize I'm standing up, not too far from where Thadée and I had been lounging and talking under the tree moments ago. He's standing beside me, pushing his glasses back up on his nose.

During the last three hours, the mortar barrage has been steadily moving closer. But this last shell is definitely of a different magnitude. Maybe it's a stray. Maybe not. I look around for evidence of the blast, but all the campus buildings are still standing. Thadée and I look at each other, and I know my eyes are at least as big and round as his are. Without a word, we shoulder our bags and start walking south.

We can still see the campus behind us, though, when Emmanuel finally shows up in the van, driving with one hand, pulling nervously on his goatee with the other, smiling as he rolls to a stop beside us.

"Forgive me," he says.

But he won't say where he's been for the last three hours. And it's not until later that afternoon that we learn that, against the advice of every other administrator, the vice rector had dispatched him and the van to stop the 500 or so students who had decided to keep on walking south toward what they considered relative safety. He caught up with them at Vunga. We return to the church and wait for the buses and armed escort the other vice rector at the university's southern campus has promised to send to rescue us all. And we wait.

And wait. "You have the keys?" Roger asks for the third time in the

. . . .

last hour. We have a plan: if all else fails, we'll load our group onto the bus and make a run for it on our own.

"Yes. I have the keys," I say, patting my pocket to be sure.

It's late afternoon when the big green buses finally arrive from Butare. The six soldiers who make up the armed escort are drunk. Only one has a gun. The students stampede before the buses even roll to a stop in the church courtyard, shoving the drunken soldiers out of the way. Some jump up the sides and pull themselves in through the open windows. When we see what's happening, we all run for our Mitsubishi.

Word of our plan has gotten around. We loaded all of our bags onto the bus hours ago, and several people noticed. So when the scramble starts, all of our designated group, many of their friends, and several stray people who nobody seems to know run to our bus. I unlock the driver's side door with the key, let Anita in ahead of me, then climb up and pull the lever to open the side door. Roger's outside, trying to calm everyone down, but when the door folds open, he's carried along in the rush and shoved through.

And at that moment, two months late, the rainy season begins, complete with hail and lashing wind.

Even worse, Marcel, a guy we already don't trust and don't like, a guy who, through his ineptitude, almost got Roger and me killed last night coming home from the volleyball tournament, tries to take a leadership role as usual, gets caught up in trying to direct traffic, and forgets he has to get onto a bus. When he realizes the last bus is about to leave, he leaps into the middle of the road, waving for us to stop. I groan and brake. The rest of the caravan disappears around a curve. Marcel climbs in through the passenger-side door, looking like a drowned possum. Anita gives him a murderous stare, but scoots up onto the backpack we'd laid over the console and lets him climb in. By the time we're rolling forward again, the rest of the caravan has disappeared.

The hail lets up, but the rain kicks in harder than ever. Even on high, the worn wiper blades can't keep up with the onslaught. Anita leans forward, squinting through the streaked windshield and copilots from her perch on top of the bag. I turn hard right when she yells that we've reached the road.

The Mitsubishi, the oldest bus on campus, was built to hold about twenty-five passengers. But in the mad rush, at least fifty have packed themselves and their bags inside. When I hammer the gearshift up to second, the Mitsubishi bucks, chokes, and then sluggishly struggles on under the overload. Everyone cheers. I glance up into the rearview mirror and all I can see are people. I try not to think about the fact that if I miss a curve in the already muddy road, or slip off the steep shoulder, or miss a gear at this next uphill curve to the right, some of those people are bound to get hurt.

The windshield begins to fog over, so I ask Anita if she can find the defroster. She switches it on, but nothing happens. She reaches up and swipes a clear spot with her hand. We've gone maybe two kilometers and still haven't caught up with the caravan, even though I've worked the Mitsubishi up to third gear. Through the slap of the rotten wipers, I can see a bridge ahead. And the two soldiers who step from the sides of the bridge to block the way.

7.

"For here there is no place that does not see you. You must change your life," Thadée says.

"The art of losing isn't hard to master," Anita says.

"It is difficult to get the news from poems, yet men die miserably every day for lack of what is found there," I say.

We came home to Kansas City and ate fast food for the first time in two years. It made us sick, but we kept eating it anyway because it tasted good and that's what everyone else ate. We found jobs teaching English, bought a car. We tried to tell our friends and families about what happened, how we lived, all about two years in Rwanda complete with pictures and slide shows. We began to notice that after about five minutes of this, their eyes glazed over. We began sentences with the phrase, "Well, in Rwanda. . . ." We spoke French to each other and called things by their Rwandan names. Whatever we were, we were no longer Americans—not, at least, in the way we'd been before. One day, we have a breakdown in the cereal aisle of our neighborhood Price Chopper, staring at the rows upon rows of bright cereal boxes, too much plentitude. Unable to make a choice, we both burst into tears. "All right," Anita's little sister Leah, who is shopping with us, says. "Fucking Lucky Charms, then."

8.

"Think of the long trip home. Should we have stayed at home and thought of here? Where should we be today?" Anita says.

"Some say the world will end in fire, some say in ice," Thadée says.

"Fool, said my Muse to me, look in thy heart, and write," I say.

. . . .

The machine gun isn't quite pointed at me. The soldier gestures with it for me to get out, the muzzle tracing a slow circle. I try to smile.

"Don't get out," Anita says.

The other soldier circles the bus, stands at Marcel's door and shouts in Kinyarwanda.

"Get out. *Sortez,*" Anita tells him.

Marcel shakes his head and greets the soldier, *"Miriwe,"* but the soldier, unsmiling and not even pretending to be polite, unslings his rifle.

"Sort," Anita orders him again. "It's raining," Marcel whines. "I'll get wet."

"Get out!" Anita yells again in French. "You're not sugar. You're not going to melt."

The whole bus erupts in laughter and even the soldier smiles through the rain pouring off the hood of his camouflage slicker. I pull out my passport and hold it up to the window for the soldier on my side to see. But he shakes his head and gestures again with the rifle. So I open the door and climb down.

And instantly get soaked. The rain's blasting from every direction at once, even upward, drenching every inch of me there is to drench, rivers pouring down my face and into my eyes. The soldier smiles, holds out his hand for my passport, glances at it, and then gestures again with his rifle. I climb back aboard, pouring water. In the meantime, the other soldier has given up on getting Marcel out of the bus, and told him to open the folding door instead. The soldier has climbed aboard and is busy checking identity cards. He grabs a woman I don't know and pushes her off the bus where she stumbles and falls into the mud. Someone hands up her bag, and the soldier throws it out behind her.

The bus has gone quiet as a funeral, and the rain beating at it from all sides sounds like a drum roll. Anita looks pissed off and scared all at once, scarlet flaming each cheekbone, eyes open wide and flashing blue sparks. I turn and look at Thadée. He's looking at his feet, but watching the soldier from the corner of his eye, his usual chestnut color gone grayish, as if he'd spread his face with ashes.

Roger murmurs something in Kinyarwanda, his voice low and pleading. The soldier whips around to stare at him, but then lowers his rifle. He shrugs to the other soldier who's walked around the bus to join him, and then steps down and motions us on. I shift into first and ease us across the creaking wooden bridge, the river beneath us boiling muddy with runoff. As soon as we're out of earshot, the bus explodes in cheers.

I don't know what happened to the woman. Roger told me later that, even though she had her identity card, the soldier found something wrong with her papers. The last I saw of her was her rain-blurred image in the side mirror, bent against the wind and rain, trudging back the way we'd come, back toward the war.

9.

"Life, friends, is boring. We must not say so," I say.

"She sang beyond the genius of the sea. The water never formed to mind or voice, like a body wholly body," Anita says.

"What instruments we have agree the day of his death was a dark cold day," Thadée says.

For months after images of the genocide filled American TV screens, we thought Roger was dead. Then the phone rang in the middle of the night. It was Roger. *"Je suis vivant,"* he said. *"Mais Remy est mort."* Then he said it again. He'd made it out of Rwanda and into Zaire then to Burundi. Still suffering from infected wounds and starving, he walked, ran, and swam across the borders of three countries. He weighed exactly half of what he does now.

When we left Rwanda, I gave Roger my old belt, which he still has. Its holes run from near the end all the way to a point so close to the buckle it wouldn't go around either one of our thighs now. He's taking it to Philadelphia with him, and says he'll keep it in the years to come. Its holes reveal the histories of both of our bodies. The hole nearest the buckle reminds us how, having survived genocide, having been shot, standing up and walking again toward the border out of the Country of Death, he was still as close as he'd ever been to not being.

10.

"Beauty is truth, truth beauty—that is all ye know on earth, and all ye need to know," Thadée says.

"I should have been a pair of ragged claws scuttling across the floors of silent seas," I say.

"I want to do with you what spring does with the cherry trees," Anita says.

We bounce around the corner and Anita shouts "What the hell is that?" swiping madly at the fogged windshield with one hand and holding

. . . .

on with the other. I downshift and squint through my fogged glasses. Something's blocking the road. Again.

As the bus slows, I slam the gearshift up into first, ignoring the grind of gears, and see a mass of people standing behind a barricade of 55-gallon oil drums and logs. We roll to a stop and I clutch, gunning the engine to keep it going. People swarm the bus, waving their arms and shouting.

"*Allez! Allez!*" Marcel screams, panicking.

"Run 'em over!" Anita shouts.

I pop the clutch and we surge forward, people leaping up in front of us and slamming into the windshield. I clutch again, and the bus rocks back.

"OK. Maybe we shouldn't run them over," Anita says.

"*La route est bloquée! La route est bloquée!*" several people shout from the crowd, slamming their fists against the bus for emphasis. I recognize some of my students.

"But why is the road blocked?" Anita shouts back.

"*La route est bloquée! La route est bloquée!*" they shout again.

I sigh, open the door, and step down into the crowd.

"*La route est bloquée!*" he screams in my face. I recognize Gatera, a student I've played basketball with.

As soon as I step off the bus, the wall of people surrounds me, melting out of the way and falling in behind as I walk toward the makeshift barricade of logs and barrels. This situation calls for calm rationality. I am calm and rational. My only mission is to discover why these students are blocking the road, and to convince them not to block the road anymore so I can drive our bus through the barricade and get on with the business of running away from the war.

"*Pourquoi la route est bloquée?*" I ask.

Gatera seems puzzled by this, wrinkling his forehead in thought. The crowd is quieter now, the closest people so close I can feel their breath on the back of my neck, those behind standing on tiptoe and leaning forward, straining to hear what we'll say.

On the basketball court Gatera was a loudmouth. And a ball hog. He'd dribble the length of the court and drive single-mindedly toward the basket, where he would usually miss the shot. After a while, nobody would pass to him, and he only got the ball off rebounds. He shaved his head, something few Rwandans did past the age of twelve. I didn't like his looks. I didn't like him.

"Because we say so," he finally answers.

"And?" I ask.

"Because we say so and because there's not enough buses for every-body. And because we're not staying here all night alone." With each phrase his voice rises until he's screaming and spitting, anger turning his face ugly. The crowd rumbles.

"We all go or nobody goes!" Gatera screams.

I can feel my cloak of calm rationality begin to fray at the edges. I'd never liked Gatera to begin with and now he's screaming in my face like the arrogant son of a bitch I've always known he was. I'm wet and cold and tired and enough is enough.

"Let us through," I say.

"No," Gatera says and crosses his arms and smirks. "Nobody goes through."

"What gives you the right to keep us here?" When I say "you," I em-phasize the word a little and tap him on the chest with my finger.

"This is none of your business," he says, stressing the "your" and tap-ping me back.

"What the hell is that supposed to mean?" I shout. "We're stuck here just the same as you because you won't let us through."

"You," he says, poking me again, "are not one of us."

"Fuck you," I say in English.

"You are not from here," he says. "Use your eyes. You are white, and we," gesturing in a sweeping motion, "we are black."

The crowd rumbles assent.

Or at least it must have. I couldn't hear its thousand voices, or even see the people, some of them my own students, those voices belonged to. I couldn't see the other buses parked in a line along the road through town, couldn't see the houses and shops that lined the road, or the people who lived there, people who had refused to sell food or tea or cigarettes, who had locked their doors and shuttered their windows when the first strangers walked into town, people who had, a month before, slaugh-tered dozens of their Tutsi neighbors. I couldn't see the steep hills behind the shops brooding over the narrow valley, couldn't see the pale blotch of afternoon sun that had broken momentarily through the low clouds dis-appearing behind those hills. I could only see Gatera and feel the need to wrap my hands around his throat and squeeze until his beady eyes bulged out of their sockets.

As I reach for him, I feel two arms snake around my own throat and drag me backward.

. . . .

"Stop it, Derick," Roger hisses in my ear. "You're crazy. They're getting ready to tear you into a thousand pieces."

I turn and see that Fulgence has me on the other side. Then I hear Anita holler, "Derr-rrick," and see her waving out of the bus window. We walk over to her.

"What happened?" she wants to know.

"I'm not quite sure," I say.

"He was being a fool," Roger says.

11.

"Let me not to the marriage of true minds admit impediments," Anita says.

"I shot the Albatross," I say.

"The world is too much with us; late and soon, getting and spending, we lay waste our powers," Thadée says.

When I ask Roger about that night we spent in Vunga, he says, "Why do you want to make me remember all that stuff?"

"Because I have to write this essay," I say. "And besides, it's not bad compared to what happened later."

He says, "Yeah," and we laugh. What else can you do when you remember those times you easily could have died but didn't. When people were dying around you, but you didn't. Then he says that he remembers the hardest part about Vunga was deciding who would go when the American Embassy rescued us. Only the American Embassy never rescued us, I point out. (They got lost in the dark and rain, and when everyone told them they were driving toward a war, they turned around and drove back to Kigali.) He says, "Yeah. And then we decided to all stay together."

When Roger decided to leave Rwanda and come live with us in Houston, we began, night after night, to hear what had really happened.

When he woke up, Roger told me late one night, the grass he was sprawled in seemed as tall as trees and everything seemed far away, like he was looking down a dark tunnel. He called out to his brother. He heard Remy take one last rattling breath, then nothing.

Roger had been shot through the arm. That bullet spun him around. The next grazed his side and he fell. The soldier came up to deal the *coup de grâce,* and stabbed Roger with his bayonet. He was wearing a raincoat, and the soldier had mistakenly stabbed the coat instead of Roger. Still not satisfied, the soldier aimed his gun at Roger's head and pulled the trigger. Roger threw up his hands and covered his head at the last instant. The only thing we can figure is that the bullet hit his little finger and exploded without penetrating his skull. He was literally a pinkie away from dying then. The concussion knocked him unconscious. His head was covered with blood from his exploded little finger. Finally sure that Roger was dead, the soldier left.

Sometime later, Roger woke up. The grass around him seemed tall as trees. Everything looked far away. He stood up and looked down. There was his wallet, empty, lying in the mud, after the soldiers had gone through it and found nothing except his identity card and passport pictures of us. Roger looked down at the bright squares of Anita and me, staring up at him from the mud. He looked at Remy's body. What could he have thought? He turned and walked back up to the road.

12.

"I know the bottom, she says. I know it with my great taproot," Anita says.

"Let be be finale of seem. The only emperor is the emperor of ice-cream," Thadée says.

"Once out of nature I shall never take my bodily form from any natural thing," I say.

Maybe when we're away from the place we think of as home, we're more willing to fall in love, to find home again in our new places. We loved Rwanda. We loved many of the people we met there. I loved Roger and all of his family, and still do. I know the names of some of the dead. They were our friends, our students, our colleagues, the family that adopted us, people we loved and who loved us back. I know the names of the dead.

I also know the names of some of the murderers.

When the genocide came, the intellectuals, both Hutu and Tutsi, were among the first to die, their names at the top of the lists. Most of our fellow teachers and our students at the National University are dead. Most of our friends are dead. Most of Roger's family is dead.

Some of our friends survived. Eugene escaped. Thadée escaped and is finishing a Ph.D. in Wales.

Marcel, like several of our colleagues at the university, participated in the genocide. When Roger returned to Rwanda, he saw Marcel on the streets of Butare, and even though Marcel begged and groveled, denounced him. The last we know of Marcel, he was being escorted away with a soldier on either arm.

Roger lives in Philadelphia now.

Fulgence, on the run and trying to hide, was caught and murdered.

13.

"Tonight I can write the saddest lines," I say.

"And gathering swallows twitter in the skies," Thadée says.

"We must love one another or die," Anita says.

When the sun sets behind the hills, everything goes pitch-black. No electricity in Vunga. Later the moon rises and casts everything in silver through the low clouds.

I'm wet and shivering inside the raincoat I dug out of the backpack for warmth. It's been raining steadily since sundown. As many students as possible have packed themselves into the buses. When I look in the rearview mirror, I can see rows of heads pillowed on bags of clothes, leaning against the windows. I can hear the murmur of Kinyarwanda from the back, and know that at least a few of us are still awake. The students who haven't managed to claim a space on the bus huddle under the overhanging eves of the few shops that have porches. A few have been pacing since dark, from barricade to barricade, from one end of town to the other, pacing, heads hung under the heavy drizzle. Through the fogged windows of the bus, they look like ghosts as they pass.

I scoot further down in the seat, trying to discover a little extra legroom under the steering wheel, lean my head against the window and close my eyes. Then open them again. There's a face, nose, and lips smashed against the glass staring right at me. I spring back upright, pulse pounding.

I open the door, and see Fulgence trying to recover from convulsions of laughter.

"Surprise," he giggles, then turns serious. "I don't think the Americans are coming to rescue you tonight."

"We know," I say.

"Don't be scared, Anita," he says to her across the bus.

"I'm not," she says. *"Ntakibazo.* No problem."

My watch says 1 A.M. Five more hours until first light. Thadée leans forward from the seat behind mine.

"I can't sleep," he says. "I feel like talking," he says. "Do you?"

So we all lean together around the console and talk for a while. What if the battle moves our way? What if the people of Vunga are gathering in the hills right now, marching this way to burn our buses and massacre us? "This will make a great story," Thadée says.

Then we begin to recite all the poems and parts of poems we can remember, all the poetry we know by heart. We quote Shakespeare and Milton and Donne, we quote Wordsworth and Coleridge and Keats. Thadée quotes and translates some Rwandan poems he'd memorized in high school. Then we quote some more. We quote Whitman and Dickinson, Auden and Yeats and Stevens and Plath. Each of us is an anthology! We quote all the poetry we know. We quote scattered lines, we quote poetry we didn't know that we knew until this moment. We keep breathing poetry until the first birds sing and we can see the road out of Vunga emerge again through the rain.

Elephant Girl

. . . .

by
DEBORAH A. LOTT

From the first day of kindergarten on, LeeAnn and I watch each other. As I sit in my chair by the window, isolated from the rest of the class, howling and sobbing for my mother, LeeAnn cannot take her eyes off me. Some of the other children, who regard themselves as big boys and girls who don't need their mothers, stare at me with contempt for so obviously needing mine. LeeAnn is different; she cocks her head in my direction, perplexed by the showiness of my display but also impressed by the vehemence of my refusal to acquiesce to authority. My defiance inspires her own; she ignores Mrs. Bell's admonishments to "pay no attention to the little crybaby" and looks right at me. In between my tears, I look right back.

We are the two smallest children in the kindergarten class, and Mrs. Bell has positioned LeeAnn in the front row on the dingy green carpet. She is shifty and itchy and out of sorts, scooting away if another kindergartner's arm so much as brushes against hers.

That morning I watched LeeAnn's mother walk her into the classroom. She was the picture of serenity, of domesticated femininity, tall and smooth and compliant, with a shoulder-length brunette pageboy. She was wearing a chintz dress with ruffles around the neckline.

"Why, isn't that a pretty dress!" Mrs. Bell said on greeting her.

"Thank you, I sewed it myself," LeeAnn's mother replied. Tugging at her arm, LeeAnn followed behind, dragging her legs and scuffling her feet in silent resistance. She was skinny and slight, with a perennially testy, screwed-up expression on her face. She was dressed for the first day of school like Shirley Temple as Rebecca of Sunnybrook Farm in a dress her mother had made, pink gingham with an apron of white crinoline. Its big puffy sleeves made her skinny arms look even more simian. Her dirty-blond hair was painstakingly set so that it fell in banana curls, held by white plastic barrettes molded in the shape of bows.

Regardless of how she was dressed, LeeAnn was not cute in any story-book sort of way. She had thick, dark hair on her limbs, which were bony and elongated despite her small stature. Freckles ran across the bridge of her nose in an uneven pattern and her nostrils flared when she laughed.

When it was time for LeeAnn's mother to go, she knelt down grace-fully, rolling one of her daughter's ringlets around a finger. Then she stepped back to admire her creation, gave her progeny a dry kiss on the forehead, and disappeared. A moment of sadness fell across LeeAnn's face, which was quickly replaced by her usual irked expression. She did not raise a word in protest.

When my own mother's exit became inevitable, I grasped and clawed and screamed and kicked, my interest in holding onto her turning into fury at her rejection. Mrs. Bell wrenched me away with her bony hands.

"Oh, honey, stop this right now," my mother said, embarrassed. And then to Mrs. Bell, deferentially, "I can't understand why she gets so hys-terical, my little cuckoo girl."

I proceed to make a name for myself by crying the entire first day. When I will not stop crying, Mrs. Bell segregates me from the rest of the class in a chair by the window. From there, I can see my mother—or more precisely my mother's car, a 1955 cobalt blue DeSoto that remains parked outside the school.

I know that my mother is sitting in the car but from my vantage point at the window, I cannot quite make out her face. I am left with Mrs. Bell's face, which is old and gnarled, her skin and stiff hair both a bluish gray. She wears glasses like my mother does, except that hers are square and severe and my mother's sweep up on the sides and have rhinestones at the temples.

When Mrs. Bell puts her hands on me and pushes me down in that chair by the window, I can feel the joints of her fingers dig into my shoul-ders. "There," she says, "if you won't stop crying, you can just sit here all by yourself." The words come out of the pinched opening of Mrs. Bell's mouth. Behind her thin lips she is hiding the sharp incisors of a witch. She stands beside my chair for a moment, squinting out the window with her arms folded in front of her, saying "Tsk, tsk" to let me know that she sees my mother's car and does not approve of her proximity.

My mother's being so near and yet so out of reach, so present and yet

.   .   .   .

invisible to me, only increases the intensity of my grief. If I cry loud enough, I wonder, will she hear me? Will she know that I have refused to let her go? I keep up a steady, nearly perfectly unbroken stream of torment, my cries a string connecting us whether my mother can hear me or not.

At first, I am among a small chorus of kindergarten criers. Ultimately, though, the other children are pushovers, allowing themselves to be bought off by the lure of story time, of finger paints and snack and recess. Paul with the bristle-brush haircut is the last holdout before me. I am imagining that if the two of us can keep it up, Mrs. Bell will have to relent and return us to our mothers. But Mrs. Bell is cagey; she kneels beside Paul and, in a singsongy voice that barely masks her impatience, tells him everything that his mother will be doing while he is in school. "She will go to the store and buy food for you and Daddy," she says cheerfully. "She will clean and dust and vacuum the house, and then she will pick her big boy up and will be so proud of him for not crying, and you and Mommy will go home together and wait for Daddy to come home from work. Won't that be nice?" Paul whimpers two final, tiny whimpers, wipes his eyes with his fists, and is vanquished.

He must not love his mother as much as I love mine, I think. His mother must not be as precious, as irreplaceable. I refuse all consolation, insisting that there is only one genuine article of solace. Besides, Mrs. Bell's sentimental family tableau holds no comfort for me—if my mother were not sitting out in the car, she would not be at home cheerfully cleaning house or shopping for dinner. She would be hard at work in the front bedroom that has been turned into my father's insurance agency. She would be distracted, submerged in chaos, each ring of the phone bringing news of catastrophe—car wrecks, stolen jewelry, roofs blown off in the wind, fires destroying houses—claims.

Whatever my mother is doing, she is thinking about something else— the next thing she has to do, the fastest way out of the present task. My father, my two older brothers, and I all want something from her, and all she knows is that she is quickly running out. In response to my father's always overwrought emotional state, she has disengaged emotionally. She goes through the motions but her self has receded to a small point inside that no one can touch.

And now, while I sit in my chair by the window and she sits in the car, she is probably organizing files she has brought with her from the office, worrying about what trouble my father will get into without her home to take care of him. She stays here because she has promised me that she would, and because, she tells me, she is afraid that I will go "totally berserk" if she leaves. Still she will not insist on staying in the classroom, will not confront the rules directly or even tell Mrs. Bell of her intent. Her presence is meant to be a secret between us.

In my grief, I keep reliving the moment of our separation: I am clutching at a fold of my mother's taupe wool coat, burying my face and sobbing into its downy surface, desperate not to be parted. The harder I cling, the more my mother stiffens and withdraws internally. She blushes at the hint of a spectacle; her goal is to get me to let go of her without making a scene, without calling too much attention to us. The more she withdraws, the more I can feel myself losing her even as I am holding onto her, the more desperately I cling. For one sweet moment, when Mrs. Bell and the other mothers are out of earshot, she strokes my head and says, "Oh, cookie, shush," softening her body against mine, a small concession to solace. I want this moment to go on forever; hearing her call me cookie is the best thing, the only thing in the world that I want. *More cookie, more cookie, more hugging,* I think. But my mother is embarrassed by the intensity of my longing, by the rawness of my desire for her.

We had rehearsed for this day: my mother brought me to the school in midsummer, lifted me up to peer into the tiny window on the door of my kindergarten classroom. In the dark, I had been able to make out the bank of windows, the green carpet. But that day had not prepared me for the smells of ammonia and poster paints, and the chirpy emissions of all those other children. It did not prepare me for the impact of my mother's absence.

That absence bores a hole through me—there is no me without her, nothing but what is missing. Then the pain lessens a bit but I make a decision to keep crying. If I stop, if I accede to the separation, my loss will become absolute. The only way I can hang onto any piece of my mother is to not let go, and to not let go is to keep on crying. And all the time I am crying, LeeAnn is watching.

So I sit in my chair by the window, sobbing for the remainder of the first day. When the sobbing exhausts me, I whimper, I howl, I hyperventilate and make little animal sounds in the back of my throat. Mrs. Bell alternates between glaring at me and pretending I am not there.

There is only one moment when I am tempted to stop: Mrs. Bell tells a felt-board story about a seal cub who goes off to join the circus and becomes a star. I feel the lure of the story—its offer of comfort, of escape. I

.   .   .   .

like the seal. He has left his mother, too, and I want to go to the circus with him and I want to stop crying and be a star too, but I will not give in, and so I give up the story because I cannot listen and cry at the same time.

When class is over and I am finally freed to return to the sanctity of that blue DeSoto, I stop crying. On the way out to my mother, and then once I have seen her face, I feel relief and the inklings of happiness. *Yes, this is what I needed,* I think, *this is who I want.* "I cried all day," I tell her. "I couldn't stop crying for you." "Oooh," she says laughing. "You are a silly, silly girl." She hugs me but the fervor of my passion is not met by equal fervor on her part. I feel ashamed.

In the midst of hugging her, I am still longing. Longing as she holds me. Longing as I look over her shoulder for that other, perfect mother, the mother who loves me the way that I love her, the mother that she becomes as soon as we are separated.

It is the third day of kindergarten before LeeAnn and I speak. I am trying to survive recess. Unlike the other children, who cannot wait to get out of the classroom so that they can scream and cheer and throw sand and bounce balls and let out all of what Mrs. Bell calls their pent-up energy, I dread the playground. Children together in a group terrify me: their unpredictability, the way they egg each other on, their arms and legs kicking and grabbing and racing around randomly. I hover at the fringes of the asphalt yard, pretending that I am much too occupied by my own activities to join in. These consist of wandering in little circles circumscribed by my pigeon-toed gait, head down, looking at the asphalt, and pretending its every crack merits my attention.

I am carrying my snack, the same snack that I will carry every day of kindergarten, Nabisco potato crackers in a brown paper bag. My bag is folded over crisply and stapled neatly, the only bag in kindergarten closed in this fashion. My mother has performed this task as one more of her many office duties, folding the bag deliberately and then labeling it with my complete name in oversized black Marks-A-Lot. I have only to look at those official, formally executed letters in my mother's hand to begin to cry all over again. What I feel is not only her absence, but a hollowness at the recognition that she cannot see me, does not even know what I am doing. She probably isn't even thinking about me. I have slipped out of her mind. All I have to hold onto is my own name, brought into being by her hand. And if I would venture to open up my bag and actually *eat* those dry, salty crackers, they and my own tears would choke me. And I have

already learned that there are no drinks in kindergarten, unless one is willing to brave the drinking fountain, which is dominated by boys making
mud. Besides, the water is warm and comes out in a trickle.

So today I do not even attempt to eat my snack, I merely carry it
around with me, missing my mother, bracing myself against the high-
pitched shrieks of the other children's boisterous play. On the perimeter of
the playground, LeeAnn is walking around in little circles of her own. We
make eye contact. She approaches. She puts her screwed-up face very
close to mine and her wide-set, gold-brown eyes hold me.

"Do you want to play?" she asks.

LeeAnn has a hoarse, gravelly voice for a little girl, which cracks as she
elongates each syllable.

"Play what?" I ask, not committing to anything.

I soon learn that for LeeAnn there is really only one game, a game of
her own invention. My classroom display has convinced her of our shared
kinship, and so she deems it safe to share the game's details with me. It is
called Elephant Girl, and LeeAnn gets to be Sheebah the baby elephant. I
will be the nameless elephant keeper whose job it is to hold the elephant's
rope and lead her around the circus rink or the jungle floor. I am to feed
her, to pat her head, to tell her that she is a good little elephant.

As the game begins, LeeAnn leans over, clasps her hands together in
front of her face, swings them back and forth until she gets the rhythm
right, until she has lost herself in the illusion that they are an elephant's
trunk. She spreads her legs wide apart, tottering from side to side, and
then begins to move very slowly, as if her body is gargantuan. Her eyes
glaze over and she begins to make noises. She is saying, "Woo-gah, woo-
gah," the closest she can get to an elephant's bellow. I am timid about joining the game, so LeeAnn emerges from her trance long enough to direct
me. She turns around and says perfunctorily, "Untie my bow, that's Sheebah's rope." I hesitate for a moment, afraid to touch the flouncy bow at
the back of LeeAnn's dress, the bow that her beautiful mother has crafted
so carefully, because I know that I will not be able to re-create its perfectly
symmetrical loops. But Sheebah nudges me with her trunk, saying, "Woo-
gah! Woo-gah!" I can see the baby elephant now, can feel her trunk pulling
me gently into the the illusion. I want to go with her. I place my snack on
the ground by the fence and hurry back. I pull the bow out with a flourish
and take the two ties in my hands. I experiment with my voice until I find
the wise and benevolent tone of the elephant keeper. "Come on now, Sheebah," I say, beginning to guide her around the playground.

Sheebah's routine is simple and ritualistic. In order to play this game, I must believe in it as LeeAnn believes in it, and in the reassuring necessity of certain acts occurring in sequence, over and over again. Sheebah picks up imaginary hay with her trunk, puts it into her mouth and chews, her mouth partially open. Sheebah spies an especially enticing group of leaves. She gallops toward it, bellowing louder and louder as we approach our destination. When we arrive, she flares her nostrils and strains her face into a half-grunt, half-smile. She lifts her trunk to pull the leaves off the higher branches and I loosen her reins while she eats and wait patiently until she has eaten her fill before reining her in again.

Once Sheebah's appetite is sated, I can give her a command to run at my side or march in time to the circus music I hum. We can both hear the calliope. Afterward, Sheebah nudges me with her trunk and I reward her with pretend peanuts. Mostly we just walk about the playground in circles that do not appear superficially so different from my own, except that we are sworn to believe that LeeAnn is the elephant girl and I am the elephant keeper.

One day, Sheebah tests the limits of our attachment by expressing a sudden impulse for total freedom. She bounds away, lurching the reins right out of the keeper's hands. She gallops and woo-gahs, and I am left to run after her. Once I catch up, I scold Sheebah and lash her gently with the reins. Elephant girl bellows. The keeper is sorry; elephant girl is sorry. We reconcile, rubbing heads together gently.

"You're going to be a good little elephant from now on, right?" I say. Sheebah tickles the side of my neck with her trunk.

Over and over again elephant girl squats to "go," briefly for "number one" and longer for "number two." During the latter act she stops swinging her trunk, grunts, and furrows her elephant's brow. Afterward, she swings her trunk quickly and moves about in small circles to express her elation, and I say, "Good Sheebah, good Sheebah," as excited as she by her accomplishment. I groom Sheebah, pat her head, tenderly brush her enormous backside. With Sheebah beside me, I am no longer afraid of the other children. What power could they hold compared to that of an elephant?

I am a good-natured elephant keeper, elated simply to have a friend. And Sheebah's routine is a pleasure to us both; she trots, I run after her, she poops, I praise her, she eats, I stroke her head. When LeeAnn says, "Okay, just this once, you can be the elephant, and I will be the keeper," I am at a loss. I can't get the woo-gah, woo-gah down, and LeeAnn is frustrated—by not playing the part well I am calling attention to the artifice of the game. I see that it is potentially more fun to be the elephant than the elephant keeper but for it to be the most fun, you have to be LeeAnn.

In the guise of the game, Sheebah gets to do everything forbidden in the world of domesticated girlhood that LeeAnn's mother so graciously but relentlessly imposes. The elephant keeper understands, as LeeAnn's mother does not, that elephant girls need to make loud noises, to squat to relieve themselves whenever the urge strikes, to eat indiscriminately and voraciously, to make ugly faces, to be bigger and stronger and more willful than any human. If both of our mothers seem determined to turn us into good, compliant, obedient little girls, the elephant keeper loves Sheebah for being true to her elephant nature. She takes an intense pleasure, even pride, in Sheebah's grunting, her limitless appetite for hay, her massive pooping on urge, her woo-gah, woo-gah bellowing.

LeeAnn and I reenact the milestones of toddlerhood: Elephant girl is fed and then feeds herself, toilets herself, separates from and reunites with the keeper over and over again, but this time we are doing it on our own terms. And when Sheebah pleases the elephant keeper by marching in a circle or standing on her hind legs on command, when she allows herself to be reined in or restrains herself from charging, it is always an act of love rewarded by an equal return of love. The elephant keeper never expects Sheebah to behave out of blind obedience.

One day LeeAnn is in a particularly peevish mood, and Sheebah is particularly willful and exuberant. She refuses to cooperate with the elephant keeper at all; she bounds away, rears her head, performs an elephant trot. She pulls branches off trees, stampedes the playground, storms up to the chain-link fence enclosure and rams it with her head until it shakes. She woo-gah woo-gahs so loudly, shakes her trunk from side to side so forcefully, that she cannot even hear what the elephant keeper is saying.

I cannot get her into the circus ring. I cannot hold onto her. I am spending the entire recess enslaved to her will. "No, Sheebah, No Sheebah," I shout with an increasingly threatening edge in my voice. I am no longer speaking in the elephant keeper's patient, tolerant tones. The voice is familiar, though. I am speaking in the exasperated strains of my own mother. Elephant girl is *my* game now, too. We both want control, and we want it now. I finally catch up with Sheebah and am holding onto her by the black velvet ties of her dress, a particularly ornate pink taffeta, with layers of petticoats, the skirt and sleeves and waistband edged in velvet, when she begins to buck and rear her head. "You're not going anywhere, Sheebah," I say. What comes out of her mouth sounds more like a groan than a woo-gah, woo-gah. As Sheebah fights my hold on the reins, I give them a sudden hard yank, and the sound of ripping fabric rivals Sheebah's bellow. The elephant girl spins out of my reach, the raggedy, torn velvet ties of her dress still in my fist.

It takes a second for LeeAnn to realize just what has happened. We have gone too far; the evidence of our rebellion leaving a mark that we cannot erase. LeeAnn cannot go home to her mother like this; the torn ties are the proof of just what sort of game we were playing. She turns on me in a fury.

"*You* tore my dress. *You* tore the pretty dress my mother made me. *You're a bad bad* girl, and I'm telling Mrs. Bell. You're going to get into so much trouble."

"I didn't mean to . . ." I start to cry. "Sheebah was getting away, and I was just trying to hold onto—" LeeAnn looks at me incredulously. Sheebah? Sheebah who? Whatever am I talking about? She is just a good little girl on the kindergarten playground whose mother has made her the prettiest dress of any girl in the class. Maybe the prettiest dress of any girl in any class. And I am a troublemaker; haven't I demonstrated that from the very first day?

She stomps off to Mrs. Bell, who is seated at the far end of the playground under a khaki-colored umbrella for shade. LeeAnn describes her plight, pointing at me and practically jumping up and down with indignation.

I knew I should never have untied her bow, I think. I should never have allowed her to lure me into playing elephant girl. I *am* a bad girl, a bad bad girl, the girl who cannot stop crying, the girl who cannot control her emotions, who cannot control her own body, the out-of-control girl, the girl whose mother doesn't really love her, the girl who will never again have a friend. I have been caught once again failing at what is required of little girls in kindergarten: to be compliant, to be nice, to be quiet, to not cry too loudly, to not allow one's unruly desires to show on the outside. I should have just stayed on the fringes and eaten my crackers. No, I should never have let my mother make me go to kindergarten.

Over the next few days, LeeAnn alternates between shunning me and storming over with her curls flying, her gold-flecked brown eyes burning. She stands right up next to me and glares, then stomps her foot and turns away. Every day I spend recess, head down, wandering along the outer perimeter of the school yard, longing to be invisible. I am as frightened of simply being seen as of any punishment, ashamed that the light of adult eyes have invaded the insular pleasures of our game. Mrs. Bell can never understand what we were doing, but I suspect from the disapproving looks that she gives me, that she has already seen too much.

After a week, LeeAnn announces that her mother has sewed her ties back on, "better than ever," and we make up. But we never play elephant girl with quite the same abandon. We go through the motions but it is as if our mothers are always looking over our shoulders, and their looking has gotten inside. LeeAnn does not run too far or buck too hard; she eats only a small amount of hay at a time, she never poops in the ring. I do not pull with all my might on her reins. We are two nice, well-behaved girls pretending, playing a harmless game. We love our mothers, and our mothers love us. We are going to succeed at kindergarten.

In class, LeeAnn and I go our separate ways. My mother is relieved to hear how well I have "adjusted" to kindergarten life. Every day, I tell her, I raise my hand and ask to paint at the easel. Mrs. Bell, probably afraid to incite another bout of hysteria, always chooses me. If I wear my smock so that it fully covers my clothes, and do not drip too much paint onto the part of the floor not covered by newspapers, Mrs. Bell does not seem to care how furiously I cover my paper with color. LeeAnn sits across the room, busily at work at the crafts table. She strings beads with total concentration and then adorns the classroom's doll with one beaded necklace on top of another.

Freud's Couch

. . . .

by
KAREN BRENNAN

The first time I went to a psychiatrist I was barefoot, my jeans were ripped, and I didn't wear a bra. I liked to imagine I had a wild, sexy look with a hint of the lost waif. It was the late sixties, and the world had turned suddenly accommodating to people like me—*anomalies,* I say, for lack of a better word, but maybe *oddballs* is better. Those, at any rate, for whom the fifties had been dreary and hopeless, whose futures had been grimly plotted along very straight lines, and who therefore felt doomed to lifetimes of crewneck sweaters and gold circle pins and heels. In the throes of the Civil Rights movement and the Vietnam War, I began to see that anything was possible, and so I restyled myself: I grew my hair past my shoulders, I smoked pot, and I got rid of the shoes and underwear. I was after a spirit of radical liberation, even though I was stuck in a bad marriage and the mother of four children.

The shrink told me I was deeply confused. Identity crisis, he pronounced. I thought it sounded glamorous and complicated, like a movie-star malady. Dr. A (I will call him Dr. A) had a series of transplants on the crown of his head that seemed to be sprouting more lasciviously each week. Like a row of broccoli or chickweed, they grew thick and curly and distracted me from the matters at hand.

Sensing my preoccupation, Dr. A suggested I lie on his couch, which happened to face the window and the large abstract sculpture Dr. A had constructed for his lawn. Although not as arresting as the hair transplants—this *objet d'art* was rectangular and painted an unappealing beet red—the sculpture was also a distraction. It prevented me, Dr. A said, from going deeper.

Therefore, I closed my eyes as I lay on the couch—brown leather with a little throw of purple chenille in case the patient began to shiver from the trauma of Dr. A's incisive probing. He wanted to know: Why bare feet? Why ripped jeans? Why did I remain in the bad marriage? Why so many kids? Why did I hate driving? Eventually, he worked his way around to sex. What were my fantasies? Did I masturbate?

Once, while waiting in his antechamber and disdaining the array of women's magazines on the coffee table, I removed a professional book from his shelf and flipped through it. *Dementia, hysteria, bipolar disorder:* the names were like little flags heralding special events, and they intrigued me. "Did you enjoy touching my penis?" he asked during our session, in regard to the books. This was the same session in which he offered me a cigar.

I was going to a shrink because my family thought I was crazy. I was listless. I wrote poetry. My children ran around naked. My husband beat me. "There's nothing I can do to get a rise out of her," he told Dr. A in one session, speaking about me as if I weren't there. "Believe me, I've tried."

Dr. A encouraged me to leave my marriage and have a fling with him. "I have had sex with several patients and it's worked very well for them," he told me. I was not attracted to Dr. A, but fearing this might be necessary for successful therapy, I chose a doctor I could be attracted to. His name was Dr. M.

Dr. M was young and muscular. He had a nice oily flip over his forehead, and behind his skinny sideburns, flat, elaborate ears that reminded me of the scroll on Corinthian columns. I thought I could bear having sex with him if it would benefit my mental health. But Dr. M took a different approach, for which I invented a name: anger therapy. I didn't know if there were such a thing as anger therapy, but if there were, Dr M was surely the practitioner par excellence. "How hard did he hit you? How hard?" he asked me, as if I were making up stories to malign my husband and, by implication, all men. He asked me to show him on the back of a phone book.

Dr. M's office was spartan, containing one diploma over a black table piled with phone books, and two white plastic lawn chairs. On his walls, simulated oak paneling had been imperfectly tacked; his carpeting was stained; his waiting room, a tiny, windowless chamber, held one chair and no reading material of any kind.

He seemed to disapprove of me, my general ambience. He asked me to slap the back of the phone book or punch it so he could see exactly how

. . . .

hard my husband hit me. This and other demonstrations seemed designed to make me a liar, and so I hated Dr. M and drove home shaking with rage.

This was not a good time in my life to be shaking with rage while driving, since the brake shoes on our car had worn out, and we couldn't afford to replace them. As it was, I felt that I was always on the lip of danger, driving home with bad brakes in our Volvo. I would have to slide cautiously up to a red light or stop sign, for example, slowing down to a crawl as best as I could blocks in advance. But one day on my way home from a session with Dr. M, I had an accident that involved a telephone pole, a curb, and a woman in a Buick. The accident left me with mild whiplash and left the Volvo at the body shop for several weeks. It also increased my driving phobia.

For all of the above reasons, I stopped going to Dr. M. One day, he telephoned and demanded an explanation. I was making Swedish meatballs in an electric frying pan and my four-year-old son was calmly cracking eggs onto the kitchen floor. This odd fact sticks in my mind, for some reason—the white eggs breaking on the blue tiles of the kitchen floor, the yellow yolks spreading one by one across the room, and, so mesmerized by this activity that I forgot to admonish him. Then the phone rang. "This anger therapy doesn't work for me," I told Dr. M, and he said, "I don't practice anger therapy."

After my divorce was finalized, I went to a new therapist, Ms. B, who fell in love with me. She was a plumpish blond with pale blue eyes that needed a little more expression but couldn't seem to muster it up. Because I lost the car in the property settlement, I hitchhiked to her office with my baby daughter while the others were in school. Once an old lady picked us up on the freeway and I warned her about the dangers of picking up hitchhikers. I told her that I could be anyone, a terrorist, a murderer, a car thief; I told her I could be carrying a gun. The old lady just laughed, but it may have been a nervous laugh.

Ms. B wanted me to regress to the moment of my birth. I curled up in a quilt. I sucked my thumb. My real baby crawled around on the floor and played with alphabet blocks. Ms. B loved me so much, she imitated me. She became pregnant, she went on welfare, and after a while she needed a shrink.

For a while I had a job as a housecleaner for Dr. Y, a psychotherapist. Dr. Y had a lovely, large home through which her unruly children scrambled, trailing their various snacks. Dust bunnies scooted down the stairwells and nestled beneath the furniture. She never washed the dishes or made the beds. My life is incredibly overbooked, she told me. We decided to trade services, and so after cleaning her house, I'd go into her study for a session in which she'd enumerate her current issues and I'd listen sympathetically. Finally she announced that the therapy was interfering with the friendship. So, in the parlance of therapists, we terminated. We sat in her den and smoked cigarettes and drank Scotch, and she'd enumerate her current issues and I'd listen sympathetically. When I began to date the man who would become my next husband, she complained bitterly that I was ignoring her.

So for a long time I didn't go to therapy. My driving anxiety ebbed and flowed. I stopped housecleaning. I married another man. My children, like Dr A's hair transplants, grew thick and curly. I went back to him once, after the divorce, and his new hair looked quite natural. He said to me, "You have divorced yourself from everyone, how can you expect to be happy?" Ms. B's little girl was ill at birth, and she blamed me for this, for my example of motherhood that had deceived her. Dr. Y and I were friends for a while, then I moved. I never saw Dr. M again, thank god, but much later I had an incredibly incompetent dentist who could have been his twin.

The years went by. We drove across country. There is a picture of me wearing a flowered red dress, standing in front of our Datsun F10 somewhere in Oklahoma. I am thin and my face has that bony, jutting look I've never liked. During that trip I began smoking cigarettes again and my new husband was disgusted with my lack of willpower.

There's a photograph of his profile, driving the Datsun F10 into our hazy future. His head with its glossy hair, straight nose, and well-shaped red lips frowning under the mustache that won my heart.

When we got to our destination I contacted another shrink, and then I contacted the incompetent dentist who could have been Dr. M's twin: the same oily flip of hair and tall, about six-three, too large a man to be making his living by poking around in people's mouths. Indeed, his hands were enormous and clumsy, and so he was prone to carelessness. Posted to his wall on white card stock was a list of procedures he refused to do, including root canals, extractions, periodontal work, and deep cleaning. That left simple fillings, which soon fell out, chiefly due to *ennui*, I now think, on his part. Really, he wanted to be a gourmet cook and I remember several enthusiastic discussions of food while he hammered away at my mouth, inadvertently knocking off chunks of enamel. To compensate for

. . . .

his lack of expertise or interest, he prescribed drugs freely, as per the patient's request.

I began on Tylenol with codeine, which made me itchy and serene in a close-to-ecstatic way; then I moved to Percodan, which made me dopey, withdrawn, and serene in a more-than-ecstatic way. My teeth hurt throughout this brush with addiction, a dim pain rumbling around in back of the ecstasy, and my husband disapproved of all of it: the teeth, the pain, the painkillers, the shrink.

My new shrink insisted I call him by his first name, R. He encouraged me to dump the husband as well as the drugs. By now, we were in a new therapeutic age and shrinks were styling themselves as your best friends, instead of distant and Freudian. He was so compassionate that he fancied he knew what I was going to say before I said it. I said, "My sister was a beautiful little girl and I was—" "The ugly duckling," he promptly supplied. It happened again when I was comparing myself to a well-dressed relative. "Frump?" he offered. Other than that, he was a nice guy.

At some point it occurred to me that I would lose all my teeth before I was fifty if I kept on at the present rate. This idea appealed to me since it would mean a future of painlessness. Because I hated all but the incompetent dentist who refused to perform extractions, I took to extracting my own teeth when necessary. Wiggling them around with my tongue for a year or so and then popping them out while watching TV with my husband. Who could blame him for being revolted?

Even R was revolted. I displayed my wisdom tooth in the privacy of our session. It had great, winged, brown roots the size of a sparrow's head. It seemed to me totemic and lucky. "Leave your husband," R advised. "You are not getting the love and attention you deserve."

The dentist, meanwhile, was deeply involved in several cuisines. While digging under my gum line, he described a mandarin bean and beef, a grilled tuna tapenade, and a pear gallette with apricot jam. It occurred to me that we might be happy together, the dentist and I. At home, I mooned around in front of the stove, sauteeing green beans with shiitake mushrooms or roasting garlic or red peppers. My husband, then on a low-fat purge, steamed cabbages and mushrooms, filling the house with the smell of nineteenth-century hospitals.

In such a hospital, Salpêtrière, Freud examined the bodies of hysterical women arching their backs uncontrollably or grimacing. His associate Pierre Janet had fashioned a number of corrective manacles for the patients—braces, he called them—meant to discipline the female body into its original grace and pliancy. One can imagine Freud walking among metal beds in the long, dimly lit ward, lifting covers with the tip of his cane in order to peer at the writhing women beneath.

Hysteria: from the Greek work for womb, *hyster.* The womb wandering disconsolately throughout the body, according to an early theory, and colliding with other organs, "causing distress." Plato theorized the womb as an "animal that longed to bear children," whereas the ancient Romans decided that hysteria only plagued the widowed and spinstered, who longed for husbands.

Freud, on the other hand, believed that hysterical symptoms were signs of a developmental story gone wrong, and thus its sufferers, having jumbled their narrative destinies, had not arrived at true femininity. I know these facts because I wrote a dissertation on hysteria in grad school, years after the incompetent dentist moved to Hawaii with his secretary, years after R pointed out that I seemed to wear the same gray sweats to every session, and what did that tell me?

Whereas Freud's hysterics, many of them baronesses, showed up for their appointments in ankle-length gowns, trussed, buckled, and laced, their hair elaborately coiffed, perhaps adorned by a fetching hat they removed in order to lie on the green couch.

Why do I imagine a green couch for Freud? And red velvet curtains on the long windows that looked into the grey streets of Vienna? In the waiting room, the hysterics sat with their hands in their laps, gloved, demure, eyes downcast. Their symptoms were clues to meanings hidden within: catarrh, nosebleeds, convulsive tics, hallucinations of rats and snakes and, in the case of "Miss Lucy R.," the offensive smell of burnt pudding. Their names, reinvented by Freud, were carefully contrived so as not to implicate their male counterparts: "Dora," "Miss Elizabeth von M."

Why do I imagine Freud's specifically *green* couch upon which women swooned, helpless in the face of their wandering wombs? My parents, I told Dr. H, had a green couch with little nubs upon which we were forbidden to sit. Although this couch has been in our family for as long as I remember, I believe I only sat on it twice. It was down filled, heavenly, and cool, situated, as it still is, in the shadowy living room, the nubs making a little pleasurable friction on my thighs. In the lexicon of my psyche, then, if green couch equals forbidden territory, the couch of psychoanalysis is for me a little lawless. Perhaps this is why I return to it again and again, incriminating the guilty self only to lavish it with forgiveness. "Perhaps," said Dr. H, the most noncommittal of my shrinks.

Dr. H, I should mention, was the only psychotherapist I fell in love with. He was short and chunky and wore T-shirts to our sessions. I suppose I loved him because he betrayed no interest in me whatsoever. Once I saw him and his girlfriend in a diner, eating eggs, reading the Sunday paper—she was blond, with a long nose and thick ankles. Not at all like me.

I first went to a shrink because I was deeply depressed. I'd lost thirty pounds in the space of three weeks and I slept far too much for a young mother of four children. Between naps, I remember sitting on our couch (more couches! but this one was grey) and staring limply ahead to where the branches intermingled outside our window. At the far ends of the intermingling branches were geometrical chinks of dull sky that seemed supremely meaningless. Still, I continued to stare as my children raced around my knees and even as my husband hit me to bring me to my senses. (Or was it vice versa: the children racing around my senses, like the lost smell of oranges, and the husband bringing me to my knees?)

As a child I'd had a dream about being sucked inside a yellow channel as wide as a rope and experiencing a complex sensation that still returns to me in moments of illness. The sensation is of having my organs shifted from within, accompanied by little flickers of both nausea and pleasure.

This dream, which I call My Dream of the Yellow Channel, has had the benefit of the following professional responses. Dr. A: "It represents your claustrophobia, your unhealthy marriage!" Dr. M: "Obviously a recollection of the birth canal! The message: grow up!" B: "A mystical experience!" Y: "Reminds me of one of *my* dreams!" R: "S&M-ish, kinky!" Dr. H: "_____." But it is obvious to me that this is a dream of the wandering womb, the hysterical dream of the hysterical dreamer. Dr. H shook his head. "You're too intellectual," he said.

The second reason I went to a psychotherapist was because I had developed a driving phobia. But since I never talked about it, no one ever helped me overcome it. Talking about it was equivalent to inducing it, and inducing panic required a stronger character than my own.

I inherited my phobia from my father, who had a fear of heights. This was astonishing in a man so *manly*. Once in the car, on what feels in retrospect to have been a midwinter February—misty, cold—he stopped his Oldsmobile in front of a bridge and made me take the wheel. I must have been about sixteen. In my memory, the bridge was flimsy, possibly wooden and spanning a small river. As I drove its short distance, I remember wondering what there was to be afraid of. I was unacquainted with the mind's formidable power. At sixteen, in those prehallucinogenic days, a bridge was simply a bridge.

Later I heard rumors of my father's refusal to take elevators in tall buildings, to sit in any restaurant with an aerial view, to fly in a plane without many Dewars on the rocks to fortify himself. In all other matters, he was aggressively macho. He called women "broads" and "dames" and was shameless in social interactions. A master of the hustle, he once convinced a Sears clerk to sell him four General tires for the price of two and was known to barter with grocery-store clerks for heads of lettuce. Still, he had this terrible fear that, even in a small way, affected his choices in life.

I was nineteen, a college student, when I was visited by a panic attack of my own. This occurred in a theater in New York City, in a balcony row my father would have forgone. Suddenly, I felt an uncomfortable compulsion to shout loudly or clap or laugh. I can still feel myself squirming in my plush seat, a sensation like cold sweat running over my limbs, my heart racing.

A few years later, married, the same thing happened. But instead of an urge to laugh or clap, I simply wanted out. I was seated in the middle of a long row of seats and the theater had gone dead silent, as had the actors, in what must have been a moment of heightened drama. For the record, I did not push my way annoyingly past the theater-goers on either side of me, but remained as I was, feeling as though I would burst into a thousand pieces, clearing my throat softly as if to assure myself of my own existence.

Until I wrote the preceding sentence I never realized that what is threatened most vitally in these panic attacks is one's own existence. In some psyche-genetic loop, I took on my father's disposition to phobias, allowing them to cast my life into a smaller, more constricted frame. But really, for most of my life, I was consciously terrified of only one thing: my father.

My macho father drank his Scotch with a splash of water on the rocks; he smoked, daringly to me, whatever cigarette brand caught his eye in the newsstand (I remember especially a brand called *Hit Parade* whose packaging was garish and taste was stale); he was fond of practical jokes among his male friends, preferred blonds over the brooding brunettes life had favored him with, adored his two younger sons, felt tenderness and gratitude toward his younger daughter, my sister, and was completely flummoxed and irritated by his oldest child, me.

I was the black sheep, I am still fond of saying. I lost my sweaters, I was late to dinners, I talked back. My father slapped me with the flat of his hand, aiming for my head. On more than one occasion, he chased me up the stairs and banged on the locked bathroom door while I sat trembling on the closed toilet lid. "You drive me to it. You provoke me," is what my father would say, and it was years before I would discover this was the textbook language of abuse.

If I were to perform a chemical analysis, a breakdown, of my father's temperament, I would say it was two parts anger, two parts fear, and one part sentimentalism. This last is complex, having its shallow and deep chords, and ranging from childhood memories of true tragedy and deep pain to his eyes filling with tears when I sang "Galway Bay" at his request. When I'd finished my performance, when the guests had respectfully applauded and resumed their conversations and cocktail sipping and hors d'oeuvre munching, the look of pride on my father's face would be supplanted by his usual look of disapproval. Why didn't I brush my hair for the company? Why was my voice so shrill?

My father's disapproval drained me of whatever being I'd been shuffling together at the time. What I mean to say is that his anger toward me was annihilating.

My phobias, which used to be free-floating and vague fears of annihilation, have found their focus—a fear of driving, especially on highways, especially over bridges, in traffic, and in unfamiliar territory of any sort. I especially dislike being caught in the left-hand lane or at a light with cars behind. At such times, I feel the familiar weakness in my legs—a kind of helpless, abandoned feeling—followed quickly by shortness of breath, a flurry of chaotic heartbeats, and a kind of paralysis as the fear washes over me and lodges in my throat, making swallowing difficult.

So, in a linguistic turn Freud himself would have appreciated, my father's fears have substituted for my fear of my father. In this way, years after my father's death, I can keep him with me. And driving itself—a metaphor for crossing thresholds, for going bravely into the unknown or uncomfortable—seems the perfect discipline to keep me in my place, not venturing too far or too dangerously. It also keeps me racking up bills for psychotherapy. All this I've figured out, though it has taken me years, and it hasn't altered my driving fears a bit.

Now, in my fifties, I recognize that being the black sheep carries with it a distinction that sets me apart from the others in my family. The *black sheep* has constituted a *black hole,* an escape hatch, a place through which, like Alice, I can crawl through to the wonderland of my usual life. Living alone, my phobia is less insistent. I drive where I can; where I can't, I bum rides, though it is a dream of mine to conquer my fear of driving, to hop in my car, and go anywhere, hours and days on end, to check into sleazy motels in the middle of nowhere and have cross-country adventures.

Two nights ago I dreamt I was driving on a long, windy, mountainous road. The visibility was so poor I couldn't see where I was going. Although the car managed to stay on the road, I knew the odds were against me: sooner or later, the car was doomed to plunge over the edge. And when it finally did, hours into dreamtime, the car soaring into murky space, lurching toward a bluer sky, I felt the purest ecstasy.

The phobia is an area wherein I stash all the horror of my life. Then I keep away from it. In this way, I manage to be a cheerful person. I tell this to my new therapist, who I'll call Ben, after my dear grandfather. "Now that's transference," says Ben when I tell him about his new name.

We sit in his office and occasionally I let my eyes stray to the view, which is of mountains covered with snow. I tell him about the men in my life, who come and go, breaking my heart and shoring it up again; I tell him about my children, who are grown-ups now and seeing their own therapists. We sit like two old cronies with our cups of mint tea, looking at the stationary, eternal mountains. He's a bald guy; I have fake blond streaks. It's a new era, post-millennium, post-September 11, and the world has lost its optimism. We have, it seems, liberated ourselves for nothing but ourselves, who forge on, beating ceaselessly against the current, pining for mental health in a time of the gravest pathology. I myself wear a fashionable jogging suit, black velvet with wide stripes up the sides of the retro-flared pants.

"And about Freud's couch," I say. "I recently discovered it wasn't green, but covered with a lavish kind of Kelim, red and gold. It must have been rough on the poor women's backs." Ben nods. "It just goes to show," he says. "Nowadays you can buy a picture postcard of it," I say. "Yup," he says. And I say, "Just the couch, *sans* the women, which is weird, come to think of it. All those women vanished into history, without last names, were the foundation of modern psychology." "You've got that right," Ben says. And then we sit in companionable silence. And then I begin to talk because, despite the easy place I occupy in a genealogy of pathetic women, talking is my cure.

The Solitary Star: Finding a Cuban Home in Poetry

. . . .

by
RAFAEL CAMPO

Home for Christmas, and I am sitting at my father's desk, in his small-ish, uncluttered, dark study, which is full of replacement things—because this is Santa Rosa, California, not Guantánamo, Cuba. My family always moved a lot, always striving for some better other place, and my parents have continued this restless exile habit even now, into their retirement years. The desk is mahogany, with a beautiful pattern of inlaid ebony and walnut, but it is only a reproduction of the battered original I imagine once graced my grandfather's study, where he penned his requests for the endless permits required by the Cuban government to run his cattle ranch. In the corner, in a faux-stone urn, fronds of a miniature silk palm whisper something not entirely inaccurate about the tropics. On the wall hangs a worthless stock certificate from a long-defunct Havana sugar refinery, stately and businesslike in its gold-trimmed frame, with its elegant engraving of some landmark building I do not recognize (but which my father must). In simpler wooden frames, two numbered prints of *campitos* by the Puerto Rican artist Cajiga, worn, stolid faces all the more tragic beneath an extravagance of blooming *flamboyanes,* gaze back at me as if from an unchartable distance. Even this holiday seems oddly unpossessed by us; another year of tinsel masquerading as icicles when a ruddy, corpulent, and altogether too jolly Santa will visit instead of the more nobly serene *reyes magos.*

Nothing here is truly old, passed on, burnished by great- and great-great-grandparents' hands, in the family for who knows how long; even this expansive house, with its brand-new "antiqued" terra-cotta tiles and wide laminate shutters, seems fashionably imprinted with a plantation look borrowed from *Architectural Digest* more than the accumulation of artifacts and memories that one might recognize as a home. Though I am home, I am not really in a place I can truly call home—I am visiting a technicality, a simulation, a semantic distinction. Cut into the side of a mountain, commanding its acres of mossy California oak and shredding-barked eucalyptus, overlooking a valley that looks vaguely familiar but isn't the view my father still remembers, the one from the hilltop in Cuba I have never seen, it offers more comfort than consolation, more the illusion of place in its expensive sunsets and lavender-scented breezes than the more bracing candor of unmanicured earth composted with manure and cane cuttings and irrigated for generations by water drawn from a river nearby in which *campesinas* pound out stains from laundry.

All my life, I have been told that Cuba no longer exists as a place, and yet it remains the intensely evocative destination, consciously or unconsciously, of my family's every story, every argument, every move and action. Cuba is at once all that was lost and everything that is remembered but cannot be spoken of, and yet of course is. Surely, my parents' swank new home expresses this paradox; my grandparents' vexing double refusal ever to learn English or to return to see the island they fled in 1960 underscores it. In some way or other, it is imagined as the cause of wounds and divisions, great and small, from any of the world's catastrophes and the assassinations of national leaders to why my *tía* Chila was disowned by my grandfather and the reason for my gayness. It is why how much *cumino*, garlic, and lime juice goes into the marinade for roast pork matters so much; so little else besides recipes, and a few creased photographs, could be saved, to be transported across that 90-mile stretch of sea.

So perhaps it will not seem so far-fetched when I say I believe this problem of language, this self-frustrating refutation of expression, is the reason I became a poet.

It seems impossible to some to speak of Cuba without speaking of loss; I suppose that poetry has a similar magnetism, an ability to say one thing and yet mean another. So much to say about Cuba, and so much to deny— and in not one, but two languages! I suppose that counts as another thing that was saved: Spanish, gigantic with emotion and meaning, could not be left behind in a drawer or confiscated by the Communist soldiers patrolling Havana's docks. I have always loved the collision of those two tongues, Spanish and English, washing into each other like great bodies of water, full of fish of different shapes and sizes but all as slippery, as each clamors to fill up my absence of a homeland. I had a dream as a child that the reason I could never visit Cuba was because it had disappeared under the surface of the sea, leaving a deep dark hole into which the ocean poured endlessly, insatiably; in another, waves pounded on an imagined beach insistently, like fists pounding a table, as if demanding to be heard, until nothing was left but a feeling of unresolved rage. Now, I can see that the hole in the ocean was really my *abuela*'s secondhand, malfunctioning top-loading washer, which would fill to the brim with water and then suddenly drain with a loud sucking noise; the pounding fists must have represented those of my uncles, arguing Miami politics across the crowded kitchen table as fiercely as they maligned Fidel. Spanish and English, English and Spanish, rising and crashing, spilling and roaring, all in the effort to create sense. To create sense out of what they would just as well destroy.

Language, and eventually poetry, has thus come to hold at least the promise of that sense of place for me. Not just language generically, but a strained, conflicted, shouted, Spanglish-mutt version of it, a dynamic idiom, capable, it seemed during my childhood, of containing all those sacred narratives that at the same time it wished to erase and replace. Not the quiet English of the hymnal, or the melodious Spanish of a madrigal, but the ungainly, sentimental, misunderstood, and way-too-honest language of my Cuban immigrant family. The way they spoke, an inflection could become an instrument of torture; if you weren't crying or laughing or screaming when you said something, then maybe you didn't really feel it. Smoke snaking from nostrils, and the slight muffling of what I came to think of as cigar-words, conveyed a gravity as heavy as those long, humid days during which they were spoken. Certain words carried entire histories of family feuds, all the meanings crowded into them like retirees on the sight-seeing buses that sometimes lumbered down Calle Ocho, as if our part of Miami had become a foreign country. As if, in carrying out language with us, we had brought along our sad yet somehow ebullient nation.

Yet for all its consolations, I admit language is not actually a homeland, it is only a vehicle of the imagination. If it is a kind of place, maybe it is one with too many seasons, too many genders, too many colors and textures and exhalations to allow the construction of a reliable shelter. I ask myself: Wouldn't it be better just to go, finally, get on an airplane bound for Montreal or Mexico City, and rush through the crowded airport terminal to catch my connecting flight, where to see Havana glowing on the Departures monitor would appear to other travelers not so magical, than to labor with these deficient words over this blank page? One need only to recall the tragically unstable Tower of Babel—which for an embarrassingly significant part of my life I misunderstood homonymously as the tower of babble—to appreciate the inadequacies of language. For just as language can bind people together, it can also divide them, or serve to punish them. Put another way: I once had the fantasy that by learning Spanish, by speaking it masterfully, I could somehow accomplish the arduous journey back to that forbidden isle, but to my dismay, reading (and even translating) the likes of Martí and Darío did not transport me there. Worse, the pain of never arriving seemed to magnify my sense of loss. Metaphor may give us the sensation of movement, the illusion of translocation; onomatopoeia may trick us into thinking we hear parrots squawking outside our windows. We must be grateful for these gifts of language and the imagination, but they are not the same as traveling *there,* arriving home.

So I sit here writing, imagining what it would be like to be writing in Cuba. I find it hard to resist that current of loss, the one that always drags me down when I try to inhabit Cuba. All I have is these languages, these words, this tremendous capacity for invention they proffer, and yet I indulge in my impulse to devalue them. My language, fluid and insubstantial, seems all too easily shaped by this familiar trope of defeat; I resent its seeming powerlessness and yet struggle to make something valuable from it. I want to say *empanadas* and be returned to my *abuela*'s kitchen again; it seems so little to ask, since I can smell and even taste them now. I want to go even farther, all the way to the places I have never been, where I have been forbidden to tread. I want my words to be able to resolve a political conflict of longer duration than most in recent history; I want them to lay bare the differences in ideologies, themselves constructed of words, and thus logically more amenable to my designs. I want them to *do* something— what Auden warned us about in his mandarin way, I suppose, when he famously wrote, "Poetry makes nothing happen."

It seems that I have stumbled here onto what may keep language—or, more precisely put, the impulse toward narrative—ultimately so unabandonable. Perhaps it is the desire to create, the will to understand, the possibility of constructing the uninhabitable yet marvelous edifice, that is what we seek. Perhaps this recalcitrant process itself is what is so particularly compelling about poetry to me, the dispossessed exile and sexual "deviant," always searching for my elusive home, looking for it in my jotted-down descriptions of every *bodega* and *panadería* here in Boston and in the cities I visit, every stuccoed 1950s Miami ranch-style house of my youth, with humming power lines cutting up the sky above the fenced-in pool out back instead of snorts of cattle and the rustle of sugar cane,

.   .   .   .

with its fireworks of untamed bougainvillea erupting beside the front
door—searching for it again in the body of my Puerto Rican–born lover,
that part that is supposed to be there but isn't, that lust to be made whole,
to fit perfectly and pleasurably into someplace as dark and warm as a night
by the sea, to be discovered and entered myself, and thus finally rescued.

The poet's uncompromising effort, of course, is what I specifically refer
to, not just any casual engagement with language but the struggling with
it, sanding and planing it, cursing it, invoking it, singing it. In giving language a particular, hard-won, physically wrought shape, as the poet by
necessity does, I must believe reader and writer alike can experience a certain authenticity, a degree of durability that suggests the reality of place. A
place like Cuba, which perforce is a place of the imagined, to which actual
travel is illegal (for U.S. citizens, outlawed by our government) and sometimes even more venomously proscribed (for many Cuban expatriates, by
their own families' elders), almost seems to demand a poetic form of ad-
dress, a structured language that allows an approach, perhaps like a bridge,
a feat of linguistic engineering, like Hart Crane describing the Brooklyn
Bridge, wondrous symbol of great promise and possibility, at once sturdy
and precarious, connecting the modern to what lay beyond it. The poem I
want to write about Cuba holds fast to it; it is crafted to the specifications
of its elusiveness. The poem, I have always thought, can speak the unspeakable; it creates a well-defined space from the dimensions of nothing
and loss.

To the modernist, that ever-so-seductive figure to the Cuban expatriate, the poem is itself the thing, the very place, unadorned, without artifice. It is so real it can be touched, or tasted, or seen—raindrops on the red
wheelbarrow (or, perhaps more appropriately here, on the red skin of a
ripe mango). How I have longed for the modernist fantasy to be true! Yet
I know it is a false promise. Cuba itself is locked in the modernist moment
and persists as a monument to an ideology that was supposed to explain
and control everything, its monolithic apartment blocks and government
buildings built to serve a purpose and not to be beautiful, its spartan *poli-
clínicas* efficiently administering vaccinations and other basic medical
care while helping round up people with AIDS for quarantine. A word
is enough to denounce one's neighbor in Cuba, enough to send a homosexual or a counterculture intellectual to prison for life. I suppose words
cannot get more real than that. Hence the functional, parsimonious, in-
conspicuous poem, poured out like concrete over jungle, would seem to be
the ideal medium for rendering such a modernist paradise. So there must

be more to the compelling utility of poetry than its deliberateness and craftedness—and more to a place than mere objects.

We "Latinos" (as some of us like to call ourselves here in the U.S.A.) ultimately prefer, of course, what has been termed magical realism to such practicality and drabness. Reflecting more closely who we are as a people—diverse in terms of national identities, flamboyant and exclamatory in temperament, and of mixed Indian, African, and European blood—we especially appreciate the hybrid quality of this brand of literary writing, where elements of what we can so plainly recognize around us are fused with our superstitions and fantasies and passions. In the strange realm of Allende and Borges and García- Márquez, artifice perhaps comes to eclipse craft per se. The many repressive forces within Latin American societies—not just the failed Communist government in Cuba and other inhumane forms of totalitarianism (such as the dictatorship of Batista that preceded Castro, and others more long lived in Central and South America), but also the Catholic Church, rampant crime, and extreme poverty, to name a few—seem to drive us to these escapist fictions. Rather than confront the innumerable dead in Pinochet's Chile, or search out the fates Argentina's *desaparecidos,* it is pleasantly distracting to ponder the bloodless allegory of the labyrinth, far more palatable to savor the preposterous notion that secret recipes can induce love. This writing takes us on a journey, but too often it is a journey *away* from truth, no matter how human its impulse to do so may be, and how ostensibly harmless.

This tension between what seem two poles in the imaginative journey to Cuba suddenly brings back one of my saddest family memories. I remember a lesser journey, one I took within the confines of my grandparents' bedroom, which was always kept curtained and dark, and thus was the coolest place in their house in Miami. The modest dimensions of the room made their bed seem enormous behind the closed door; the usual riot of voices and smells drifted in to me but seemed weirdly distant, as if from a broadcast picked up on a radio in a weak signal from another country, a kind of reverse Voice of America—as if all the way from Cuba. The bulky dresser, low enough that I could make out some of its enticing, talismanic objects—my *abuela*'s hairbrush, my grandfather's keys, a glow-in-the-dark plastic rosary. And in a basket, some papers in envelopes, some postcards—it was the busy-ness of words, not even the images of Cuba, that attracted me to these the most. What messages, what secret codes, what stories did they contain? Soon, I was poring over them, insatiable reader that I was, even then. Private words and thoughts galloped

. . . .

through me, racing like my heart. After a short while, I learned my grandfather had cancer. (Although most of the details were contained in language I could not yet understand, I remember that word so vividly that I
assume now I must have only recently learned its meaning.)

At that awful moment, amidst all my confusion and terror and guilt
and excitement, I can distinctly recall feeling pulled in two directions: one
was toward the security of knowledge, the odd comfort of knowing, un-
embellished, this piece of information, and the other, toward the fantasy
that it was not true, that I could somehow revise what I now knew by re-
casting it as a story, as make-believe. The letter from the doctor, the hospital bill—serviceable, neatly typed, raw, containing just what they meant.
The postcard from my aunt in Cuba, the letter that I guessed had been
returned from someone whose name I didn't recognize—wild loops of
handwriting inflated by emotion, denial, hoping for a cure, imagining the
worst. I suppose that even then, for the first time, I yearned for a form of
expression that was neither of these, neither heartless fact nor groundless
fancy. I wanted to feel whole again, to be transported to a familiar territory, a nation whose language was truth.

In the light of these inadequate, or at least unsatisfactory, models for
creating place in language, it is fascinating to consider how the Cuba
forged out of a novel poetry—a postmodern poetry, shall we call it for the
moment, for lack of a better adjective—is perhaps not only more accurate,
but even somehow preferable to, more authentic than, the real place.
Cuba, the unreachable island, must be a different place to me than it is to
the woman of Yoruba descent who cannot read at all but whose chanting
voice echoes during her daily prayers amidst its interior's mountains, to the
mestizo fisherman who sees the verdant countryside sprawled out every
day before his rickety boat as he pulls it into the sea, to the white Com
munist Party minister who dines nightly on steak served on fine china
stolen from a successful merchant family who escaped. The chorus of
voices harnessed in such a poetry animates the place in its stew of distinct
traditions and mixed metaphors and half-truths born of myths or fantasies. Surely the postmodern notion of the fragment also has literal expression in current-day Cuba, in the crumbling grand old buildings that
line the *Malecón* and the streets of downtown Havana, in the brokenness
of the Soviet empire of which it was once a part, indeed in the disconnec-
tion of its own people both within the country (the modern-day myth of
its classless society proven false) and across the most charged of political
and national borders. Even the stubborn Descartian dualism of body and

soul, so emblematic of the Cuban plight, may yield itself to this new poetry. Decades later, after my grandfather died of the disease we never discussed (just as we never discussed Cuba), I wrote a sequence of sonnets in his memory, during a year off between my second and third years of medical school—poems that had the effect for me of finally locating myself closer to that beloved, immortal place, poems that began to heal the twin wounds of his death and our exile. The cacophony of Cuba, the irresolvable arguments and the shrieks of children, the clash of *son* with the incessant chittering of insects—perhaps in the poem that is labored over but that ultimately leaves itself unfinished, the poem that sounds like Spanish but is written in English, the poem that proudly recalls its origins but humbly recognizes it comes from many places—perhaps this poem is the one that is Cuba.

Down the hall, I hear the commotion of my family finishing dinner and reconvening in the family room, honk of chairs pushed back from the table, clinking of glasses and silverware being cleared. Someone puts on a CD: the Buena Vista Social Club. Cuba is suddenly the rage now, all over again; Americans, like entitled teenagers, often crave what is forbidden to them. Night has fallen, and a solitary star shines over the valley, as if privately alight for me, teasing me as if aware of its metaphorical powers. I close my eyes to it and picture my grandparents dancing, conjured back to life before the liquid black pool of a spinning LP on a phonograph. I imagine what hung on the walls of their house, what the floor was like, what they heard out the window, whether there was some breeze. I am almost there; the music is so familiar, the lyrics so nearly perfect, it is like I have been there before. When I try to write again, all that comes forth is a few tears—not for what was lost, no, but for what it is yet possible to create.

"This grass is very dark to be from the white heads of old mothers."

. . . .

by
MICHAEL JOSEPH GROSS

I couldn't have been more than ten years old when I first read this line. I found a cheap yellowed paperback copy of Walt Whitman's *Leaves of Grass* in our house and liked the pink and green colors on the cover and wise-looking old man whose picture was there. I scanned the pages but the order of the words was strange to the point of being incomprehensible. Then I found that stretch of "Song of Myself" where Whitman asks what death is: "What do you think has become of the women and children?" His answer was closer to believable than anything I'd heard in the Methodist church where Momma took me every Sunday:

They are alive and well somewhere,
The smallest sprout shows there is really no death,
And if ever there was it led forward life, and does not wait at the end
    to arrest it,
And ceased the moment life appeared.

All goes onward and outward, nothing collapses,
And to die is different from what anyone supposed, and luckier.

It was a sweaty day when I read this. The pulpy pages were sticking to my fingers, but these words had an energy that was exactly the opposite of the day's. They shot into me, seemingly without my having exerted any effort of understanding. Excited, I took it to Momma in the kitchen and read it out loud.

I wished that she would tell me what I believed: that it was true, that I was right to let it make me feel safe. What she did say I've forgotten. I remember her standing by the kitchen sink smiling, looking scared and proud of her boy. I think she just did not know what to make of it.

My mother, who used to weigh 130 pounds, dropped to 95 after we put her in the nursing home. This was my first time seeing her in the sixteen months that had passed since then. One morning in May, I flew from Provincetown to Boston and from Boston to Chicago, rented a white economy sedan, and drove four hours into southern Illinois to the farm town where I grew up. I dropped my bags at home and drove with Dad to the county nursing home, which sits directly across the street from the town's tombstone dealership.

In the fluorescent light of the nursing home's one long hallway a young attendant, a woman I must have known in high school but can't remember, said, "Glad ya could come home, Michael," in a surly voice, in a way that may or may not have revealed her judgment but certainly sparked my guilt. I saw Mom sitting in a chair, in a row of old people sitting in chairs. Her white hair was thin and half fallen out. Her arms and legs were stringy with ligaments and tendons.

All day she sat in this wide red vinyl recliner with high armrests, and all day she twisted her limbs around each other like vines, and in this twisted state tried to curl herself into a fetal position. Her eyes were big in their sockets and usually unfocused, and sometimes she clutched her hands to her forehead and ground her teeth, slowly and deliberately. When she was more relaxed, her eyes sometimes focused on the person she was with.

I tried to act normal, as if I wasn't shocked to see her, as if looking at her didn't make my eyes burn and the first thing on my mind wasn't the fact that she was going to die. When I sat down next to her and reached out for her hand a smile broke across her face. For a minute or so, she beamed with a look that I'd like to think was recognition. Then she assumed a neutral expression of heightened awareness that is distinctively hers. It is a willed brightness. It says, *I am not going to let you know how hard this is for me.* Looking at her, I wondered how old she was when she learned this look, and who she ever thought she was fooling.

She probably learned this look as a girl. After her father died when she was seven, she moved with her mother and younger brother from Kansas through Missouri, Illinois, and Indiana, at least ten times in eleven years. The inscriptions in her high-school yearbook say things like, *Jean—You seemed like such a nice person. I'm sorry we didn't get to know each other better.*

.   .   .   .

She probably refined this look for my dad, whom she often addressed as Daddy, and from whom, as far as I was able to see, for as far back as I can remember, she successfully hid practically all of her thoughts and feelings. I am not aware of a single occasion on which Dad asked for her advice about childrearing, vacations, finances, or any important question affecting our life together. Growing up, sometimes I asked Mom why she wanted to be married to someone who wasn't interested in anything she had to say. She always gave the same answer: "He doesn't hit me. He gives us everything we need."

I am not going to let you know how hard this is for me was also, and probably most importantly, a tenet of Mom's faith. Her favorite book was *The Power of Positive Thinking* by Norman Vincent Peale. She believed that any difficulty could be overcome by willing herself to righteous action, and she believed that righteous action consisted of always placing her own interests last. Because her self-effacement was real, she was easily taken for granted—by me and my sister, by our neighbors, by anyone who ever received a coffee cake or loaf of bread she stayed up late to bake. She never expected reciprocation for her generosity, and it was rarely offered.

Mom's habit of self-sacrifice was so abject that I will probably always wonder whether her rapid decline into Alzheimer's was entirely biologically based. When Mom called me at college in Massachusetts three days after my sister's suicide attempt, she delivered the news ten minutes into the conversation, leading with, "We're all happy now, but your sister's in the hospital." Mom had been forgetful before. After this she became even more disengaged from the world; but I still hoped that she was just depressed and might pull out of it.

Almost three years later, when she was fifty-eight and I was twenty-six, Mom was diagnosed with early onset Alzheimer's, and my father has been her sole caretaker since then. I've come home to visit about once a year, no more often than I visited before. My sister and I agree that visits work best when they're scheduled leapfrog style. She arrives in Illinois (from San Francisco) one day; I arrive the next; she leaves the following day; and I leave the day after that. Neither of us wants to spend more than two or three days at a time here, and neither of us can stand to be here for very long without the other around. Dad is not easy to get along with.

"Tell your shrink that your dad's a *classic narcissist*," said his sister, my aunt (a psychologist), when I started psychotherapy three years ago. "That will save you some time." She explained that a classic narcissist is a person who cannot understand that other people have an existence independent from his own.

On Christmas morning in 1999, the second year that I did not go home for the holiday, when Mom and Dad showed up at the hospital emergency room, the doctor could not imagine how Mom could have sustained the bruises on the bones beneath her eyes when, as Dad explained, she fell next to the toilet in the bathroom. The doctor filed a report with the state, alleging physical abuse. Around the same time, several other reports were filed independently by neighbors. She had been walking around town with black eyes for months. He had been yelling at her in public, calling her stupid and saying that she was trying to drive *him* crazy.

Social workers investigated the complaints. I learned of the investigations from an offhand remark in a letter from a relative, then called to tell my aunt and my sister, and together we arranged for Mom to enter the nursing home. Dad resisted; he said the charges were false. We said he had no choice in the matter. When she was institutionalized the investigations were dropped.

Months later, in a conversation with Dad, he said to me abruptly, "I loved her so much. We had such a good life together."

I said that I could not imagine how hard it had been for him to take care of her all alone, that he had done more than most men would do to take care of their wives, and that I admired his commitment. I also said I knew that sometimes people lose control in situations like his; they do things they wouldn't normally do. I meant all of it. His staying with her makes me think their love must be more complex than I can see. But I was also trying to make him feel safe so he could tell me the true answer to the question of whether he really did hit her. I didn't want to scare him by asking point blank, but I did want to know. I wanted to be told what I already believed. He said, "I never did anything but love her."

One of the most frightening and unsettling things about Mom's disease is its cruel logic. Her current situation is consistent with the whole emotional trajectory of her life with Dad. She has always wanted to disappear, to become an instrument of his will. He has always treated her as his property, as if she existed solely to please him.

The night of that first visit, Dad told me that he went to the nursing home every day at five to hand-feed Mom solid food for supper—"to put some food down her," as if she were a hole. Feeding Mom, Dad did not pick up

. . . .

any of the crumbs that fell down the front of her sweatshirt or wipe any of the bits of cheese from the corners of her mouth. With crumbs of food on her face and clothes, she would not look at me. With a napkin I wiped her mouth, her nose, and then she would look at me again.

To prepare me for this visit, Dad had said that she was "a vegetable" now. She had not spoken in months. Then, surprising everyone, she spoke one word while my sister and I were with her.

When we saw her on my second day home, her face was fearsome with the effort of shaping her lips to speak, and then she said it. She said, *"Hesus."* Her voice was labored, relieved. Then her focus collapsed, her eyes seemed deeper in her skull again, exhausted.

After we left, my sister and I asked each other at the same time if she meant to say "Jesus." We laughed a little bit, awkwardly. It broke the tension.

Which was necessary—because really, what do you *do* with that? We talked it out. Was it a random thought? An instruction to believe? Or maybe something more fantastic. Was it something she saw, Jesus with her in that room? Is this word, which names for her the greatest love, a name for her own love for us? A name for our presence with her? In that moment, she was Jesus? We were Jesus?

I told my sister about a poem that came to mind, one that, on first reading, hit me with the force of Whitman: "As Kingfishers Catch Fire" by Gerard Manley Hopkins, in which ". . . Christ plays in ten thousand places / Lovely in limbs, and lovely in eyes not his / To the Father through the features of men's faces."

I told her that was the poem I recited to myself every day of the summer when I was twenty-three, a seminarian preaching in a Siberian Yupik Eskimo church in Nome, Alaska.

Each mortal thing does one thing and the same:
    Deals out that being indoors each one dwells;
    Selves—goes itself; *myself* it speaks and spells,
Crying *What I do is me: for that I came.*

We remembered what a good Methodist Mom was, how the Jesus she introduced to us was a man of love, though not, like Hopkins's Jesus, particularly encouraging of self-awareness. Hopkins promises that to be fully oneself is to "act . . . in God's eye what in God's eye he is: Christ." Although Mom seemed never to have that kind of confidence in her own

goodness, she did teach us that Jesus loved us more than we could imagine, with a love that is superior to all others, but never judgmental or
condescending.

All this, from *Hesus*. It could mean anything.

The summer when I recited Hopkins to myself was the summer when I finally figured out that I was gay. It was Hopkins, with his promise that to
be what you ought, you must be who you are, who gave me the words to
reconcile my life with Christ's. Although this was two years before my
mom's diagnosis with Alzheimer's, it was the period during which her disease was becoming a fact that no one but she and my father could ignore.
Simultaneous transformations: something inside her was killing her; something inside me was bringing me alive. She, always the sacrificial character
in our family, lost vitality as I gained it.

The gift of awareness was hard for me to accept, however, because
Momma, who defined love for me, was also the person who first defined
gayness for me—in the form of a warning, even a threat, that if I kissed a
boy, she would be hurt beyond measure.

In first grade my best friend Andy and I liked to play a game in which
we took the roles of whichever boy and girl in our class were deepest in
boyfriendly-girlfriendly love. Steve and Lisa were the hot couple on the
last day we ever played this game. We rolled around on the floor on the
yellow carpet under the piano bench in my living room, hugging, petting
each other's hair, kissing each other on the cheeks and nose and forehead,
saying, "Oh, oh, Steve"; "Ohhhh, oh! Lisa!" and then I (Steve) would try
to kiss Andy (Lisa) on the lips and he would refuse.

After Andy left that afternoon my mom, who never punished me, sat
me down on the piano bench, very upset, and said nervously, "I heard
what you were doing."

I looked up at her, not understanding.

"You were trying to kiss Andy," she said. "You must never, ever do that
again."

I was confused. I think I tried to explain: it was Steve and Lisa, not
Michael and Andy.

She kept on, stammering: "I don't want you to become a—a *fruit*."

Now I was more confused. "A what?"

A fruit, Mom explained, was "a man who kisses other men. It's very,
very, very bad, it's an awful thing to be, and I don't want you to be one.

. . . .

You have to grow up and marry a girl, and have babies, and I'll be a grandma."

I agreed, but I didn't understand. I had never stopped to wonder whether Andy and I *really* wanted to kiss each other. It was a fun game. Why was this the one thing that made her angry with me?

"Never, ever do anything in your life that you can't do in front of me," she said, looking for a long time into my eyes. I promised I wouldn't. I hugged her and things seemed mostly okay.

This happened in the only house I ever lived in growing up, a rambling turn-of the-century Victorian that sits on three acres on the edge of town. It was built by a bank president as a present for his wife, who is said to have reluctantly left Chicago for the cornfields of southern Illinois. When I go home the house is always a little closer to dereliction, and on this visit I noticed that the back steps on the front porch had collapsed and vegetation had grown up over the rotting boards. Lengths of gutter and trim dangled from the roof. The rock garden by the back porch had been dispersed: the steer's skull (which used to sit next to the old wagon wheel that leans against the latticework where I grew a patch of morning glories every year) was sitting in the middle of the backyard, where the dome climber used to be. Of the three cars in the driveway, one still ran.

Inside, my father's collections covered almost every surface of the house. There were copper kettles, trilobites, MacDonald's Happy Meal prizes, Native American kachina dolls (and baskets, drums, ladders, rugs, arrowheads), baseball caps from grain elevators, crockery, sharks' teeth, pale blue Danish plates, and more. Two nineteenth-century sleighs (the horse-drawn kind) sat in the garage. Rows of empty glass showcases stood in the basement.

On this visit home I found two shotguns leaning in the corners of Dad's bedroom and a pistol on the floor next to where he slept. I didn't look to see if they were loaded. I asked him why the guns were out and he said, "I've got 'em. I want to see 'em." He said he didn't keep them in display cases because "what if somebody breaks in?" But the lock on our back door was so old and worn that it no longer required a key. When I first arrived, he showed me how to open it with a rusty knife that he kept on the porch.

It's hard to go back home. I feel that I almost cease to exist, because there is no room for people in this house anymore. The living room, dining room, kitchen, and all of the bedrooms are now storage rooms for Dad's collections, piled just shy of the toppling point. Before I arrived Dad had cleared an 18-inch swath around the perimeter of the bed in my old room. In the dark before I closed my eyes to sleep, I saw the stacks of boxes that rose a couple feet above mattress level like the miniature skyline of a miniature city.

Before Mom got sick, the house was almost as full but not as cluttered. Mom used to devise ingenious ways of hiding Dad's collections in the closets, but she would also fantasize about radical housecleaning. In a puttering, mock-crazy voice she'd say, "*Stuff!* Stuff stuff stuff stuff stuff stuff stuff," although she never got rid of any of it.

She couldn't get rid of it. She lived in Dad's definition of a family, in Dad's definition of a home, in Dad's definition of her self. She had no close friends and rarely permitted herself the luxury of a long-distance phone call to keep in touch with relatives out West. Her confidants were our dogs—a succession of poodles and other small breeds that Dad would bring home from his veterinary practice when he came across a dog he couldn't bear to put to sleep. I was her other confidant. Sometimes she would make a cup of Constant Comment tea and call me to the kitchen to talk—conversations I loved, because growing up I never felt closer to anybody, and also resented, because I wished somebody else would be her best friend. "You listen to me," she would say thankfully, "I can talk to you."

By the time I came out to my dad four years ago, Mom's thoughts and behavior had grown completely unpredictable. One day she cried because "all the good people died" the same year that her father had died, "especially the triple one." After an hour of coaxing and guessing, we figured it out: Franklin Delano Roosevelt. She loved to quack like a duck and giggle at the noises she could make.

Dad's first response when I came out to him was to ask, "Is this because of something *I* did? Or didn't do?" He asked me not to tell Mom, and I agreed that it was best not to risk unleashing fear in her mind. But like most rationalizations for the closet, this proved an unsustainable silence, because the impulse to romantic love is woven into the center of a person. It affects the shape of every other love in a person's life.

Communication with home trailed off. The telephone was mysteriously traumatic for Mom: she said hello and dropped it on the floor. Conversations with Dad were no better. He didn't tell me about Mom's doctor's appointments or current condition; he balked when I asked questions because he had it all under control; and after a while, I stopped asking. Also,

. . . .

at that time coming out was my central emotional occupation, but any mention of men I was dating or even new friends I was making met with silence on his end.

There was not much left to talk about. I gave brief updates about my job writing speeches for a politician. He told me what he'd found with his metal detector. Every time I talked with him I felt prickly adolescent hatred because it seemed like I had nothing to say but everything, which couldn't be said.

When I stepped in to help with Mom's move to the nursing home, things with Dad started, slowly, to change. After that, I was a little more present in our conversations, he was a little less overpowering, and then I started having a wish that I couldn't understand.

I wanted to tell Mom that I'm gay. I didn't know why, except that when I imagined her dying without my having told her, it made me feel intolerably alone. But to tell her now seemed foolish, even disingenuous. I lectured myself. I had waited too long, lost my chance. Now she couldn't understand, so my disclosure would be only for my benefit. Without her understanding, wouldn't this confession be just a cheap imitation of courage? A domestic theatrical skit— "Boy Tells Mother He's Gay."

A friend helped me untangle those thoughts: "It won't hurt her," he said, "and it might make you feel better." He helped me remember some things I believe: that coming out is not, fundamentally, a confession, even though it often takes that form; and its ultimate purpose is not to help anyone else understand. Coming out is a discipline of reclaiming ourselves from oblivion by getting rid of the fears that cut us off from who we are.

That first night visiting the nursing home, after Dad finished feeding Mom, I asked if we could have some time alone. He left the room and I held Mom's right hand and told her that I wanted her to know about my life. I told her about the beach where I lived and the places I'd been traveling and my friends and my work and I told her that I'm gay. I said I'm sorry I didn't tell her earlier, but I hadn't known how she'd take it and I hadn't wanted to worry her. I said I didn't know how she'd take it now, or whether she'd understand, but that I hoped she'd at least see, at least sense, somehow, that I'm happier, stronger, more confident than I had been before.

She looked at me the whole time I was talking. When I stopped, she started smiling, and she smiled for a long time. She reached out the hand I wasn't holding, and, one at a time, she touched every feature of my face— cheeks, eyes, forehead, nose, lips, chin.

When Dad came back into the room, I wondered if he sensed that anything special had happened. I probably wouldn't have told him anyway, but before I could say a word, he noticed Mom gripping my pointer finger. "Watch out," he said, laughing strangely, "she's going to break it off."

Before I came out to anyone, I had a dream in which I saw myself talking in a completely new way—at one with my words, which came fluently, effortlessly—something I'd never experienced in waking life, where I was always searching for the right phrase and rarely feeling I'd gotten it right.

I don't remember what I was talking about or who I was talking to. The setting and the words didn't matter as much as this fact about the dream: my dreaming self knew, watching my dream self speak, that the reason I was able to be inside my words was that the person I was talking with knew that I loved men.

I remember waking up hopeful, imagining that if I could find the courage to come out, maybe someday I could speak that way. I also remember thinking, *If you talked that way in this dream, that voice is inside you already.*

Entering the lobby of Chicago's venerable Palmer House Hotel, I was surrounded by squads of shirtless men in black leather: armbands, harnesses, jeans, chaps. Tattooed slogans in six-inch Gothic letters arched across naked backs: SLAVE, STRENGTH THROUGH PAIN. I saw a man on all fours barking like a dog, his neck straining against a metal leash held tight by his Master, snapping his jaws at the chew stick with which his Master teased him, to the amusement of all gathered near. I wasn't completely sure that I belonged here, but it was where I wanted to be.

I had timed my visit home so that I could go to Chicago directly afterward for International Mister Leather (IML), the world's largest annual gathering of leather men. Held every Memorial Day weekend, IML is at heart a kind of beauty pageant. Contestants from sixty countries compete in the categories of Physique Posing, Fetish Costume, and Personal Interview. Throughout the weekend, the hotel also hosts a Leather Marketplace, where I watched porn stars sell used jockstraps to fans; I browsed long rows of butt plugs ranging in size from baby carrot to traffic cone; and I watched photographers take souvenir portraits of men in full regalia. One who advertised "Free Bondage with Photo!" snapped shots of a Minnesota couple. The bottom was handcuffed, naked, on his knees; the top, in harness and chaps, stood impassive like the farmer in *American Gothic,* holding a whip where Grant Wood painted a pitchfork.

This was my second IML. The previous year, my first, was a mostly solitary experience. In the mornings I would go to the Art Institute or take architectural tours of Louis Sullivan buildings, which were among the first American skyscrapers. At lunchtime each day I read *Kindergarten Chats,* a book of Sullivan's essays, the most famous of which is written in the form of a Socratic dialogue between a master architect and his pupil. Sullivan's architectural mantra—"Form ever follows function"—was grounded in his anthropology: "It stands to reason that a thing looks like what it is, and, vice versa, it is what it looks like," he wrote. "And so does the form, man, stand for the function, man." In the same way that a man's appearance projects his character, Sullivan believed that a building's appearance should be determined by the function of its interior space. Reading this while wearing a leather jockstrap and chaps, eating chicken Caesar salad, I wrestled earnestly with the question of whether to believe that "that which exists in spirit ever seeks and finds its physical counterpart in form, its visible image."

Of course I didn't just read. I spent the afternoons and evenings cruising, but I devoted less energy to connecting with other people than to the project of constructing a plausible argument about why I had chosen to be there, and why I was drawn to the idea, but frightened by the experience, of sexual submission.

Procrastination is not always a waste of time. Part of the process of experiencing desire is questioning where it comes from. Freud's smothering-mother/distant-father theory is an insufficient explanation of the origins of gay desire, but the idea is still compelling for a boy like me who identifies with his mother. When loving men was still an impulse that I would not name, when it was something my body did over my will's objections, even then I wondered: Do I feel this way because my dad doesn't love me enough? Maybe, I hoped, searching for any explanation but the obvious, I'm just needing my daddy.

For me, the anxiety of coming out contained a huge measure of anxiety that I was gay because I'd been unable, as a boy, to develop attachments to my father and other men. The men I want instinctively are the big strong men, with a relaxed phallic vitality that *makes* and *does* and *is.* As I quickly learned when I started coming out, when this kind of man wants to have sex with me, he usually wants to fuck me. Then I panicked, because I feared what it meant to be wanted that way: that it meant I was a girl of a man.

More than any words that a man can say, the experience of getting fucked is what viscerally defines him as gay. When I came out to one female friend from college, she asked if I'd yet been "you know, the receiver," and when she learned that I hadn't, she was relieved; she said it meant I was still straight. Talking about sex with straight male friends, I find that they can relate to me as a man only if I talk about being a top. No matter how tenderly phrased, any mention of getting fucked will make most straight men wish you'd disappear. It's a deeply strange position to be in. When a man admits to bottoming, he's erased from the whole straight world, and at exactly the same time, he writes himself onto that world as queer, in great big flaming letters that can never be put out.

Straight friends aren't the only ones who help sustain the shame. I've never known a group of gay men who didn't constantly tease each other about the feminine associations of bottoming. A huge amount of prestige attaches to the "total top"—usually a big strapping thing who says he's never been and does not want to be a bottom. He is supremely alluring because supremely masculine. And the straight world's double standard regarding sexual reputation applies equally among gay guys I know: getting fucked all the time makes a man a slut; fucking all the time makes a man a stud.

The good Daddies I have known have had one thing in common: they use humiliation to paradoxical effect, revealing how absurd shame actually is. Daddy calls boy his bitch; he brings the bottom's hidden shame into the open and plays with it, makes shame a source of pleasure, beauty, and even power. The first leather top I met taught me a maxim of the leather world—that the bottom is always in control, because the bottom chooses a safe word at the beginning of the scene. A good top knows how to read his bottom, to take him to his limit of pleasure or pain, and then push just beyond it. For the times when Daddy's judgment fails, however, the safe word is the bottom's power. I say that word, the scene is done.

I've never had a relationship that involved dominance and submission—a taste for leather is not among my prerequisites for dating—and with most men I'm as happy to give as to receive. For me, elements of leather sex provide specialized terms in a larger vocabulary of sexual practices. You don't say "flummox" every day, but sometimes it's the only word that works.

I planned to be at IML after visiting home this year because I wanted to

. . . .

blow off steam, to enjoy a weekend of animal existence. After seeing my mother on the verge of disappearance, after endless conversations with my father and sister about how difficult this was and how much we missed her, with an undercurrent of unavoidable awareness of our own mortality, I knew I'd want to go someplace where I didn't know anyone, where I could do exactly what I wanted to do and think later about whether it was right or wrong. This year, I decided that I wasn't going to spend the weekend reading architectural theory and indulging the grandiose fear that my submissive side means that I am unspeakably fucked up.

And this year, when I talked with people at IML, I wanted to listen with my whole body, and not to fear what my responses meant before I felt what those responses were. When I asked one sexy, single Master whether he and his slave would ever break character when they were in public, he said, "I don't think of these as roles. This is who we are. Most people in our lives would not know that we are Master and slave. But I would dominate my slave in subtle ways in public. He would open the door for me as we enter a restaurant. When I realized that I'd forgotten my glasses in the car, he would retrieve them." I got an erection while he was telling me this.

Within three hours of arriving at the Palmer House I had found myself a Daddy for the afternoon, a big tall Italian man whom I'll call Tony, with a nose-filled face, a light dusting of hair on his shins, an arm-swinging, oh-I-didn't-even-notice-my-shirt-was-off swagger, and a disarming come-on-smart-boy-relax affection for me. He's a dog breeder. Boxers and Jack Russell terriers, he said at first. Later he revealed an expertise with less butch breeds when he told me that one of his clients is a 1970s movie star who is known for having adopted an enormous number of children. As it turns out, she also collects poodles. Very small ones. I imagined her at home in Connecticut, frantically seeking more and more smaller and smaller babies to take care of. "You cannot make a poodle small enough for that lady," Tony said.

We had a nice time. "You know you feel empty without it," he said, when, wanting him to fuck me, I told him I didn't want him to fuck me.

Afterward he told me that his last relationship had been a three-year Master/slave arrangement. He said that he had thought being a Master was the ultimate safeguard against being abandoned. "I thought if I owned him, he would never leave me."

I asked him if he wanted to go with me to an orgy that night. He said he'd rather not, and I went by myself.

The party, called Pig Fuck, hosted by a porn studio, took place in an empty warehouse in a bombed-out neighborhood just beyond the Loop. Off-duty policemen provided security. About 500 men paid $40 each for tickets, which included unlimited beverages (beer and water) and clothes check. In the entryway, men stripped down. Most were naked except for their boots. Clothes-check claim numbers were written with black markers directly onto each man's skin. Mine was B-12.

Beyond the clothes check was a maze of rooms and corridors with raw concrete floors, walled off by sheets of plastic and fabric hung from the ceiling. Some rooms were empty dark spaces; others, with slings, were well lighted. There were four Porta Potties, but on the way to the Porta Potties were two inflated kiddie pools, guys standing in circles pissing on the guys laid flat out in them.

Dance music played. I watched three men moving their bodies in time, pressing their three faces together in a kiss, to a remix of the Beatles singing "All the Lonely People." Probably no one heard me chuckle for all the grunting and "Fuck yeah!" and "Fuck me!" and "Fucker!" that filled the room. Somebody said, "You fucked all three?" and somebody else said, "Nah, just one," and lit a cigarette.

In one dark room I immediately found a man my size, around my age, with my build and my haircut—a skinny, smooth boy with a buzz cut; the kind of man I am almost never attracted to—and we reached out and put our arms around each other and kissed, and he kissed just like I did. We just stood there kissing and holding each other for the longest time, two little boys clinging to each other, or to ourselves, and we didn't say a word.

Then I went to find a big man. I saw the one I wanted, a fireplug mound of muscle getting a blow job from a boy on his knees. I touched his chest to see how he'd react and he pulled me to him and pushed the other man's face away from his cock. He had pecs like saddlebags, bigger than tits, a thick meaty cock I gagged on, and when beer came burning up in my throat, I sat back to catch my breath and he leaned down and touched my face, kissed me, tongue in my mouth even though it couldn't have tasted good. I pulled a condom from my sock and put it on him and he raised me up to bend me over, a crowd of men around us watching. I remembered the morning after I kissed a man for the first time, waking up finally knowing I was a body, and not just a personality and a mind *inside* a body, and here in the warehouse, looking up at the circle of hard cocks, hearing voices groaning *G'boy,* I felt something like that again, felt new, all the way to my core, free and full. At the end I stood and turned, face to face, licking sweat off each other's cheeks and foreheads, noses, chins, eyes,

.   .   .   .

feast of armpits, hug and kiss and then he said he had to go and find his boyfriend. He gave me his business card and said that I should e-mail him and keep in touch. He held my head against his shoulder, petting me, calling me names that would look nasty on paper, names I wouldn't let anyone call me most days, but if any words could have made me feel more powerful in that moment, I have no idea what they are.

By writing the things I've just written, maybe I'm taking revenge on Mom for making that rule about never doing anything that I couldn't do in front of her. Maybe I'm also drawing closer to Mom than I've been before. Mom always got Dad's glasses from the car when he forgot them on the dashboard.

After I left for college, Mom wrote letters to me constantly. When she moved into the nursing home, I organized all of the letters I had received from her that I had with me at my apartment in Provincetown. The file is five inches thick: thicker than *War and Peace,* thicker than *Don Quixote.* I put the letters in chronological order and started reading them studiously. She always said that she was happy. Every description of every day was circumscribed by a deliriously humble, maddeningly opaque optimism, tight and tinny like a song by the Andrews Sisters. Then I found an extravagant litany of hope, edged with open anxiety, which was so beautiful it stopped me from reading any more of the letters: "Every day I wish & pray for so much for you—for happiness & health & challenges & contentment & friends & peace & for life everafter & pride & compassion & for coming home once in a while."

On this visit home I found under my bed another cache of letters written in Mom's neat, tiny hand, and a kind of scholarly impulse kicked in. At first I wanted to take them home, to organize them, to have them, regardless of whether I would read them. But my suitcases were full, and I knew that I wouldn't read them, at least no time soon, so they're still under the bed in that room, and there's a mousetrap sitting just outside the door.

I used to wish that Mom would come into her own and be free after my sister and I left home. She would stop being the servant of our household. She would travel and spend her own money and have fun. Now when I get upset because none of that will ever happen, I try to remember that my fantasy was not hers anyway. She lived with a very clear sense of the limits of pleasure she was allowed, and it showed in everything she said and did, even in her smile, which was sometimes easy but never full. At the top of her smile, the corners of her mouth always turned down a little, as if even that were too much pleasure to permit herself. As if she couldn't be inside the moment of the reason for that smile—worrying backward in time, whether her pleasure was justified, or worrying forward in time, that the pleasure couldn't last.

In my room at the Palmer House, Tony stood naked behind me in front of the mirror because he wanted to look at us together, and I recognized, as I sometimes do, that same shape on my own smile. "What's wrong?" he asked. I smiled again, a little fuller than before.

Holding Momma's hand, my sister said, "It's soft," because Mom's hands were always dry from all the dishwashing, no matter how much lotion she put on them at night. I held the other hand. My sister petted Mom's hair and said, "Momma, your hair's so *white*," because our mom always was embarrassed that her hair, gray since she was thirty-five, was tinged with yellow, and so she used her special Silver Fox shampoo to try to make it whiter. "You would be so happy," she said, "your hair is finally white." We also noticed that somebody at the nursing home had been plucking all the little hairs from Mom's chin, the hairs so fine she couldn't see them. When we were children, on Sundays before church she would ask one of us to pluck them with tweezers for her, and even though we hated doing this, and we were mean enough to tell her so, one of us would always do it anyway.

The next morning, after my sister had left, I went back to the nursing home alone for my last visit with Mom and read to her from Revelation, the New Jerusalem passage, in which God wipes every tear from her eyes, and there is no more suffering. She was grinding her teeth and beating her forehead with her fist, and I could hear her bowels moving. She didn't seem to hear a word I said, and that night, after driving four hours north across flat land on which storm clouds trailed rain like jellyfish trailing tentacles, I am in the dark of that warehouse, amazed I am licking the sweat from the smile of this man, licking with happiness and pride and compassion, full of gratefulness that I can choose to be exactly where I am. This moment's no epiphany, but still it has a point, and it's a point that I'll come back to, a place where nothing's wasted and whose name is always true. Here, *here* is the point. Like deer finding salt in the deep woods, the fact of these, our tongues and tastes, the sole point, the whole moment. *Here.*

Seeing Is Believing

·   ·   ·   ·   ·   ·   ·   ·   ·

by
CARMEN BOULLOSA
translated by Alfred MacAdam

All my adult life, I've been nearsighted. Very myopic. So much so that glasses were totally useless. If I tried to wear them with the correction I really needed, walls would begin to curve and straight hallways would metamorphose into round but not transparent fishbowls. My limited vision was a genuine handicap. For me, seeing—what other people do as involuntarily as breathing—was possible only at the cost of tremendous effort. It sounds ridiculous to say "effort" about wearing contact lenses, but that's what it was. Eye irritation was a prelude to conjunctivitis and scratched corneas, heavy prices to pay. To see or not to see, that was the question.

Then I was the beneficiary of a technological advance: soft contact lenses. The kind I used for almost twenty years restored my sight. All I had to do was pop them in when I wanted to see and take them out when I wished to hide in my nearsightedness. I would alternately see or not see, and seeing or not seeing stopped being a problem. The soft lenses were perfect. Soft enough not to irritate my eyes and solid enough to provide the necessary correction.

If I was sleepy or tired, fed up with the madding crowd, I could take out my lenses with the flick of a finger and, because I'm so myopic that without lenses I'd never find the emergency exit, the lights would go out. If I put my contacts in, I could see bees flying. If I took them out, I could hide and take refuge in a dense, liquid mantle. Behind my nearsightedness, the world went on, but things would lose their sharp edges. Inside the mask of my blindness, everything would mix together without turning into chaos. Objects fluttered about, light and ethereal.

I shuttled back and forth comfortably between the world of sight and my reclusion in the darkness until, in a technological caprice, my soft lenses were taken off the market. Overnight, they were replaced by lenses with the same name but with II added. These Junior contacts were not as soft as their predecessors. My corneas simply would not tolerate them. I was desperate; I couldn't find an equivalent to the Senior version. The disappearance of my comfortable lenses meant I was blind. I couldn't leave the house unless someone led me around. And since, as I've said, glasses were no help either, I was forced to try laser surgery. I had company during the operation: Liliana Felipe, the composer and singer, was with me. They dressed us up as if we were going into outer space: germ-free white robes, socks and caps of blue cloth. They had us stretch out to wait on seats more comfortable than anything in first class and covered us up with blankets.

I went into the operating room first. Before my face was covered and my body again wrapped in a blanket, someone put a teddy bear in my hands.

The operation was practically painless. The most annoying part took place when they propped my eyelids back so I couldn't blink and then, for a few seconds, I smelled the odor of burned bone—the moments when the beam hit the eye. I hugged the teddy bear as hard as I could.

Each eye responded in a different way. In my left eye, the first, the beam was bright, an intense red. In my right, I saw it more diffusely. In my right eye, my sight came back quickly and precisely; it took a bit longer to come back in my left, as if I were stunned. The only thing I saw the same in both was blindness. The doctor announced it: "Now you won't see a single thing. It's normal," he said, as he lifted the cornea. I pinched the bear hard. The absence of light wasn't black or white or gray—it was color without color, thick, evaporated. Hostile? I perceived it as hostile, but now that I remember it, I recall huge blots, all uneven—I think a person might see that way whose eye hadn't learned to see in his mother's womb. And it wasn't smooth; there were swirls or blots, and it lacked dimension. It didn't seem to contain either nearness or distance; it was alien to space.

The entire operation lasted only a few minutes. When I got up out of the chair, as if by a stroke of grace or an act of magic, I could see.

I was seeing much more than my adult eyes had ever seen without lenses. The days that followed were extremely strange. Although my eyes were reasonably faithful for distance, I couldn't read, and bright lights hurt me. Saying "faithful" is saying a lot. During the first days, my eyes changed, began focusing, learning to see more acutely. I shut myself up in

·   ·   ·   ·   ·   ·   ·   ·   ·

my house, first because my vision was so unmanageable and second because I felt I had a new body—well, if not brand new, at least renovated and, in a key area, remade.

I discovered a certain strangeness in every object. Seeing the leaves of the trees, seeing them whole, seeing them when I woke up without any sort of help whatsoever was for me a totally unknown experience. No, it wasn't just my body: everything appeared to me now as if newly born, fresh. Opposite my window, the park, the volcano Iztaccíhuatl, the sky, the clouds, the buildings next door, the passersby walking along the sidewalk, everything was different. Including myself. I would close my eyes, and there I was, but when I opened them I saw, without any assistance, without my extra leg, without the other member I'd gotten so accustomed to—that was different, and unexpected.

I dedicated myself to remembering, and as I strolled through my memories, I tripped over one that I'd kept buried for years. I remembered how I'd lost most of my vision. I became nearsighted when I was fourteen or fifteen, but it wasn't serious. It was when I was twenty that I turned into a mole. It was because of sadness and pain. My sister María José, five years younger than me, died in a car crash when she was fifteen. Her death combined with my mother's, her best friend's, and those of others. María José's death brought the others back to me; they all merged; life was cruel. It robbed me of those beloved beings, attacked me, surrounded me. I fell into a deep depression. When I emerged from that black pit, when I accepted things and could return to the world, I no longer saw anything. I was separated from others by a thick, aquatic mantle of nearsightedness. My depression had stolen more than 20 percent of my vision in both eyes.

Could sight be just one more manifestation of joy? Can our involuntary senses be affected by our emotional state? Had I stopped seeing because I no longer wanted to see death pursuing my loved ones? Had that desire changed the shape of my eyeball? I can't answer any of these questions, positively or negatively. The death of my sister blinded me. Twenty-five years later, two tiny darts of light restored my vision almost magically, and I responded with celebratory joy. The world would go on being the same, but now it was entering me more through my eyes. When I made my entrance into the realm of the seeing, I felt a blow of joy. As the days passed, the wave of good fortune didn't diminish, and slowly I began seeing in greater detail.

Exactly one month after the operation, when the surgeon intended to make what he called a "minor adjustment," using the laser to bring my vision to perfection, I moved to New York, having accepted an invitation from the Center for Scholars and Writers at the New York Public Library. As far as I was concerned, the minor adjustment could wait forever. I was seeing more than enough for my eyes to guide me through the world without the aid of lenses, and if I wanted to see perfectly, in order to check the depth of snow on the volcanoes, I could use some low-power glasses. Besides, I had the matter of the move on my shoulders, and in New York there are no volcanoes. Seeing with my own body, without the help of contact lenses, was a stimulus to begin my new life, my New York life, joyfully.

I felt, believed, perceived, intuited that I was going to grow in this city, that the city was going to give me vitality. I'd been visiting it for years, surrounding it, until, finally, the siege worked, and I entered. And here I am in Babel, verticality, vertigo, in all those things that make up New York.

What we want is one thing, but what actually happens is something different. I was heading for an intense relationship with writers in a place where I'd be doing my work, so I focused my social appetite on what the Center could supply. But before the program in the Library began, I made new friends, not all of them writers. One, with whom I could chat and laugh endlessly, is a painter, an artist obsessed with New York: Robert Neffson. Neffson paints New York cityscapes; he seeks to depict—in faithful realism—an order that reality lacks. He reorganizes the world, betraying it, and fixes on his canvases an idyllic, harmonious New York—Arcadia. And in that city, he finds ecstasy, illumination, peace, the instant when we hear the beating of angels' wings, the sighs of the gods—all of what was once called the sublime.

The buildings, the streets, the passersby, the cars—what mountains, lakes, sunsets, and landscapes were for nineteenth-century painters—represent a ray of light in the mystery. In Neffson's cityscapes, there is neither sunrise nor sunset; time is stopped at some undefined hour, a hypothetical midday when the sun does not beat down directly but falls refracted as if from different angles. For a Latin American like me, his project is frankly exotic. It contains a good dose of hyperrealism, but with another intention: to depict New York as a utopian city.

The soul has been cut out of its corporeal prisons and scattered over the urban landscape. On top of that scene, a rigorous order has imposed itself. So it may be more than the truth: Neffson's utopia, the city from which pain, sickness, old age have been extirpated, flows like a cold drop, which the details (a theater poster, graffiti on the side of a truck, shopping

. . . .

bags in the hands of pedestrians) cannot warm. There is something frightening in that paradise, in the rigid, beautiful harmony of his canvases. The whistle of silence takes control. There is no explicit betrayal of reality; we look into a mirror, and the mirror makes subtle changes by making use of other mirrors, constructing a new order. Not a betrayal, but in the pursuit of harmony, certain compromises take place.

In an unfinished canvas, I saw how Neffson added and subtracted characters. One disappearance: a Hispanic woman wearing tight, violet slacks, her hair tied back in a ponytail. She radiated self-confidence. Which city could she be from? Some Latin American capitol, but which? She had her back to the viewer. She was almost in the center of the picture and slightly in the foreground. She had a major role. She was there until Neffson finished the first version of the painting, until the entire canvas was covered with paint.

But one day I came back, and she was gone. The painter had erased her. Why? She was warm. She was agreeable. She satisfied the eye. I asked the painter. "She attracted too much attention and blocked out the depth of the intersection; she broke up the harmony of the group of three next to her." He added more reasons, but did not convince me he was right until he added another character in the rear of the composition, changed the shirt on a third, and then I understood his motivation. She stood out from context. In these canvases, totality prevails over any details, even if they are treated with care. Another female character also disappeared from the picture, a gringa with a gym body. Wearing a cap on her head and a bag attached to her belt, she was hailing a cab. She'd put her shopping bag on the sidewalk and was bent forward slightly, impatient. She disappeared from the canvas and never got into her taxi. Her shopping bag also disappeared.

Seeing Neffson's work, visiting his studio to see a half-finished painting, talking with him—it all gave me a splendid welcome to New York. What intrigued me was this nondistortion, this against-the-grain return to realism. While I struggled with the chores of moving and getting set up in a new city—not an especially easy or simple city at that—I was using my new eyes to watch another window on utopian New York develop on another canvas, Neffson's New York. For the first time in my life, surrounded by cardboard boxes, I assembled tables, chairs, and a desk. I discovered, despite my awkwardness, the wisdom hidden in things. I had blisters on my hands, but I quickly saw my house all in place.

I'd decided to live in Brooklyn, in Carroll Gardens. Our neighborhood is quiet and fun, too. Several writers live here: Francisco Goldman, Mike Wallace, Sara Kerr, among others. There is something immodest in my neighborhood, or perhaps immodest only to a woman born and bred in Mexico City. In Mexico, we think that when we're out on the streets we have the right to be no one, anonymous souls lost in the mass. In this corner of Brooklyn, old people sit around fanning themselves as they watch the sun set from their rocking chairs. Writers sit shoulder to shoulder on the subway correcting their manuscripts, and neighbors greet one another by name, asking how the family is. For me personally and for my culture there is too much exposed intimacy, so exposed that on my street corner, in the front yard of a brownstone townhouse, they sell dresses right out in the open. They come in all colors, cheap dresses to wear to work, with or without flowers, with sleeves or sleeveless, long, short, full, straight, each on a hanger, swaying in the breeze.

On Tuesday, September 11th, at 9:30 A.M., I was getting ready to go to my cubicle at the New York Public Library on Forty-second Street and Fifth Avenue. But I got distracted and began to daydream. What was I thinking about? I jotted in my notebook the sentences I would use to begin what I thought would be these pages, "Neffson's New York." Out of my daydream, I extracted the first words. They were, "There is only one ego larger than the Argentine ego: the New York ego. The canvases of Robert Neffson, a native New Yorker, depict just that, the gigantic, outsize ego of New York. Has anyone seen the images in his paintings in real life? A New York without pollution, untouched by chaos, an ordered, perfect city, harmonious and sweet, a city that offers itself to the spectator as paradise, impenetrable, vulnerable, sealed."

An explosion jolted me out of my reverie. "Mommy, what was that?" On Tuesdays, María goes to school (the Stella Adler Conservatory for Actors) late. "Maybe it was thunder?" "Thunder? How could it be thunder, Mommy, look at the weather, the sun's shining." I muttered some other, equally stupid answer, something like, "This is a port; in this city you can't tell what's going to happen." I couldn't invent any more answers for María because it was late and I had to run to catch the subway.

On the way, I had an attack of maternal conscience and tried to call María on my cell phone. It didn't work. I stopped at a pay phone. María frantically told me that a friend had called from Mexico City to ask if we were all right, because there had been an attack on the Twin Towers. I hung up and saw, out of the corner of my eye, on a television set in a beauty parlor, the image of a plane smashing against one of the the towers.

. . . .

But I didn't stop. It looked like a total fiction. The hands on my watch were moving and I was going to be terribly late getting to the library. I wasn't thinking about anything. I went down into the subway, passed through the turnstile, but when the F train pulled in, it stopped without opening its doors. The driver leaned out of his window and shouted to all of us, "There is no service to Manhattan! It's hell!"

Manhattan, a hell? I went up the subway stairs, walking beside one of those many Carroll Gardens neighbors who look like writers. He looked me in the eye and said, "Welcome to the twenty-first century!" I tried to use the cell phone again to warn María not to leave the house. It was useless, and at the two pay phones, lines had formed. I got in line. The television set in the beauty parlor was visible from there, too. The sky darkened. The air filled with ash and small fragments, and then some not-so-small pieces began to pour down on us. Without getting off his bicycle, a messenger was explaining to a silent boss that it was impossible for him to reach his destination, that he'd tried every route. When my turn came, María didn't answer. I stepped aside and waited for her. It was still raining white on us, the particles falling with an airy slowness, making their way down hundreds of stairs. Their indolence didn't spread to us, but it certainly slowed us down.

The intersection of Smith and President got bigger. The streets looked like wide avenues. From the sky came a warning, a threat. Ash was still falling, and, even more slowly than the ash, papers slid through the air, whiter than everything else that was falling, like mirrors reflecting the light, which by then almost wasn't reaching us—the radiant September light, the intense light that precedes autumn. The papers reflected the light, dancing in the air, absurd survivors; below, where we were, there was less and less sunlight. Midmorning seemed a bizarre, sinister late afternoon. Even our speech seemed slowed. María appeared from behind the cloud. We made our way back to the house. The parked cars had turned white. We were able to make a few telephone calls before the lines also began to fall.

During those first hours, I returned obsessively to Neffson's paintings. Manhattan impervious, orderly Manhattan, unpolluted Manhattan, persistent, overwhelming, arrogant, magnificent Manhattan, the arcadia the painter painted and repainted on his canvases, reproducing one of those dream cities that exist behind this city, the exploded Manhattan. Now the cold drop of its arrogance was not there, not anywhere to calm the flames of the earthly inferno. The fall of the Twin Towers buried thousands of people and burst the dream of this city, a Babel where countless ethnic groups live together. How many thousands?

María and I walked out of the house toward the Brooklyn Bridge. The wind was still carrying the residue of the towers—no longer the first white feathers, now it was dust, cheek-slapping blasts of harsh, thick dust. The towers had been scattered. Thousands of people fleeing from the explosion were walking along the street, many covered with ash. Not white ash like that covering the cars but cement colored. Some were weeping. Most seemed unable to believe what they'd lived through. Nervous. Distressed. They walked like insane robots, not knowing where they were going. There were Latin Americans, Asians, Arabs, Jews; there were Italians, Irish, people from different African nations, French, Hindus, Pakistanis. Who wasn't there? The crowd seemed selected to represent every ethnic or national group in the world. Most of those passing were survivors of the attack.

The air smelled of plastic and bones. It was like the smell that invaded Mexico City days after the earthquake. Here it smelled that way right from the first day—of dead bodies, fire, collapsed buildings, violence.

The genocidal murderers didn't hate the United States only because of its imperialist aberrations. As the father of one of them said, "We hate the United States because it's a country that allows marriage between homosexuals and tolerates the lowest sort of behavior." They hated each and every one of the women working there because they did not have veils covering their bodies. They hated the intelligence of those women, their sensuality, their vacillations, their problems, their very lives. They were disgusted by this interethnic city where credos, religions, and dreams—including those in Neffson's paintings—live together. They hated his serene utopia. From the terrace of his studio in Brooklyn Heights, Neffson saw the second plane smash through the second tower; minutes later, he saw the first tower fall, and, moved to tears, he asked himself, "What are they doing to my city?" They were showing it their hatred.

One of the remarks intercepted before the terrorists attacked: "Finally they're going to pay." Who's going to pay, who and what? Here on the corner near my house, the colored dresses being sold in the front yard have been replaced by T-shirts that are all the same, each and every one white, with the American flag printed on the chest. This change is also the product of hatred. We who think of ourselves as citizens of the world have no reason to pay for their hatred, any hatred.

They hated my eyes.

. . . .

When I could stop thinking for a moment about this nightmare, as happened to me years ago with another cloud of sadness, I'd already lost some vision in both eyes. Now I definitely need glasses. My eyes demand them. They've taken refuge in their sanctuary. My eyes dimmed, but luckily not the eyes of all artists. Weeks later, I saw Neffson's painting finished. I was surprised by the luminosity and serene joy his Columbus Circle radiated.

This Place / Displace

.   .   .   .

by
REGINALD SHEPHERD

SOMEWHERE

A few years ago, the Pet Shop Boys, a group known for their ironic, even camp, approach to pop music, though they themselves claim to be utterly in earnest, released a version of the classic (dare I say "gay classic"?) "Somewhere," a song both highly specific in its promise of a place for us and utterly vague about just where this place might be or how or when one might get there. And who exactly is this "us"? Not anything to which I've ever belonged. The extended remix is some ten minutes long; the actual song doesn't begin until seven or so minutes into the track and fades back into the remix after about two and a half minutes. I find this a very appropriate aural image of whatever that place would be for me: it takes a long time to get there and it's gone almost before you notice you've arrived. By the time you reach it, you've already left.

BE THANKFUL FOR WHAT YOU'VE GOT

Robert says that place doesn't determine happiness, but it does structure it: it defines the parameters within which happiness can be achieved or not. For me, large cities offer at least the possibility of happiness: they provide the resources, social and material, out of which happiness might be constructed, a critical mass of potential. Small towns offer nothing but claustrophobia, boredom, and the insanity bred of too-long confinement in too-tight a space. A therapist of mine in Buffalo, a man who wore large rhinestone pins on the lapels of his tweed jackets, told me that one could

170

be happy or unhappy anywhere, that place didn't matter. It all came down to me. (Or was it that it all came down *on* me, crashing even?) I replied that a place can't make one happy, but some places make it easier to be happy, and some places almost force unhappiness upon one. A place is as much produced for one by one's relationship to it as by its objective elements. But it's those elements with which one has a relationship. Place doesn't in itself determine happiness or unhappiness, but any given place does define their terms.

Place is a kind of fantasy, an asymptote like the self: there's a place for me, somewhere a place for me, and I know there is because I can imagine it. I also know I'm never there. No place is the place that I've imagined, that I've imagined it could be (utopia means nowhere, after all), just as no real man is the lover of whom I've dreamed. And I am never the self I've imagined, the self I've longed to be. But sometimes a real man can be better than an imaginary lover, just because he is real (which I used to think disqualified him); a real place can be better than an imagined one. Or so I like to imagine.

TONIGHT IS FOREVER

I have often felt at home, experienced a sense of belonging, in gay clubs late at night or early in the morning, sometimes even dancing to a Pet Shop Boys song. This despite the constant experience of being snubbed or ignored or patronized because I was black or not buff enough or too smart or not cool enough or just generally not quite what was wanted. I remember a Wednesday night at the club Spin in Chicago several years ago (the place has gone through several names since then) when I was deciding whether to accept a teaching job in West Virginia. I had applied for a position teaching poetry writing and they had offered me one teaching African American literature, for which my only background was biological. It was something that I knew I didn't want to do (it was, after all, West Virginia), but it was also something I thought I *should* do, the sensible, practical thing to do (get a job; work is everything—isn't that the American way?): a sure recipe for disaster in my experience, and I have experienced many disasters as a result of such decisions. British diva of that bygone moment Gabrielle was singing that dreams can come true if you have hope, if you can live for tonight, and beautiful boys not all of whom were white were dancing without their shirts, happy to be young and gay and potentially having sex with each other, and I knew that I couldn't leave, not that night anyway.

MY WAY

I lived in the Bronx until my mother died when I was fifteen, when I moved to Georgia to live with my mother's relatives, people who thought of reading as a bad habit—you're not making money and you're not having fun, so what good is it? Going to my aunt's house was better than going to a foster home, the horrors of which I'd seen in too many TV movies and read about in too many young adult novels. Since my escape from Georgia I have led a highly peripatetic life. One might say that dislocation has been my location. My wanderings have been motivated by a combination of choice and necessity, by choices that felt like (and sometimes were) necessities and by necessities I tried to imagine as choices. Mostly they've been motivated by the need for money and the wish to avoid a lifetime of underpaid semiskilled labor. They've also been motivated by a restless dissatisfaction with wherever I was and a conviction that wherever I went next could be better, though as I've gotten older, and as some of the places I've gone have gotten more out of the way, that hope that the next place would be better has faded.

Gay space has been crucial in my life: gay bars and clubs most especially, gay social and political groups, gay bookstores, gay boothstores and back rooms, gay baths, even cruisy toilets and streets and parks (in which I've spent a lot of time, as many men who wouldn't admit it have)—the spaces where gay men come together both literally and figuratively, either as gay men or just as men who are looking to get off with other men. Such spaces have been central to my sense of how I related to a place, of what place had to offer me, and what my place in that place could be. I've made so much of the promise of music and the promise of sex and the promise of belonging somewhere by means of sex and music, in a club's crowd of men dancing together or apart, all dressed up in their bodies, in a bed or a car or an alley or a bathroom, with one other man, having sex together, dressing up my body with someone else's for a while.

Sometimes a place had nothing more to offer for gay space than a cruisy toilet or park, and perhaps a monthly gay coffee house. Such places, those with the most limited choices of gay space, have been those in which I have been most unhappy.

YOU CAN'T GET WHAT YOU WANT TILL YOU KNOW WHAT YOU WANT

Several years ago I somewhat facetiously came up with a set of criteria for an acceptable place: not a place in which I would necessarily be happy (happiness is never to be expected), but a place in which it would at least be possible to imagine being happy. It would have to have a subway, for one thing, though Buffalo made me realize that even if this was a necessary condition it was a far from sufficient one. I've only very recently, and quite late in my adulthood, learned how to drive, so this was a practical criterion for me, but it was also, even more so perhaps, symbolic. A subway represented a certain density of population and development, and a certain urbanity to which mere buses couldn't attain. An acceptable place had to have at least one good bookstore (by which criterion Iowa City was paradise) and at least one good record store (by which criterion Buffalo scored well, having two). It would have to have good gay clubs (by which criterion Buffalo again scored very well, and Ithaca didn't even register), and preferably would have other gay organizations. Though I've lived in cities with extensive nonbar gay resources (Boston, Chicago) and have always been disappointed in the various social and political groups, their presence is a marker of the development and diversity of a gay community. Up until quite recently, I always found myself returning to the bars and clubs—they were simply more *interesting*. Plus there'd always be music. And even though I don't go out much anymore, I still like to know that I could. The sense of possibility is crucial to my ability to be happy with a place.

DOWNTOWN TRAIN

My brief sojourn in Buffalo, New York (home of the redundantly named Buffalo Bisons), made me realize that at least one of my criteria might need some revision in the direction of specificity: the place needed not only a subway, but a subway that went from somewhere to somewhere, with stops at various somewheres in between. In Buffalo the subway went from nowhere to nowhere through nowhere, from a downtown full of empty and half-constructed buildings (relics of a brief and abortive economic boom in the eighties) through an empty semiurban wasteland (the city had lost almost half its population since World War II) to the old campus of the university, now half abandoned, too. I was told that the suburb in which the main campus was officially located (it was really in a drained swamp off the highway, neighboring more nothing) wouldn't allow the subway to be extended that far, for fear of urban black incursions.

The subway had just recently been built, a shiny automated system almost no one but black people used, except for the odd university student and a few business people at rush hour. It ran up and down Main Street, the dividing line between the black and the white sides of town. I always thought that the subway had been built not just as a boondoggle for the local construction industry but more importantly because Buffalo, utterly lacking in imagination, needed a literal set of tracks for the black people to be on the wrong side of.

But the gay clubs in Buffalo were open till 4:00 A.M. and full every night of the week (people drove in from Rochester and even Canada), and they always played good music.

HE'S THE GREATEST DANCER

I don't drink and I don't smoke and I never have, but I do dance (or at least I have for most of my life), and the moments of losing myself in a song, of immersing myself in the diva's voicing of desires fulfilled and frustrated, of love lost and love found, in the rhythm's promise of ecstasy in the next chorus or the body of the stranger dancing beside me, have been some of the most powerful in my life. In those moments, many of which were moments of intense misery, loneliness, and isolation that the music raised up, sublimated into something grand, noble, and beautiful, I could fleetingly feel the possibility of uniting body and soul, flesh and mind. When I was dancing, even or perhaps especially when I was dancing by myself, as I usually was, I could forget myself for a moment, I could feel glad to have and be in a body, even if I usually went home alone, one body closed back into itself, trapped in my skin and my flesh, which never lived up to the shiny-skinned ideals I longed for in the club. I was often torn between dancing and trying to meet someone. (I do love that euphemism of gay clubs and bars, "meeting someone" whose name you've often forgotten by the time you two get home). Sometimes I forgot to cruise, or didn't have time to, because I just had to dance to this next song. Some nights every song was my favorite song.

My progress through the world is often awkward and clumsy, my physical presentation somewhat off, but when I'm dancing my movements are graceful and smooth. When I'm dancing I feel attractive, I expe-

. . . .

rience my body as admirable, even masterful. In the days of my constant clubbing, men who would never have slept with me would approach me to compliment me on my dancing, buy me drinks (I always chose soda or orange juice), befriend me, even. Sometimes a man would sleep with me because I danced well, though the dance floor brought me more friends than lovers.

FAMILY AFFAIR

Family is a kind of place, I suppose, a space where one is meant to feel safe, where one is meant to belong, no matter what. For me that sense of safety was always precarious at best. My mother and I were alone together (even after my half-sister's birth when I was eleven), and when she died she left me nothing but alone. She had few friends and so did I; we were bonded not just as mother and child, but as fellow misfits, as confidants, and as frequently bickering cellmates in a prison only partly of our own design. Afraid of losing me, my mother always told me that people couldn't be trusted, that no one would ever love me but her, but then she left me, and all I had then was the conviction that I could never be loved again.

At thirteen or fourteen, thanks to the good offices of Family Services, I met my father for the first time; they wanted to reunite families, but I didn't understand how I could be reunited with someone I didn't know. I spent the day at his house in Far Rockaway reading about the history of Ethiopia in the *Encyclopaedia Britannica* (which we could never afford, though I lusted after a set for years). At the end of the day he invited me to spend the summer with him, then called up the next week to say that he'd be busy. I was disappointed—he lived only blocks from the beach, and I had been looking forward to swimming. I also couldn't help but think that if he could afford a house and a car, he could afford the $33 a week in child support that he never paid.

I won't discuss the stepfather who on one occasion attacked my mother with a butcher knife (luckily the wound was superficial) and on another occasion cut all the wires inside a tape deck she had just bought for me because he'd decided that she spoiled me. A recent immigrant without a green card, he had a wife and several children in Jamaica when he married my mother, as she found out some years into the marriage, and after my mother died he brought his Jamaican family all over to New York and bought a house in Hollis, Queens.

NATIVE NEW YORKER

The first place I remember living was a high-rise building with a balcony for each apartment and a little cement playground, a housing project I'm fairly sure; in memory it felt like paradise. We lived on the thirtieth floor or so, or perhaps the thirteenth (I've never been good with numbers) and I was always afraid to go out on the balcony—I've always had a fear of heights, and to be so far up with so little to support me terrified me. I've never believed anyone would catch me if I fell.

My only real memory of the place, besides the fire, of course, is of playing with a friend among a small maze of wooden picnic tables with attached benches (no one ever went for picnics in any neighborhood I ever lived in) and having him push me against one of the tables. He didn't mean to hurt me, but I hit my head against a corner of the table just at the spot where the plates in my skull met and I cracked my skull. I remember his panicked reaction, and my mother's, and sitting in a public clinic waiting room with a green towel, which was turning red from all the blood, wrapped around my head while my mother screamed at the indifferent receptionist that someone needed to see me *now*. I don't remember what happened next, but I assume that I survived. Besides that, it was a lovely place, clean and quiet and thoroughly ratless.

We had to leave that particular paradise because of me. I'm always kicking myself out of Eden. It was near Christmas and my mother was sick, as she often was, and I was trying to light an electric candle; I was a smart child, but not very practical. I didn't understand why it wouldn't light, but I kept trying, and eventually I set the sofa on fire—actually, it was only the mattress in the sofa bed. I'm not quite sure how that happened, but the firemen came and broke down the door and they dragged the mattress onto the balcony and hosed the fire out, and the next day the building management told us we had to move. I didn't understand why we were leaving just because of a little fire the men put out in no time; the building was supposed to be fireproof, after all. But I was a child and there were lots of things that no one would explain.

Money was short and time was even shorter, so when we fell from what came in retrospect to seem like paradise (from morn to evening, all a summer's day), we ended up in a two-room tenement apartment in what I'm still quite convinced was the South Bronx, though I couldn't tell you now and couldn't have told you then exactly where it was. During the day I had to wear shoes in the apartment because the wood floors were so worn and full of splinters; at night, when I would get up to go to the bathroom, I had to wear them because of the rats—I'd carry a broom to bang on the floor and warn them I was coming, if not to ward them off altogether. Other things I remember about that apartment: the night I was sitting on my mother's lap and a giant dust ball rolled by, which she explained to me was a rat. The rats lived in the walls and used to eat my books from the inside, chewing through wall and bookcase to get at them. If not literary minded, they were definitely literary mouthed—almost every book we owned was marred by a serrated oval indentation in the middle. Apparently they weren't interested in beginnings or endings—they wanted only the pith of the book, the story's heart. One night a piece of the ceiling collapsed right over the spot where I'd been standing seconds before—I walked away and it fell in. A very considerate ceiling.

And then there was the Puerto Rican boy next door who tormented me for years. Once I picked up a package from the post office for my mother, who was sick again. He caught me in the lobby, took the package and threw the book-club books around the floor, and slapped me. My mother decided this was the last time that he would abuse me and confronted his family, who claimed he'd been with them all afternoon. "Is his face red?" they said. "It would be red if our boy had slapped him." They clearly had a taste for irony, or perhaps it was merely sarcasm. My mother, whom kids at school teased me about because of her weight, chased the boy around the block until she ran out of breath; all his people laughed and I stood wishing that I hadn't told her at all. On another occasion my baby-sitter sent me upstairs to see if my mother had come back from work; the baby-sitter's son was a junkie who stole her television set, and his pregnant girlfriend was in a human interest story in the paper. My mother wasn't home yet, but I lingered listening at the door, thinking I'd heard something inside (we'd already been robbed once, when they'd stolen my plastic pumpkin full of pennies). I guess I lingered too long, or the boy next door heard me, because he came out and tried to drag me into his apartment. I managed to break away, but I always wondered what he planned to do with me in there—there was always something vaguely sexual about his aura of threat. Or perhaps I'm just projecting, trying to shed a little glamour on his brutality.

It felt like rescue when after years on a waiting list we moved into a brand-new housing project not far from the Bronx Zoo, where for the first time since I was small I had my own room and the carpet couldn't give me splinters. But eventually the mice moved in (not yet chased out by rats), and the maintenance men from the Fortune Society stopped replacing the lights in the stairwells and started breaking into apartments, and a little girl was raped and thrown from the roof.

I have a memory from my very early youth of my mother, a very lonely and unhappy woman who drank too much and spent whole weekends nearly comatose due to Tanqueray and various sleeping pills and tranquilizers, in the hallway outside our apartment after a party slumped over a pool of her own shit, but I can't remember which of our buildings that was, or whether it was actually our apartment at all.

I'M COMING OUT, VERSE ONE

When I was thirteen or so I told my mother that I was gay and she screamed that she couldn't have one of "those people" living in her house. Of course, it was an apartment in a housing project, not a house, and it hardly belonged to either of us, and she was always threatening to kick me out for some reason or another, to send me to reform school where the boys would rape me and then I'd be sorry I'd been bad. We yelled at each other for a while, she went to the bathroom, and I threw a red plastic ashtray at the closed door. Where it came from I don't know, since neither of us smoked, but my childhood was full of things being thrown—telephones, aerosol cans, whatever came to hand. When she came out of the bathroom I told her that I was kidding. People will believe whatever they want to believe. Of course, I didn't stop reading books about gay liberation or buying *Blueboy* and *Mandate* during my lunch break from school in midtown Manhattan and *Playgirl* at the Puerto Rican convenience store across the street. I always wondered what my mother did with those issues of *Hustler* and *Penthouse* she brought home. For a while I thought that she was buying them for me, to make me straight or something like it, but she got angry when I would keep them for myself.

OVER THE RAINBOW

New York is one of the worst cities this side of Calcutta in which to be poor. When I was young, what I wanted most of all (right after not to be poor and not to be black, which at the time seemed to be equivalent) was to escape the city and live in the white-picket-fence world I saw on television shows like *The Brady Bunch*, where everything was clean and everyone had a front lawn and a backyard, where no one had cans of

Campbell's cream of celery soup from the local church food box for dinner because they couldn't afford groceries that week and there were never, ever any rats. No one I went to school with had ever heard of rats or welfare, except perhaps on television: after barely surviving second grade at P.S. 6, I took a station wagon, then an orange-yellow van, and finally the subway to scholarships my mother had wrangled for me at private schools in Riverdale (the Bronx, but not the Bronx at all) and then Manhattan; another borough might as well have been another city, another galaxy, where all the stars stayed lit, maintained in constant working order.

My mother, whose ambitions for me were fierce and unrelenting, also longed to escape New York, and most of all she wanted me to escape it. For me to escape the city was for me to escape poverty. Most summers and many Christmases she would send me to stay with her sister in Macon, Georgia (where she grew up), just to get me away from the city and its dangers. She attained her ambitions after a fashion: she died and we both left. After her death, when I was forced to leave the city, what I wanted most was to return to it, or rather to an imaginary New York in which I had never lived, a city I read about in books and saw in television shows and movies about smart, hip, sensitive people dressed in black who hung out in shiny cafes talking about T. S. Eliot and Susan Sontag and then went dancing at the latest club. Wherever I wasn't, that was where I wanted to be, and the place I wanted to live was always a fantasy.

Few people remember that the Brady Bunch put out records. One single was called "It's a Sunshine Day"; another was "Time to Change." The actor who played the father died of AIDS.

WHERE THE BOYS ARE

All through my adolescence, in my twin bed with Bugs Bunny sheets in a Bronx housing project, on my rollaway bed in the den of my aunt Mildred's crowded house in Macon (the TV and two cousins who shared the sofa bed slept there, too), in my dorm room amidst the snow and neuroses of Bennington, Vermont, the place I dreamed I would finally belong, the place I thought would finally be mine, was the gay community, about which I'd read so much in books that were already out of date by the time I read them in the late seventies. I watched *Word Is Out* (I bought the book, too) and read *The Homosexual Matrix* and *Lavender Liberation,* I learned all about gay liberation and the joining together of oppressed minorities, and I knew that gay men wouldn't be racist or sexist or classist because they were oppressed. They understood oppression firsthand, so they would never oppress anyone else. My experience of black people, in my various neighborhoods and my various schools, in my mother's family, should have taught me that oppression doesn't improve anyone's moral character, and furthermore that people tend to be jealously possessive of their own undeserved suffering, unwilling to acknowledge anyone else's, but I was naïve and desperate to believe. Gay men, of course, are no more accepting and tolerant than anyone, and certainly no less racist: white gay men are white men before they're anything else, but I didn't know that then. The place where I imagined my gay life would begin didn't exist and perhaps it never had, but planning my trip there kept me alive for years.

THIS MUST BE THE PLACE I WAITED YEARS TO LEAVE (INCORPORATING I'M COMING OUT, VERSE TWO)

To the extent that I've ever officially "come out," I came out in Macon, to my relatives, to my teachers, to my schoolmates. I was never less (and rarely more) than a Martian to everyone in Macon, probed and stared at and taunted; my relatives, including the aunt and six cousins with whom I lived (she had more kids than that), called me by my last name (not theirs), as if to emphasize our difference. Sometimes my cousins called me "Mikey," after the kid in the Life cereal commercials, because supposedly I'd eat anything. "Hey, Mikey, he likes it," they'd say. I never bothered to explain to them that Mikey was the kid who *wouldn't* eat anything—that was the commercial's point. And people in Macon seemed to me like members of some unwashed tribe of troglodytes, with distasteful rituals and undeveloped frontal lobes. I wanted to ward them off as much as they wanted to avoid or mock me. By announcing to all and sundry that I was gay, I could keep them at a manageable distance: I wasn't one of them and I wouldn't be there long. In Macon, Georgia, in the late seventies, even in the public high schools, there were several sissies, like my cousin Stacy, who had permed hair and long painted nails and pants so tight they once split when he was getting into the car to go to school, who stayed out late on Friday and Saturday nights having sex with strange men in the park. (I don't know how you think you can name a boy Stacy Maurice and not expect him to turn out a fag.) My aunt and other cousins tsk-tsked and said it was a damned shame the way he carried on, but no one ever tried to stop

· · · · · · · · · ·

him; I kept hoping they'd kick him out of the house, but hoping never made it so. I thought those sissies were sordid and disgusting, and I was not like them. They made gays look bad. On the rare occasions when he wasn't stealing my clothes and my gay books and my money or beating me up just for the hell of it (sissies can be vicious in a fight), Stacy would invite me to go with him to the local gay bar, called We Three (lesbians, gays, and bisexuals, you see), but I was afraid of getting carded, and more afraid of what the place would be like and who the people I would find there would be. More of Stacy and his friends, a roomful, a bar full? I preferred my fantasies of an ideal gay world, somewhere out there.

Despite the classmate who told me that I only said I was gay because it was trendy, in Macon, Georgia, in the late seventies there were not, to my limited knowledge, openly gay men who weren't sissies, who didn't fit into the compartment they had for "those sorts," and in Macon, Georgia, in the late seventies if you didn't fit into a box no one knew what to do with you, which was fine with me, since most of the things they knew were rather frightening. Someone stood up in homeroom once and announced, "I saw Reggie reading a book called *Ho-mo-sex-you-a-lity and Its Play-Sures.*" I responded, "No, it was called *Homosexual Oppression and Liberation,* and it's about how ignorant, bigoted people like you oppress gay people." Someone stopped me in the hallway on my way to class one afternoon and said, "You a faggot? I think all faggots should be taken to an island and shot." I replied, "Actually, the word is gay, and I don't remember asking what you think." Someone once yelled, "Hey faggot," in the school parking lot as I was leaving school and I yelled back, "Yeah, you wanna make something of it?"

The bravado came easily: I had no real ties to anyone in Macon, and since I didn't fit into the box labeled Sissy, people were in general baffled by me, which was a kind of safety. But I did quite apparently fit into the box labeled Black, however much my relatives who ridiculed the way I spoke and the crazy white-boy music I listened to thought the contrary. I was much more impressed, and wounded, by occasions such as the time in art class when I overheard a white-trash boy named Billy Somebody say in the course of a conversation I didn't catch, "But that's Reggie. Reggie's a nigger. I ain't no nigger," as casually as you'd say "Reggie has brown eyes" or "Reggie's left handed." Quotidian racism was a way of life there.

I haven't seen Macon in over twenty years, but to this day I still have nightmares about being trapped in my aunt's house surrounded by my

abusive, stupid cousins. For some reason, I've returned of my own voli-
tion and now I can't leave (there is no bus, the airport's closed, I have no
money, or just because). I keep trying to explain that I'm an adult now,
with my own life, but no one ever listens.

I WILL REMEMBER MASSACHUSETTS
(INCORPORATING I'M COMING OUT, VERSE THREE)

Taking extra classes before and after school, I graduated from high school
a year early in order to curtail my sentence in Macon; every A brought
me that much closer to escape. I got a scholarship to Bennington College
(about as far away from Macon as I could imagine at the time), a small
progressive school on the outskirts of Nowhere, Vermont, populated by
the neurotic and artistically inclined children of the wealthy professional
classes, and the occasional Getty or Iranian princess. A fellow scholarship
student joked that you could always tell the kids on financial aid: they
were the ones who dressed well. The trust-fund kids wore filthy rags, but
they were expensive filthy rags. Another friend nicknamed the school the
Bennington Institute for the Emotionally Gifted; he later dropped out, as
I did, though he was there when I came back. I thought I would find
the artistic and intellectual community I had never known, and that the
school's small size and isolation would foster that sense of community, but
all it fostered was neurosis in various forms. I still have dreams that I have
to return to complete one last course. The fact that I have two master's
degrees never seems to matter, and I can never find my room—the dorm
turns into a labyrinth through which I can't find my way, and from which
I can't escape. I pass the same rooms over and over, but none is ever mine.
My dreams have always been refreshingly obvious.

Though I got a good education there (not without some struggle) and
made a few friends I still have twenty years later, the hothouse isolation,
sexual frustration, and continual psychological trauma that was life at
Bennington (and I did live there year-round, having nowhere else to go)
eventually drove me to drop out after my junior year. Oddly enough, I did
eventually graduate from Bennington, though four years after I should
have; an entire class had come and gone in my absence, but one person
from my class returned at the same time I did and graduated with me, so I
didn't have to feel *completely* like a man out of time.

I took the settlement money that had been sitting in a trust fund since
I'd gotten hit by a car when I was four and moved to Cambridge, which

was close and which a friend had said was a friendly, intellectual city. I hadn't realized that he was joking; if I'd only seen that the joke was on me. For a city of its size, Boston / Cambridge (there's little distinction physically or socially) is remarkably rich in resources—bookstores, record stores, cafes, restaurants, gay clubs and bars, and gay social and political organizations of all sorts—and it gets shinier and glossier with every passing year. And Boston was certainly much better than most places I've lived since; I missed it dreadfully after I had returned to school in the boondocks. But Boston, though politically progressive, is also one of the most unfriendly, puritanical, and socially conformist places I've ever lived: everyone, no matter what their social position, seems to exist behind an unbreakable glass wall of propriety and contempt for outsiders. Friendly people who had just moved to the city would metamorphose within a month into cold fish who wouldn't speak to me. Even the punks with their black thigh boots, white pancaked faces, blood red lipstick, and high-stacked hair dyed black adhered to the same standards of etiquette: never express a genuine feeling (other than disdain), never be spontaneous, and above all never say or do anything different from what those around you say and do. It takes little deviation to seem like a freak in Boston, and I've always been more than a little deviant. But *de trop* as I have so often been, I know it wasn't just me: one of my bosses at the Boston Public Library, where I did data entry for two years, once asked me if I had been able to make friends in the city, since she (a middle-aged and quite proper heterosexual white woman) found it so difficult to get to know people. I made a few friends even so; two of my oldest friends have lived in the area all their lives, and both have always found it a very lonely and isolating place. Boston is also the most pervasively racist place I've ever lived, outside of Macon: the racism merely gets more polite the higher you go on the social and educational scale.

The gay scene was little different, or, given my hopes and expectations, it was worse. The old joke in gay Boston is that you can tell if a man in a gay club is interested in you because he's the one who's most assiduously ignoring you, and that's if you're lucky enough to be white and socially presentable. It's no joke that Boston is the only place I've ever lived where I met men who were insulted by my telling them that they were attractive. Boston was the first place in which I encountered large numbers of gay men, a "gay community," as it is sometimes jokingly called, and I still haven't recovered from the trauma.

BLUE IS FOR BOYS

My first summer in Cambridge I asked a handsome man to dance at the gay club Campus (Cambridge is quite collegiate). He said thank you, not right now, but maybe later, and so I approached him about an hour afterward, in case he wanted to dance by then. I'm sure he must have thought me somewhat slow, but that night was better than the many nights I spent staring at beautiful men I couldn't have, fantasizing about the persons their beauty must embody, afraid ever to approach my slightly wooden idols (all of whom were white, like the marble statues I compared them to). I did eventually go home with someone that night, though he never returned my calls. A friend asked me a few years later, "Don't you get tired of humiliating yourself?" and perhaps I should have. But I believed in my own pain, and sometimes I got poems out of it, poems I don't have anymore: I threw most of them away as mere personal documents, though sometimes I think back wistfully on their naïve intensity, nostalgic for past purities of suffering: back then I was really *feeling*.

To talk to any of those men was usually a disappointment, but there was always another god across the room, and I had a talent for self-deception: I could make almost any man interesting if he looked the part well enough. "Somehow I never learn," went the song. I sang along to it all summer, much longer than I should have. My life has always had a soundtrack.

LOSING MY RELIGION

One Sunday afternoon in the mid-eighties, desperate to find ways to meet men besides bars, and clearly very bored, I went with an acquaintance to a Metropolitan Community Church service on Beacon Hill. Sometime before the service was half over, it occurred to me that there was something absurd about finding myself, a lifelong atheist or intermittent agnostic at best, sitting in a church because I was looking for a man. The last time I'd been in a church was at my mother's funeral, and frankly I hadn't enjoyed the experience. To go to church *because* I was gay, when I would never have done so had I been straight, seemed to undermine the whole point of opting out of social norms and expectations. It further occurred to me that if I did somehow meet this hypothetical man at this service, he would most likely be some variety of Christian believer (someone, indeed, who believed enough to go seek out a gay church) and that we might have a certain lack of things in common. Belief in god being high on that list of lacks. (Robert points out that I might have met someone like me, who was just there to meet men, but who wants to hang out with a hypocrite?) When we went up for communion the priest or whatever they have in gay churches hugged me and said some kind of blessing I couldn't quite catch. Not knowing the proper response, I said "Thanks." One needs all the blessings one can get.

I WOULDN'T NORMALLY DO THIS KIND OF THING

Deciding once again to try to meet men in a context other than the bars, and deciding furthermore that I might try to do something for my community, I went to an ACT UP meeting in Boston with my best friend, Jim, who had been going for some time. This was in 1989, during my second sojourn in the city of cold shoulders. The meeting was long and tedious and populated, as such things usually are, by those too socially challenged to get dates, but I wanted to rise above my shallowness and make a contribution. I had no interest in doing anything that might get my head bashed in (I certainly don't need to give the police any excuses to beat up a black man), but a particularly whiny and weedy bald guy announced that they *desperately* needed volunteers to help sell ACT UP paraphernalia, and that sounded suitably out of harm's way. So after the meeting I waited and waited to volunteer while he tried to pick up my very buff friend. "I have a bunch of pictures of you from the last demonstration. You look really *angry*." Anger can be sexy, in which case I must have been very sexy indeed at that much-too-long moment, being snubbed while trying to volunteer my supposedly desperately needed help to someone whose chances of sleeping with Jim (or anyone, I suspected) were somewhat less than his chances of going surfing on the moon. I put good works behind me and went back to the clubs, where I could at least be snubbed by *attractive* men, to the sound of a good beat.

RED, RED WINE

I've always wanted to live in the middle of whatever there was to be in the middle of, however much middle there was, so when I moved to Buffalo I moved into Allentown, which someone described to me as the Greenwich Village of Buffalo. That meant that the neighborhood was filled with winos and antique stores, and men searching my late-night street for sex with other men. It happened that North Pearl was one of the cruisiest streets in town, as well as an excellent title for a poem.

The bums found their way into several other poems, but I never worked in the antiques. The line that comes most immediately to mind is from a poem I later discarded: "and drunken winos stumbling senseless into dawn." I've always wanted to use that line again, but I've never found the proper place.

I WANT YOUR SEX

Though I lived in Buffalo for only six months in 1991 and hated the place passionately (I felt that I had ruined my life by going there, but I didn't know what ruin really was), I look back on the place fondly. Buffalo is the place where I shed much of my sexual Platonism, my belief that a beautiful body meant a beautiful mind, that there was some necessary relation between beauty and virtue, that beauty meant anything at all. Such notions are very useful for poems, but in life they are invitations to humiliation and self-abasement, an invitation I've accepted all too often. *Shall we dance?* self-hatred has asked, and I've taken his well-manicured hand. In Buffalo I began to have sex for the sake of sex, rather than sex for the sake of the person I could become if I had the right kind of sex with the right kind of man in the right kind of place. I not only had more sex, I had it less inhibitedly and, since it was less psychologically fraught, enjoyed it more. "Less fraught" and "less inhibitedly," of course, still leaves a great deal of room for inhibition and emotional freight. Everything, as they say, is relative.

WHAT HAVE I DONE TO DESERVE THIS?

I found out I was HIV positive in Chicago in 1994, just before my first book was scheduled to appear. Devastated, I was convinced that I would be dead within a year or two (this was when AZT was the only antiretroviral medication available) and that my first book would be my last, my testament. Feeling alone and very frightened, I sought out a community of those who would understand what I was going through, with whom I could share my experience. I went to an HIV support group run by Test Positive Aware Network (an organization that does an enormous amount of good work, I hasten to say).

The one support group meeting I attended, for those recently diagnosed HIV positive, was full of men who had devised a whole New Age philosophy around HIV, transubstantiating it into a blessing in disguise.

. . . .

Contracting HIV, they said, had forced them to examine themselves; it had made them put their lives in order, had forced them to give up drinking or taking drugs or various other bad habits: it had given their lives meaning and direction. I thought contracting the virus was something that might drive me to drink or to drugs.

Since about all I've ever done in my life is examine myself in the minutest detail, and since I've never liked alcohol or alcoholics, drugs or drug addicts, it occurred to me that while this virus was a lot in itself, it wasn't very much to have in common with anyone. It certainly didn't make us alike. I found the group's near-celebration of HIV rather ghoulish; I can't see a virus that may foreshorten my life as some kind of gift, let alone as the basis on which to redefine my life or my self. It's just an unpleasant thing with which I have to deal, an obstacle to get around as best I can. I have been lucky in that, for me, HIV has been largely abstract: I know that I have it because doctors and lab reports tell me I do, and because of the fourteen pills I take each day. So far I have had health insurance and no opportunistic infections. But even if that were not the case, HIV would not constitute my identity. I don't know what the meaning of my life is, but I know it isn't HIV. I don't find HIV meaningful, or even very interesting, and a virus isn't really much to talk about unless one is a doctor or a scientist. It's certainly not something on which to build a community, let alone a sense of self.

In the sweetly condescending manner of the true believer, the members of the group patiently explained to me that I might feel that way at the moment, but that I'd come around to their way of thinking. Since I never had that lobotomy, I never did come around. I never came back to that support group, either.

SPACE ODDITY

" 'Pleasure is not the only reason for travel,' he said." I've always wanted one place I could stay, but I've never stayed anywhere long. All my adult life I've wandered from place to place, from school to school, a deeply unheroic Odysseus less in search of a home (that was long gone, if it had ever been mine at all) than fleeing a place (any number of places) in which he feared being trapped. Having nothing behind me (no family, no financial resources), I went forward, following the trail of funding to who knows where, terrified of having to go back to doing data entry or worse. Sometimes I managed to convince myself by sheer force of will that the next place would be better; sometimes merely that wherever I went couldn't be worse than where I was. Until I got to Chicago I almost always managed to convince myself that wherever I had left was, in retrospect, better than where I'd ended up. In the words of the gifted poet Amy England, who also wrote the line with which this section opens, "To love a place forever, don't spend too much / Time there."

NAÏVE MELODY

Early in his adulthood the poet Wallace Stevens confided to his journal: "Life is an affair of people, not places." But for me life is an affair of places, and that is the problem. After years of going to various schools in the middle or even on the outskirts of various nowheres, I decided it was time to live in a real place again, so after I finished an M.F.A. at the Iowa Writers' Workshop I moved to Chicago. I adored Chicago as a place, its eclectic and impressive architecture, its highly varied cityscapes, its utterly rational street grid, which always let one know where one was in relation to any other place in the city and which overcame even my great talent for getting lost (I loved saying things like, "I'm at about 3000 North and 500 West" and knowing what they meant), its dense texture of sidewalks and subways and street life, its physical resemblance to New York in all except its affordability (and the easier availability of sex). I adored the lakefront, by which I never ceased to be inspired—large bodies of water have always fascinated me, the vanishing of the horizon into a meeting of water and air. If an ocean isn't available, any body of water large enough that the far shore can't be seen will do. And the lake always told me where I was—if that's Lake Michigan, that must be east.

Chicago is a city with what might be called an exposed exoskeleton: an industrial city in a way that New York no longer is; with factories adjacent to condominiums, its workings are visible to the naked eye. I found Chicago's physical presence, the city's embodiment of social relations, to be inspiring for my work—society was a body here in the most literal sense, which could be seen, touched, heard, and smelled (even if the smell was sometimes unpleasant). The lakefront embodied this meeting and merging of man and nature, the collision and collaboration of the natural and the artificial, because it was constructed. The neighborhood in which I lived for my entire six years in the city, appropriately called Lakeview, had originally been a swamp or even underwater. Much of the lakefront, fringed by a ribbon of green called Lincoln Park, was dredged up out of the lake and built up of landfill, rocks, and cement, punctuated every few miles by an artificial beach with trucked-in sand. I never got over the sight of people in bathing suits sunning themselves on concrete slabs, or at best on flat blocks of rock, sometimes with a towel to cushion their backs, sometimes not.

While I loved the city and would happily go back there, the people in Chicago left me cold, and left me often. (By several odd twists of fate and logistics, my friends tended to leave the city for places like Denver and Utah, some of them to return after I, in turn, had left.) Though I lived in the middle of the hip, gay neighborhood during my entire residence in the city, and though finding sex was often as easy as taking a walk down Halsted Street at one or two in the morning (or, when I lived above a bar, as easy as going downstairs), and though I met, at age thirty-one, the first person with whom I ever fell in love, a brilliant and impossible boy-man with whom I had an intense, all-too-fraught and crisis-ridden, but quite substantial, relationship for some five years, as lovers, as roommates, as friends and antagonists, I found Chicago, an easy place in which to meet people, to be an almost impossible place in which to get to know them. The Midwest, as I first discovered during my sojourn in Iowa, is full of self-consciously nice people, nice people who will cheerfully lynch you if they decide that you're not nice. And I was, in the words of someone who had met me for all of five minutes, relayed to me by a Midwestern friend, "that really rude East Coast guy who thinks he's really cool but really he's just an asshole." I refrained from asking how nice it was to convey such tidings to friends, or for that matter to decide such things about strangers.

Despite my difficulties in playing well with others, I would happily have stayed in Chicago for the rest of my life. It was the first place I felt that I actually *lived* in many years. But my job, at a school a three-hour commute away on the Greyhound bus, made me utterly miserable, and I couldn't imagine any living I could make outside academia. So, after six years of nightclubs, Tower Records and Reckless Records, Borders Books and Unabridged Books, and delicious, inexpensive Thai food, I left Chicago for what seemed to be a good job at a good school, in a small town in upstate New York that had all of the disadvantages of a college town and none of the advantages, because that seemed to be the thing that I should do. I'd experienced enough consequences of doing things because I "should" to know that things done because one convinces oneself they're for the best never work out well, but I'd convinced myself I had no choice.

Unsurprisingly, I was miserable in Ithaca's grim, poverty-stricken backwater. Surprisingly, it was there that I met Robert and fell in love, at thirty-seven. It was only for the second time in my life, and it was the first time I discovered that love needn't be constant tumult but can be simply two people who care for each other and enjoy being together. I don't much believe in fate, but sometimes I think I went to Ithaca so that I could meet the person I didn't know that I was trying to come home to.

The list of places I've lived, or at least existed, grows longer and longer: the Bronx; Macon, Georgia; Bennington, Vermont; Boston (and Cambridge), Massachusetts; Amherst, Massachusetts; Providence, Rhode Island; Buffalo, New York; Iowa City, Iowa; Milwaukee, Wisconsin; Chicago, Illinois; Ithaca, New York; and now Pensacola, Florida. The South is about the last place I'd ever expected to have ended up, short of Montana or Idaho: when I left Macon at seventeen I vowed never to venture south of the Mason-Dixon Line again. Those people had fought a war to keep slavery, and losing didn't seem to have much changed their minds. Living here has brought many changes, not all of them welcome. For one thing, I have bought a car and learned to drive, in that order, even though my identity was built around being a pedestrian and I still hold the automobile responsible for the destruction of urban life in America. But not everyone here is a Confederate, and the rifle racks on the pickup trucks are mostly empty these days. And Robert is here and is from here, so I know some good has come from the place.

When I began this essay I didn't know where it would lead or what its shape would be. But then I realized that it's a sort of story after all, and the story is a comedy: it begins with trouble and ends with love. To the extent that I have a home now, it is Robert. I don't know where my journey will take me, but I know that he will be with me. Life turns out to be an affair of people after all.

The Last Safe Place

. . . .

by

KATHLEEN CAMBOR

From the time I started kindergarten when I was not quite five, I liked everything about school—the smart, plaid dresses that were bought for me, so different from the frayed and mismatched play clothes I was accustomed to; the boxy saddle shoes I wore; the smell of paste; the vibrant sheen of the finger paints; the soothing cadences of the little rhyming songs we learned; and the improbably long walk to school with my slightly older brother. (For years, until I actually went back and measured it, I wondered if, in a distortion of memory, I had exaggerated the distance from my house to the public school I attended that year. Could my parents really have allowed us—hardly more than babies—to walk more than a mile through busy city streets alone? Did my mother and father really believe that the world was *that* safe, or was this just one more lapse of attention, one of the early signifiers of the failure of focus, the trouble in our house?) Prior to starting school, I had really not been anywhere to speak of. My family didn't venture out much. We didn't take trips or vacations; we didn't have friends in other parts of the city. Except for church and my grandparents' house, the occasional trip to the doctor (although he most often came to us; it was the age of house calls), I'd never left my neighborhood. Then the state declared that I was ready for school, for the world, and I was set loose on it. I remember how immediately and completely I loved that walk to school, the games I devised for myself during it, the elaborate lengths I went to in order to avoid stepping on cracks, the dandelions I plucked from the lawns we passed, the admirable restraint and caution with which my brother and I, holding hands, waited for traffic lights to change. We picked up other kids on the way, spilling from houses and streets along the route to school. Merle and Sissy Neuse, Anita Burns and two of her rowdy, redheaded brothers; the beautiful, dark-haired Susan Waelchli. They were my first friends beyond our block.

In a short time I found that my gradual mastery of schoolroom labors—rough crayon drawings, the manipulation of short, blunt scissors—gave me a growing sense of myself as competent. The trek to school, the sense of order and achievement I felt in my life there became a kind of balm to me. School provided me with a stretch of four hours every day in which I could be distracted from the worry that gnawed constantly at me: about my infant sister and my young, fragile mother whose depressive illness had begun to penetrate the walls and floorboards in our house, invading every crevice, like an invisible, odorless, but deadly gas.

I don't believe it ever crossed the minds of educators then that we should be learning to read in kindergarten. Intellectual preparedness was not part of the agenda. We were there to be socialized, to sing, to learn to sit still, and to pay attention to our sweetly earnest teacher, the patient object of our abject love, our first surrogate outside our families. We were *read to,* gathered in tight, squirming circles, all of us in thrall to the sound of Miss H's voice and the words she shaped with it. The *sound* of language came first, like music, and we tilted our faces to Miss H like so many flowers yearning toward a bright, life-giving sun. My classroom was small and in the basement of an old and overcrowded building. Often the heat was insufficient for the cold winter mornings, and we had to wear our coats and mittens throughout the school day to keep warm. Our below-ground space was windowless, so that even when the spring came we never saw the sun. In spite of those things, that classroom seemed to me to be a place of rare and subtle beauty. I wanted to live at school where, I felt certain, Miss H lived. I could imagine no other life for her but the one she shared with me.

I carried that goodwill toward school with me to first grade, to Catholic school, and to the tasks set forth for us there, where the goal *was* to acquire skills. I learned to add by counting on my fingers. Then, an early addict to achievement, I worked assiduously to calculate without the crutch of my hands, to do math in my head. I attended to my reading texts in the way that a religious scholar studied papyrus scrolls, sounding out each letter, laboring to attach the sounds of them, one to another, until they became words, then sentences. The Readers, as we called our texts, had as their central characters Dick and Jane and the loyal pooch Spot. As real to me as if I knew them, they took their important places in my imaginative life. The neighborhood where I grew up was a polyglot ethnic mix. We were Irish, Poles, and Slovenians. Those Readers and their stories of the vibrant little family in which Dick and Jane lived were a revelation to me. I had never seen a blond child before I saw a friend of Jane's, whose name escapes me now, in the pages of my Reader.

In my family, we had always been encouraged to be modest in our wants, but my Christmas list in that, my first-grade year, was unusually brief. Books. I was deeply earnest in the expression of my wish. No dolls, thank you, no toys, no frivolity. I wanted to attach myself, commit myself to the school life that had already given me so much. My parents chose two volumes that they must have thought would please me. *Heidi* and *The Five Little Peppers and How They Grew.* What I didn't realize until I opened the books on Christmas morning was that real books were quite different from the discrete, short tales of Dick and Jane. I remember how hefty my Christmas books seemed, how amazingly full of words they were, surprisingly lacking in illustrations, those great space-fillers I'd become accustomed to at school. There were no illustrations in *Heidi,* none in *The Five Little Peppers and How They Grew.* And the chapters, it appeared, were part of a continuum, each one leading to another. As I flipped through their pages, my excitement about my gifts soon gave way to a slowly mounting nausea. (My stomach, a barometer, always signaled me when there was trouble coming.) I feared I wasn't up to the work I'd chosen, not worthy of these things I had acquired. And then there was the actual mechanical problem of reading.

I pondered and pondered how to go about this. The longest segment of Dick and Jane lasted a mere three pages. The margins were wide, the illustrations large, each short section calibrated to the attention span, the phonetic prowess, of a tentative beginner. I had never seen either of my parents read a book; there was no one in my home to whom I could turn for guidance. And then there was the issue of which book to read first, the problem of being seen (by whom? I wonder now) as playing favorites. Was that allowed? Was it a reader's prerogative, was it *my* prerogative, to make a judgment, declare one book to be more important, more urgently in need of reading than another? Worry about my mother, about what would happen to us all if her unhappiness continued to deepen, as it threatened to, had already made me a young insomniac. Now I spent sleepless nights in a kind of bibliophilic ethical crisis. How could I choose one of my books without giving offense to the other? I had attributed tender, human feelings to those books, and I feared that, by choosing, I would inflict a wound.

Wounded myself, sensing already that I did not quite fit into my family, that I was the least desired of my parents' children, I was eager not to give injury. And so in an effort to be fair, I read one chapter in *Heidi* and one in *The Five Little Peppers and How They Grew,* and in that way labored through their pages. I remember the long weeks of the enterprise, how confused I was, how unhappy, struggling mightily to make sense and keep track of the two utterly disparate story lines. My head and brain were small; there wasn't sufficient room for all the characters and information I was gathering. I turned what ought to have been pleasure into an ordeal. I curled into the green armchair in our living room, my work illuminated by our one good lamp, which I had moved to a place beside me. The Pittsburgh winter kept me indoors and at it, until after weeks and weeks my index finger, my reading finger, grazed beneath the final words of *Heidi.* I remember how tired I felt, and at the same time, how triumphant, aware that I had taken on a hard task and by the sheer force of my determination seen it to its finish. It was not the reading pleasure I had imagined for myself, but there was pleasure nonetheless. From those two books I learned things about myself. I learned that I was iron willed, relentless, and capable of being scrupulously fair even when it strained my meager resources.

This marked the beginning of a feeling I had that books could raise me, could help me to create a self, could become my parents, my advisors—objects that took the place of the people whom I might have looked to for advice, information, solace, but who were unavailable to me. A distracted father, undone by a marriage to a barely functioning depressive; a mother who slept most of the day, and who alternately wept, fretted, and despaired when she was awake; siblings who depended too much on me because, in the arbitrary ways that roles are assigned in families, I had somehow been designated the capable one. When it came to seeking life instruction in Catholic school, I found that religious doctrine as it was elucidated in the Bible, catechism, and Daily Missal provided me with a rigid, tortured moral sense. But I soon came to understand that the nuns, with few exceptions, were too judgmental to be truly helpful about the stuff of daily life, that even the most well meaning of them had stones for hearts, all the softness that should have been part of a spiritual life made hard by the punitive and unforgiving rhetoric that was so much a part of church lore of that time. Of course the truth was that I couldn't have been easy to instruct or comfort. I was tender, raw nerved, too sensitive for anybody's good. My world was one in which a sturdier child would probably have fended better, found some safety in denial. But I was overly, exquisitely, at-

· · · · · · · · · · ·

tuned to everything around me, every sea change. My inner life was an overwhelming, overwrought tumult of feelings, and uncertain where to go with it, where to look for help and understanding, I turned into myself to try to find a way to manage. And then, once I began to understand how much they had to offer, I turned to books. I found the school library, then the public library nearby, named for Andrew Carnegie, someone who would come to figure large in my own life years later. I never cozied up to a librarian, never sought advice as I worked at developing a reading plan. I was not in search of human friends or helpers. I had assessed the possibilities for help from humans and decided to trust my instincts about books, to let books raise me.

■ ■ ■

I made my first real sacrifice for art, for knowledge, when I was six. I had begun taking piano lessons at the beginning of my second-grade school year, and the fact that my family didn't have a piano—couldn't afford a piano—had somehow not been considered to be an obstacle when the initial negotiations about lessons began. I don't recall why I'd asked for piano lessons. No one had suggested to me that music was a lofty enterprise, and I had never been encouraged to have whims; my parents were anything but indulgent with me. They were practical, strict, and because of my mother's depression, they always had the kind of frantic, edgy look of two people under siege. Still, the piano lessons were somehow deemed a good idea. But after about a month of them, it became clear that I was doomed to a dauntingly slow progress if I couldn't find a way to practice. My piano teacher was a nun, housed in the convent across the street from my elementary school, and it was she who suggested that I could come into one of the convent dayrooms, a room containing a piano, during my lunchtime, in order to practice my scales and simple exercises. I was already, at age six, an overly earnest child, eager to succeed and please, but I liked to eat as much as anybody. And yet, for some reason, the idea of going without lunch didn't trouble me. Something felt oddly *right* about it—the joining of music and hunger, of art and difficulty. I don't know where that feeling came from. I had no models when it came to thinking about literature or music—the yearning toward it, the need for it. Such notions were not part of the *zeitgeist* in my family or neighborhood. *We* were working people; *we* didn't put on airs. But nonetheless at six, in the convent dayroom, I knew that I was engaged in something that mattered very much to me. I knew I had been singled out, that I had been given a special privilege—access to the convent when it was largely empty—and that it felt right to be the only child there, hungry and alone at the dark upright piano, the image of Christ crucified hanging on the wall behind me. In addition to the sounds of the music I was making (elementary as that music was) there were, as well, the random, mysterious midday sounds drifting from the rooms and hallways of the convent beyond the closed door of my practice room. A chiming clock. The occasional echoing click of a single pair of shoes on the buffed wood floor. A surprisingly girlish, careless laugh that rose charmingly—a young nun, I supposed, happy in a house of women. Everything I felt about what I was doing, in relation to the piano, in relation to who I *was,* was connected to that place, that room, the way my hands felt, fingers curved, thumbs on middle C, ready to launch me up and down the keyboard. I remember the feel of my skinny bird-legs dangling from the tall piano bench, swinging in time with the music.

Because I counted so little on the adults around me (or at least convinced myself that I did), for a long time places became, in many ways, more important to me than the people who inhabited them. The library, the dayroom in the convent, my grandfather's basement workshop where he kept assorted saws, clamps, levels, and Mason jars full of nails, the stuff of his woodworking hobby. He and my grandmother, my mother's German-speaking parents, took my siblings and me in when things became impossible at home, and I remember them with a hopeless, inflated, utterly idealizing love. If they had flaws, which they certainly must have, I won't, *can't* directly acknowledge them. They kept me safe during times when I understood that I was in real danger. I knew in some absolutely basic, instinctual way that I owed my life to them. But what I've come to realize over time is that even as they kept me safe, and even as my heart is filled with gratitude for that, they also denied me something that I needed badly—some sort of frank discussion of the reality of my experience at home. When my father took me to them—bundled up in a blanket in the backseat of our old Buick, in the night and in a hurry, for the twenty-minute ride to their house and safety—we all acted as if it was a surprise, a holiday, a lark, as if there had been no frantic phone call. Perhaps it can be attributed to Germanic reserve, but neither of them spoke directly about my mother's illness, about her erratic behavior, her inability to care for me. No one ever said, "This is not the way your life should be. It must be hard for you." And because of that, in the end, it was my grandparents' house, even more than my grandparents, much as I loved them, that became the real place of safety for me. Until I left for college at age seventeen, I never once slept through the night in my own home. I sat outside my parents' bedroom door; I sat on the bathroom floor, the cold porcelain bathtub anchoring my spine; I sat next to my sister's bed and monitored her breathing, as if her very life depended upon me. Anything to stay awake, to avoid letting down my guard. But I slept the sleep of the just, the innocent, the baby, in the little room my grandparents kept for me. In my one recurring dream about my childhood, my grandmother and grandfather are never there. It is their narrow little row house that I see, and it's bigger than it ever was in life, a place full of secret rooms, hideouts, all for me. One room for reading, one for writing, one for thinking. An embarrassment of riches. All the space I could ever need.

■ ■ ■

My father ran his own small business as a heating and roofing contractor. He essentially worked alone, although on occasion, for a job too big for one man, he took on a day laborer, usually some panhandler he'd come across in his travels around the city. His work took him everywhere in Pittsburgh. Because of that, he seemed like my worldly parent, out and about in his truck, venturing into little-known neighborhoods, narrow cobbled alleys. Occasionally on a Sunday, he'd load all of us into the Buick and take us for what he called a ride. It was a way of getting my increasingly housebound mother out. Our destination on these Sundays was always a house in need of a new roof or furnace, a job that my father was hoping to get, and once there he left us sitting in the car and went inside to negotiate with the homeowner and bid on the work to be done. My brother, sister, and I were numbed by the boredom of it, and the long time spent waiting in the car in such close confinement with my mother set us all on edge. But these rides, these visitations, also gave me a sense of the far-flung places my father's work took him, and of how large the city actually was.

I, too, was worldly in my way. My walk to school had acquainted me with a whole inner-city neighborhood that I could access by myself, on foot. There was a movie theater on the boulevard we crossed to get to school, as well as Isaly's deli/sandwich shop where I could stop on days when I had a little money and could buy myself a Klondike bar. My dentist's office was above a five-and-dime. The library was around the corner from my school, and no one seemed to care, or even notice, how much time I spent there. Often I lost track of myself in the stacks, and I'd glance out the window to see streetlights blinking on and realize that my brother was long gone, that I'd have to walk home by myself, in the dark.

There was a little hospital at the end of my street with a long, sloping hill beside the parking lot that proved to be a terrific place for winter sledding. In the summer, sunflowers grew along the border of the slope next to the sidewalk, the tallest flowers I'd ever seen. Summers meant freedom, and my brother and I got up early every day, gulped down cereal and milk, and then raced for the door. If we overslept (a rarity; we were eager to get going) Merle and Sissy Neuse summoned us by tossing stones at our second-floor window. We had no restrictions, no limits placed on our wanderings. Rules were beyond my mother's mothering capacity, and for once her illness worked to my benefit. She didn't stand in my way. I left home at dawn, didn't return to it until moments before the last light faded. I caught bees and fireflies. On a dare, I rode a scooter at breakneck speed down a steep and winding hill, and I crashed with such force into the sidewalk that a pebble from the cracked cement where I landed is still embedded in my knee. My brother and I had collected a great assortment of friends, and we played hide-and-seek and ate bologna sandwiches in the houses of pals we'd made whom my parents didn't know. I thrilled at the thought that they might not approve, that I was defying them, that for once I was not being good. We lived then beyond the scrutiny of the adults in our house. We enjoyed a heady, careless freedom.

Then, during the summer after my ninth birthday, we moved. Our house had long been too small for us, with my brother, sister, and me sharing one tiny bedroom, but in order to get what my father thought we needed—three bedrooms, a good-sized yard—we had to relocate some distance from the city. The house my parents settled on was ranch style, brick, and lacked the dilapidated charm of the little, yellow two-story we'd lived in since my birth. The subdivision in which the house was located consisted of three short streets, surrounded by paved, heavily trafficked highways. There were no sidewalks, there was no possibility of walking, and no place to walk in any case. The county park, our school, the roller rink we might have frequented were miles away. To leave, to escape from our hemmed-in little three-block world, required a car, a driver, and a mother able to get up and go. We were, all of us, except my father, prisoners there. A school bus picked us up at the Fox Trot Inn, a roadhouse in a clearing on the highway's edge, and we became slaves to its schedule. We had to wait in

. . . .

the school cafeteria at the day's end for the bus to take us home. There was no freedom to drift or to gain access to the school environs. So even though I could see the public library from my fourth-grade classroom window, I couldn't get to it. I remember looking at it, longing for it, when I ought to have been learning long division—its redbrick façade, its lopsided, welcoming sign. I was like a traveler in a desert, disoriented, thirsty, a victim of tricks my mind played on me, seeing a mirage. Eventually the bookmobile paid twice-monthly visits to the Fox Trot Inn parking lot, but I soon realized that bookmobiles must be a kind of Siberia for librarians, the place they're stationed just before they're fired for incompetence. The nail-biting, worried redhead assigned to mine never remembered to bring the books I hesitantly asked for, and soon enough I took pity on her and stopped filling out the requisition cards. Eventually my relationship with her grew into a kind of kinship, born of the realization that we both had been marooned in a desolate, provincial outpost. I read what she had on hand. At eleven I was arguably too young to be reading Ibsen, but Irene pressed *A Doll's House* into my hands, a book that became a watershed in my reading life, and one that provided me with a chilling, daunting glimpse at the vagaries of womanhood and marriage.

About two years after the move, for reasons unknown to me, my father became an avid reader. He bought paperbacks and stacked them in the front hall closet. (*The Rise and Fall of the Third Reich* is the tome I remember best.) After he came home from work each night, he ate his dinner at the kitchen table quickly, perfunctorily, as if it was a chore to be gotten through, then moved to the living room, where he read until long after I had gone to bed. It took him from me, from all of us, this insistence on uninterrupted time, this preoccupation with the written word. But it also, in some way, restored him to me. He'd never been a very engaged father—thirty-seven when he married, tired already from caring for his family after his father died when he was just thirteen. By the time I was old enough to be truly conscious of him, it was as if his energy, his capacity for joy, had withered or been spent. I was very sweet in his presence, quiet, never a problem, and in that way I did nothing to increase what I thought of as his great unhappiness. But I had no idea, really, how to actively engage or cheer him. Yet when he began to read, I felt as if he belonged to me, and I to him, in a way that was new for us. His passion was history, mine fiction, and we never spoke to each other about what we were reading. There were no exchanges of confidence, no shared moments of intimacy, no acknowledgment that we were alike in some important way. But before his reading life began, I had been possessive and anxious about mine. The value I placed on my inner world of thought and feelings seemed out of sync with everyone and everything I knew, and I suspected that the kind of rarefied and privileged life I longed for, an interior life, was a genetic, hereditary gift. Since, as far as I could tell, no one related to me felt as I felt or thought as I thought, I feared that I would one day be cruelly exposed for what I was—a great pretender. And on that day the books I had saved for and bought and the music I played would be abruptly, arbitrarily, coldly taken from me. The first time I saw my father read anything but the daily paper, I felt a kind of peace wash over me. It was not the great, lighthearted happiness that I suspected some other children felt at various moments in their lives, but it was an unspeakable relief to me to discover that my father found meaning and value where I had found it. It was the first time since we'd moved that I felt anything but utterly alone.

Who in America knows the history of Memorial Day? The story of how that holiday began? What I knew of it, growing up, was that it was the day of remembering and honoring the dead, the day that my family traveled as far as we ever did—to the other end of the city—to plant flowers on the graves of my father's parents. It was a long drive, an adventure for us. Did we sing in the car? I doubt it, we were not given much to singing, but I like to pretend we did, to remember it that way. Unlike my German grandparents, these grandparents were essentially unknown to me. My grandfather died when my father was a boy, and his mother, my grandmother, died when I was not quite six. I remember Mom, as we called her, but only in swift, fragmentary flashes—the sweet lift and fall of her Irish brogue, her faded, oft-washed housedresses that smelled of sun and soap. Mine was a sensory knowledge. What I actually *knew* about her and my grandfather was that they had been striving immigrants, as so many Americans were in the early twentieth century—Irish, Catholic, full of overly enthusiastic, misplaced hope. And then reality imposed itself on the misplaced hope, and the young husband, my grandfather, who'd become a coal miner by default, because it was the only work that he could find, died, leaving five children and a wife who would live three decades more without him, without his great, expansive love. It was a long time for her, but finally they were reunited, buried together, and once a year my parents, brother, sister, and I joined them, and picnicked with them. On no other day did my family spend so much uninterrupted time together; on no other occasion did we enjoy such plenty, eating alfresco, in sunlight, an elaborate

·   ·   ·   ·   ·   ·   ·   ·   ·   ·

lunch packed by my father, with a dizzying array of food—ham sandwiches, potato salad, apples, bananas, a chunk of yellow cheese, a thickly iced chocolate cake. On that one day there was a feeling of lightness, of abundance: for once there was more than enough for us all, and I felt grateful for it, grateful to these grandparents whom I didn't know, whose presence, even after death, brought this kind of goodwill and ease to a once-beloved son. I liked to sit close to their headstones during these picnics. I imagined, as only a child might, their spirits floating above us, watching, as we assembled on the old quilt we used as a picnic blanket, its edges anchored to the windswept hillside with stones we'd gathered from the cemetery driveway. On those days, even my mother seemed energized, willing, bent to the task of turning the earth at the base of their gravestones with a little handheld spade she'd brought. Readying the earth for planting. My grandparents had lived and were buried in Carnegie, Pennsylvania.

Fast-forward thirty years. Again it's Memorial Day. Again there is a car, a journey, but one that is of the most ordinary sort. A mother running errands, going for groceries, videos, library books, tending to life's mundane requirements, her children buckled safely in the seat behind her. This time I'm at the wheel, a grown woman in Texas, and on this May afternoon there will be no graveside visitations. Texas is where I live, where I'm raising my family, but except for them, my husband and two babies, I have no relatives, no history, and no roots there. The ribbon of freeway stretches straight out before me, and the lack of contour in the landscape, the extraordinary flatness of southeast Texas, is something that I have never grown accustomed to. I've learned to pretend that the vast, uninterrupted expanse of sky is compensatory in its beauty, but I'm kidding myself. I miss hills. And on that Memorial Day, a day set aside for memory, I feel uneasy and rootless without a grave to visit. The afternoon is hot, the children doze, and in the rearview mirror I can see the pink flush of perspiration on my daughter's cheek. It's a holiday, but it seems quite different now than it did when I was young. Less sacred, less memorializing, more a convenient addition to a weekend break, an opportunity for working Americans to take a little time. The radio sends its soothing buzz of sound into the car, and I'm about to turn it off, to enjoy the very particular silence that comes with sleeping children, when the commentator begins to read an essay about Pennsylvania and another Memorial Day, May of 1889. It is the story of the Johnstown Flood, and it tweaks something in my memory. I know this story, or at least I know something of it, and now, attentive, I listen and learn more.

On that May day in 1889, in the waning years of another century, the people in Johnstown knew what the Memorial Day agenda ought to be. Work stopped, shops closed. Veterans of the Civil War were still alive, and they made plans to honor brothers, comrades who had not survived the war. Memorial services in Johnstown's twenty-seven churches would begin the day, followed by a long, elaborate parade, with several marching bands, a single piccolo player tooting out the notes of "Yankee Doodle." The Grand Army veterans took their places among the marchers. Mountain wildflowers had been woven into wreaths and garlands; buntings had been hung along the parade route. Late in the afternoon, as the sun slid down the western sky, candles were lit, hymns sung. In the cemeteries there were graveside picnics.

Johnstown was a thriving small metropolis in the Allegheny Mountains of western Pennsylvania. There was steel mill there, a barbed-wire factory, and a woolen mill. Work was plentiful; the railroad brought commerce and travelers to the city. There were electric streetlights, an elevator in the new hotel. Everyone was justifiably proud of his prosperity. They'd built a city, a good place. One could imagine, plan a future there. As Memorial Day ended, citizens and patriots drifted home as a chilly, drilling rain began. Lulled by the sound of the rain, they slept. And awoke to a relentless storm, and street flooding, to a day that began with what seemed to be mere inconvenience, the kind spring flooding caused—a ruined rug, soaked curtain hems—and ended prematurely, horribly, at 3:10 P.M., when an earthen dam fifteen miles above the city burst, unleashing twenty million tons of water, a great devouring wall of water, into the narrow valley that led to Johnstown. By nightfall, two thousand innocents, wives and husbands, napping children, were swept away, drowned, or burned alive in the ensuing fire, their hopeful, happy lives obliterated

I never aspired to write a historical novel. I was working on another kind of book when the story of the Johnstown Flood beckoned to me. And a beckoning is what it felt like. I thought of Saint Paul, knocked from his horse by a summoning, demanding God. In my car that day it seemed to me that I had been drafted into the service of a cause.

It was good that I didn't know then how much there is that works against the success of historical fiction. There seems to be, there seems always to have been, a great deal of controversy about the value of histori-

.   .   .   .

cal fiction, its place in the literary cosmos. The critiques of it are many: the accretion of period detail, which is one of the hallmarks of this fiction, the proof that the author did her homework, often feels artificial and arbitrarily inserted; imaginings about people who lived in times so utterly removed from our own are doomed to inaccuracy; the writer of historical fiction is cheating, acquiring a false legitimacy by associating herself, by virtue of her subject matter, with Dickens or Austen, who already described the manners and mores of their time with such great artistry. In a letter, Henry James warned Sarah Orne Jewett against the whole unwieldy undertaking.

What I also didn't know was how much I'd come to love the work that had chosen me in spite of the great difficulties attendant to it. All writing has at its root the writer's willingness, her need, to take an imaginative leap, to give life to the story she wishes to tell. There are characters to invent, a world to be described and peopled. If she writes about contemporary life, the writer is somewhat aided by the reader's basic knowledge of the world as it is now. Because of that knowledge, there already exists between writer and reader some degree of familiarity. The reader nods as he turns the pages. That's right, he says. That's how it is. That understanding, that nod from the reader, is not available to the writer of historical fiction. What is available, however, and what is part of the pleasure for the writer, is the opportunity to give life not only to characters, but also to another time, a time in which the world was quite different from what we know it to be now. When I began, I suspected but did not really know how complex a task that would prove to be. Nor did I know to what degree it would return me so forcefully and intimately to myself and to places to which I had a passionate and deep connection—the hills of Pennsylvania and the dusty recesses of the library.

Around the time that my first book was published, another novel appeared that took as its fictional subject various intrigues surrounding the building of the Panama Canal. It was a splendid story, and was praised, as it deserved to be. Much of the book was set in Paris, which was described in impeccable and vivid detail, and the author was singled out for special notice because he had never been there, to the City of Lights. Library research and his rich imagination had enabled him to fully create a place he'd never seen.

I was among the admirers of this imaginative feat, and when I began to write about Johnstown I thought that such a thing might be possible for me. I pored over photographs, read painstaking first-person narratives about life in Johnstown and in other parts of the country both before and after the flood. I made maps and time lines, studied biographies of the industrial giants of the day, the Robber Barons, who had owned the dam and whose inadvertence led to its collapse. Henry Clay Frick and Andrew Mellon. Andrew Carnegie, endower of the libraries that had been the refuge of my childhood. I learned as much as—more than—it seemed possible to learn, all kinds of things about the era: what people wore and what they read, what goods merchants were selling, what songs were sung, the way it might have felt to be alive then in America. But I soon realized that I had to travel there, to spend time, that for me there is a kind of knowing that can only be grasped by the body, a very essential physical sense of a place. I knew I had to stand at what had been the breast of the dam, to walk through the streets, so different now than they were in 1889, but also, I suspected, so deeply, essentially the same. I had to look at, feel, the encroachment of the steep hills that surround the city, clogged still with the trees and underbrush that would have made escape in May of 1889 so impossible. I needed to kneel, to feel that earth as my characters would have felt it, so dear to them, the physical representation of all they meant when they thought, when they uttered, the word "home." I wanted to breathe their air, see the way the tree limbs in their valley clawed the great blue dome of sky.

"Nora remembers well the excursions of her childhood, the gradual upward movement as the train charged from the city toward the mountains. The sense of rising. Of coming out of herself, out of her life, things falling away behind her." So I wrote in my novel, and so it was for me as I drove into the Allegheny Mountains from Pittsburgh, as I became physically aware of the distance traveled, the change in elevation, the surprising drop in temperature, the bone-penetrating chill of mountain air. Vistas like these were my girlhood vistas—western Pennsylvania, familiar and yet oddly foreign to me, a landscape that I'd fled, thrust from my mind and memory because it was associated for me with so much unhappiness, with the shipwreck of my family. Johnstown is not Pittsburgh, and yet, when I went there it felt so much like my place, it seemed utterly available to me, as did the men and women who had lost their lives there. Death was random and greedy in 1889, as death always is, and businessmen, lawyers, and clergy were among those who perished in the flood. But Johnstown was a hub of industry. It sprang to life and thrived because of labor, and for the most part those who died were working people. My people. The Czechs and Poles, Croats and Irish I grew up with, who befriended me

. . . .

when I was five, who became my companions, my pals, my soul mates on my long, long walk to school. Grandview Cemetery, where so many of the those who died in the Johnstown Flood are buried, is situated on a hill that overlooks the city proper, as if designed with an understanding that even for the dead, a view is a good, a necessary, thing. On my first visit to Johnstown, I spent a long day there, and in a kind of homage I read every name on every plain flat marker, hundreds upon hundreds, an overwhelming stretch of grass and graves, and I felt a profound, awed sorrow at the enormity of it, so much bright life wiped out so suddenly. During that visit, I removed my gloves, ran my cold hands across the weather-worn, chiseled engravings on the gravestones. "Lost. Flood." I traced the varied names. Andrew Dudzik, Lee Sing, Sophia Sarlouis. Benjamin and Mary Hoffman, and Bertha, Minnie, Marion, Florence, Joseph, Helen, Freda—all seven of their children. The next spring, on Memorial Day, I returned to Grandview Cemetery with a bottle of spring water and a ham and Swiss cheese sandwich, and ate it slowly, mindfully, while sitting on the grass among the markers, and in that way, without the benefit of ceremony or overflowing picnic hamper or spread quilt, without the company of my father, long dead, who had allowed me, in the end, to have my reading and writing life, who taught me the exquisite value of remembering and honoring the dead, I picnicked there.

I had been using libraries throughout my life, but now I was spending all my time in them, enjoying both their arcane and their more ordinary treasures. In the Johnstown Library I unearthed street maps, a list of businesses—butchers, grocers, blacksmiths from 1889. In archived records I found names and addresses of people who lived there then. I sought help from a librarian and he gave me all the help I needed. In New York, in Texas, I lost myself again, as I had as a girl, in the stacks, the microfilm. I studied the art that Henry Clay Frick loved, read biographies of Andrew Carnegie, and many of his letters. I gave myself over to another time and to another way of being. I would have said that my work was the work of reconstruction, and it was, but in more than one sense. Because even as I struggled to bring my characters and 1889 America to life, I was at the same time reconnecting to some almost forgotten part of myself. I already knew that the work of writing makes great demands of its practitioners. Now I was reminded that it also offers lavish, unexpected gifts.

Not long ago, I was asked to appear at a book festival on a panel about the place of research in writing. I agreed to participate. I was their guest. I'd do my part. Once there, I discovered that my fellow panelists and I were an unlikely group, disparate in our interests, our only bond being, I quickly realized, that we'd all had to learn something we didn't know in order to write our books. I'm not sure what the audience learned, but I learned 1) how to get a CIA agent to confide in you (from a mystery writer), and 2) the nature of the special code of honor among Texas rangers (from a man who made his life's work collecting their letters.) Research, that large encompassing word, meant different things to each of us, and I began to doubt that anything of what we said that day would be particularly helpful to our audience. An eager would-be historical novelist in the auditorium asked how you know when you're finished, when you've completed all your research and it's time to write. There were as many opinions as there were panelists, but I found myself remaining silent. How could I tell this hopeful writer that you're never finished with your research, that you can never know enough? To imagine that you know enough is to stop questioning, to cut short the search for an understanding of what it is that links us, one generation to the next, one century to some far distant one, and makes us all, in any time, so recognizably, so achingly human.

When I was writing about Johnstown, my aunt Sue, my father's sister, big-hearted soul, discovered her local library. She was seventy-five years old, the aunt who had always seemed most buoyant, most inspiring in her love of life and of her children. When I was growing up, she lived simply, as we all did, but she and her husband somehow saved the money to take their three girls to Ireland on several long, glorious trips. She always came home with shopping bags full of gifts—crystal rosary beads, cake pans shaped like shamrocks, plastic replicas of the staff Saint Patrick is said to have used to drive the snakes from Ireland. Aunt Sue was the only person I knew who ever went abroad, and I remember the wonder I felt—at her sense of adventure, of possibility, at the sheer extravagance of it. Her husband and her parents had all been born there, and she wanted to know the place, wanted her children to know it. Her four siblings, severe, hard working, miserly by almost any standard, criticized and mocked her for spending money this way, for being foolish and indulgent, but she waved them off. She had a life to live, great dreams for her children. She wanted the whole world to be their home, and she didn't care if it was an impulse others could not understand.

After I moved halfway across the country and then married, in spite of the fact that we had been great favorites of each other, Aunt Sue and I lost touch. But then she discovered the library, and then she heard that I was writing (something that she felt linked me to every Irish writer, alive or dead), and she sent me a letter. When she was younger, her life had been too active, too overstuffed, for the stillness reading required, but then age slowed her, or perhaps her lack of education made her nostalgic for what she'd missed. Whatever it was, the library beckoned. She applied for and was given a card, and she set out to explore the building's many rooms and shelves. It seemed that everything about the venture suited her. A local branch of the Carnegie library was close by; she could walk to it. The fact that she had almost no money was not an obstacle; the books were free. Aunt Sue had been a library regular for about six months when she wrote to me, confident, knowing, eager to share, bibliophile to bibliophile. She'd just finished reading Brenda Maddox's *Nora: The Real Life of Molly Bloom,* a biography of Nora Joyce, and she wondered if I knew the book or had heard any of Nora's story. "She was married to James Joyce," Aunt Sue wrote. "You've probably heard of him—the Irish writer. A drunk and a bum, but a great writer, I hear." After a brief appraisal of the Brenda Maddox's literary effort, a short burst of questions about me, Aunt Sue ended her communiqué with a psalm of praise for the library. "All these books, and I can take whatever I want. I have my card, I can choose anything. It's all here for me." As far as I knew, she'd lived the life she'd chosen for herself, had never longed for, never *wanted,* anything. Now she wanted the world of books, and the world of books opened itself to her. She said that she felt like the luckiest person alive.

My father's sister, my secret sharer. I wished that I could be with her; I wanted to touch her hand. Instead I wrote. Yes, I said. I understand.

Notes on the Underground

. . . .

by
MARY MORRIS

On mornings when my work isn't going well, when I can't get much done and mind and body are restless, I go underground. Usually I can manufacture an excuse. A sweatband my daughter needs, a doctor I should see, an exhibit I want to catch. Then I pack my backpack as if I am setting out on a journey, which, in a way, I am. I put in my journal, the book I am reading, some notes scribbled for a story, and I am off.

Destination is irrelevant. It's the subterranean world I seek. The trains I long to ride. I am the maven of maps, the queen of transfers. I pride myself on knowing how to get from place to place with minimal effort. I know when to get on the back or the front. If an overcrowded train comes, I wait. There's usually an empty one right behind.

Perhaps because I am a writer, I prefer the trains whose names are letters to the numbered lines. The meandering N and R; the J, Z, or M, which combine to sound more like a rap group than a subway, whose origins and endings are mysterious to me. There is something impersonal about the 4 and 5, the 2 and 3. And I've never made my peace with the 9. The 6 and 1 make too many stops. Those are the commuter lines for people who have somewhere to be, a job to perform, not a chapter to read. My spirits soar on the swift W or Q that take me out of the tunnels, across the bridges, where I gaze into the harbor, spot a barge. I view the Brooklyn Bridge. The Statue of Liberty. This is the sightseer's line, not forever hurtling through the darkened tunnels, but allowing a glimpse of the skyline, a gaze into the curtained apartments as we dip back into Chinatown.

In my underground journeys, I have tried to fashion a route that spells out words. I long for the A and the C to connect to the B. The M to the A to the D to the E. The F to the A to the C to the E. The latter is almost possible, but I can't spell love. There is no O. The subway becomes some Scrabble game whose letters are incomplete. But some days I try.

In part I know all this because the subway is my preferred place to work. I like it better than my own office at home and much better than the library, where I feel confined. Here there are no beds to make, no dog to walk, no dishes piled up in the sink.

I have always worked well in motion. Stasis depresses me. I often do my best work underground. Sometimes I lose myself there. Forget my stop or even where I'm going. A few years ago, I gave up the gym. The subway is my StairMaster. I dash up its steps; I run from train to train. I never take the escalators. I wonder about old people. When I am old, will I be able to get to transfer at Pacific? Or Times Square? I stay fit, do deep knee bends. I practice going up and down.

If I have a book to read, a story to edit, a student manuscript to work on, I'll get it done faster underground. I like the company of strangers. The knowledge that if the train is in motion, I don't have to be. My concentration is complete in the capsule that is the subway, that mass of humanity hurtling toward its destination without distraction.

For a long time I thought that perhaps there was something wrong with me. It seemed like a strange compulsion until the *New Yorker* came out with its cover last spring of a subway car with a library table in the middle, a Silence Please sign hanging above the doors.

When I am not working, I gaze around me. There is something about the feel of people I do not know. The carpenter with his belt of tools, the student honing her management skills. I like to glance over people's shoulders, read what they are reading. A catalog from Kitchen and Bath, *Tattoo and Piercing* magazine, *Billboard, The Complete Bird Owner's Handbook.* And, of course, the novels. Terry McMillan was doing well for a while. Now Grisham seems to be back in vogue again. I never would have known about the Egyptian system of spiritual cultivation if I hadn't glanced into the lap of an elderly Hispanic woman as she made painstaking notes from the *Metu Neter.*

In a pause from my own work, I read the ads, the Poetry in Motion poems. It is soothing to gaze into the eyes of a child or a tired man, pondering lines from Emily Dickinson, Mandelstam, or Billy Collins. Some cars have many ads: "At Least Your Armpits Can Travel in Style," "Manhattan Mini©Storage: Premium Space at a Premium." "Watch the New

York Rangers and Win." "Adoption; it's an option." "Chances Are, Mr. Right Is On Another Car." "*¿A quién se llama en caso de heridos?*" I don't like the cars where all the ads are devoted to Jack Daniel's or the Bronx Zoo or Smoke Quitters or Feria Designers. I want to see Dr. Zizmot, the dermatologist whose picture informs you that he will remove your dark spots and warts and moles and peel back your skin. The reminder that "Domestic Violence Is Violence Too." The Absolut bottle tucked in its Christmas sock. The question "Want to learn English?" in a dozen languages. Or all the places Metro-North can take you for a weekend away. The cooling sights of an empty Jones Beach, Bear Mountain, Tarrytown, martinis in the Hamptons.

I like to dream. I don't sleep on the subway anymore, though I have. Once, after a shopping expedition, I drifted off on my husband's shoulder on the Q and we wound up in Queens, having gotten on the train going in the wrong direction. So I try not to sleep, exactly, but rather to imagine places I'll be, where I'll go. If I am not deep in work, I'm deep in thought. So I don't like it if someone's headset bleeds or if people are talking across the aisle. But I love the sound of the trains, the churning of their wheels.

I press my face to the glass, gaze out at the darkened tunnels, wonder at what lies beneath. The moles, the homeless, the subway workers in their reflector suits who work at night. Day and night are interchangeable to them. I wonder at this maze of subterranean life like the ant exhibit at the Central Park Zoo. If I press my face tight to the glass, shading out the light with my hands, I can make out graffiti artists' tags painted on the walls: STAG21, Cheezewiz; INDIGO, SCARBOY LIVES. How do they make their way through the tunnels to write their names? How fearless do you have to be put your tag down here?

Once, coming back from Harlem, I have a manuscript with me, a draft of a novel I am working on. It has just been read by a friend. The train is almost empty as I spread it out on one of those little two-seaters by the door and begin to read my friend's comments. I don't notice people getting on or off, the milling of feet, of legs. I keep thinking that when someone needs this seat, he'll ask. They're New Yorkers, after all. Somewhere near City Hall I look up. The subway is packed. I haven't noticed. I have been working the whole time. But no one has asked me to pick up my work so they can sit down.

I can lose myself underground and often I have. To me it doesn't matter. I don't have that many places to be. But I have stared into the glazed faces

.   .   .   .

of Manhattanites as their local N bypasses lower Manhattan and suddenly they find themselves on the bridge. The police officers headed to City Hall groan, the Russian woman looks bewildered, an office worker shrieks. Brooklyn, they groan, shaking their heads. But I don't mind going into the unfamiliar. As I do with the train lines, I favor the station stops that are names, not numbers. These stations exist on the outer reaches, not in the bustling heart of Manhattan, where numbers rule. For the sheer pleasure of a name I have traveled to Gun Hill, Ozone Park, Gravesend.

If you are not careful when you come to Pacific Street, the train will go express to Thirty-sixth. That's about fifteen minutes out of my way each way. Then I have to cross over and return the way I've come, but I don't care because I pause to admire the Owen Smith mosaics, entitled "An Underground Movement," depicting the men designing, the workers building, and the straphangers riding on the trains.

In some stations, I allow time for the underground entertainment, free but for your contribution. The steel drum band, the Japanese string instrument with its haunting sound, the man who dances salsa with the dummy of a woman tied to his feet. The puppeteers, the Andean musicians playing the cana pipes. The soul singers and blues guitarists, the rockers and gospel singers, the sad man in the tunnel at Sixth Avenue and Forty-second who plays one note on the harmonica, his trousers rolled up, swaying back and forth, day after day.

Or on the trains themselves, which provide their own amusements (the toothless contratenor who sings Monteverdi to an awestruck N train at evening rush; the break-dance boys, the vendors of squeaky keychains and AAA batteries, the blind concertina player, a not-bad saxophonist whom I sometimes catch on the 2 or 3).

And then there are the stories. The almost always sad stories—the homeless, the exiled, the legless, the vets, the incurables. And the con artists—the grandmother whose house seems to burn down at least once a month, the cripple who suddenly walks off the train. We have all submitted ourselves to the subway's truths and lies. We have given our pocket change for a good story or a dollar for one we believe.

I have come to understand the demographics of this city best by traveling underground. Early morning rush and the trains carry the black and Hispanic office workers, janitors, construction workers. After nine, it's mostly white people in suits. At Thirty-sixth Street I take a longer look at those mosaics I admire and notice that the designers are white; the builders, black. The straphangers get an integrated ride.

The W, formerly the B, will be carrying the Chinese from Chinatown Brooklyn to Chinatown Manhattan. If I stand near a seated Chinese person, preferably reading a newspaper in Chinese on a crowded W, chances are good I'll get a seat at Canal Street.

It is a Wednesday morning, the usual rush. At DeKalb a train pulls in. A Hasidic Jew is standing there and, as the doors open, he races in. A large black man, standing in the doorway, pushes him out. He crashes into a Hispanic woman with a newborn strapped to her chest. The Hispanic woman screams. The Hasid shouts curses. The black man slips into the Q across the platform.

On the afternoon of May 1, 1992, I ride the subway into the city with my daughter. We are going to Penn Station. Normally this trip wouldn't have bothered me at all, but that morning the Rodney King verdict came down. I was living in Brooklyn and had to get to Princeton with Kate. My husband called and told me not to get on the subway, not to go anywhere in the city. I am a fairly cautious person and I listened to what he had to say. Then my traveler instincts took over. I'm taking the subway, I decided. Nothing will happen there.

It was the subway, in fact, that made me feel that nothing would happen in New York. I've lived in Los Angeles, a city whose apartheid is fairly complete. But New York is different. Whether we like it or not, we bump up against one another every day. It's not an intimate relation, but it is a connection all the same.

New York won't riot, I told myself as I got on the F to Herald Square. On the subway people gazed around. We looked one another over. Then we took out our books, our newspapers, our headsets for the rest of the ride.

The subway has its dark side. I have been mugged, fondled, accosted by the insane. I have seen a man's throat cut. I saw a woman smash a man in the face who had molested her. I have watched mothers abuse their children and seen the helpless faces of passengers who didn't know what to do.

One day a man in a tuxedo gets into a fist fight on the platform. I watch in horror as he throws a left, then the other man smashes him in the nose. Blood pours down the man's starched white shirt as he flings the other man to the ground. The man in tux leaps on his assailant's back, pulls something out of his pocket, and handcuffs him, then flashes his badge. He is an undercover cop on his way to the opera. He climbs off the thief he's just collared and hands me back my wallet.

There is something that draws me to the self-contained little capsules, the forward momentum of the train. I love its darkness, its smell, the bod-

· · · · · · · · · ·

ies rubbing up against one another. The ambient noise people make, the chance meetings I overhear. I like the little mice that scurry along the tracks. I love the packages people carry and the way they try to stick them under their seats. The man who brought an eight-foot Christmas tree on, the Seeing Eye dogs, the dogs for the hearing impaired, the families carrying huge packages of bedding, the bikers, the musicians with bass fiddles, the students with their book bags, the people with their dress bags carrying their formal wear.

But there are things I do not like. I do not like large people who try to shimmy their way into seats where they clearly won't fit. (Our subway cars were designed by the Japanese and the seats made to fit the bottoms of Japanese people who are, obviously, not built like a majority of Americans.) I don't like the smell of urine, or the psychotics who stalk the platforms. I do not like being stuck in tunnels. Or the fear which I rarely allow myself to feel that something terrible will happen. That it could. That I will be trapped, that I will burn here.

I didn't like it when I heard the terrorism expert say that if a bomb goes off in the subway a fire storm would rage through the tunnels, or when the sarin gas attack happened in Tokyo. I don't want to think the unthinkable: that it could happen here.

When I'm not working, I talk to strangers. I relish the little subway encounters; the rubbing up against one another. The way people roll their eyes when a crazy person comes on. Once a woman leaned against me, reading my book. All around me, the train was laughing. Another time a mouse ran through our car and the whole train jumped onto the seats.

I meet a little girl named Mocha. She has just gone to see Santa with her dad and is going to meet her mother. Father and daughter are curled up together, arm in arm. I ask Mocha what she wants from Santa and she says she wants him to let Daddy spend the night. Then she pleads with her father to stay and he just bends forward and shakes his head.

I change the subject and ask about school. She is in second grade and likes biology. When I almost miss my stop, her father jumps up and pulls the doors apart with his arms.

On September 12th, 2001, I ride the subway. I have to go to work, as many others do, it seems. The train is full with its usual mix of humanity coming from Brooklyn. I am on the Q and everyone is quiet, but at the moment when the train comes out of the tunnel, people look toward the sky. They stare at the space where the World Trade Towers stood and they begin to cry. Inexplicably, silently, the entire car is filled with weeping people.

When we arrive in Times Square, a large white man picks up his backpack and hits a black woman hard in the face. The passengers look stunned. The man turns to the woman. "I am so sorry . . ." he says. And the woman puts her hand on the man. "It's really all right," she says to him. "It doesn't matter at all."

Two days later, a miserable rainy day, I have to take some packages into town. They are heavy, and midway up the subway steps I do something I normally never do. I pause. I am only vaguely aware of a half-dozen people stopping behind me. I turn and see the line. No one tells me to hurry. The woman right behind me says, "Can I help you with those packages?" And before I can answer, she does.

I don't like subways in other cities. In Prague I worry that because I cannot understand the announcements I'll miss my stop. In Paris I want to be above ground so I can see its streets. In Mexico City I'm anxious about pickpocketing. What I like about the New York subway is that it's so noncommittal, so utterly ordinary. I like the fact that I can't hear the announcements, because then I have to ask the person next to me, "Did you understand a word of that?" Then that person will shake his head and say, "No, man, I didn't understand a thing." And for a moment we will bond over our common complaint.

I don't like the new trains—the ones where everything is automated. You are now approaching Newkirk Avenue. You are now arriving at Newkirk Avenue. You are now leaving. . . . And so on. The new trains with their computerized voices interrupt the flow of my thoughts, my concentration.

And I am left to wonder. Why is it the woman's voice that tells you where you are, what station you are approaching, and the man's voice, the voice of authority, that tells you to stand clear of the closing doors?

A number of years ago my mother gave me a watch. On the watch is a picture of my dog, a bichon. I can't tell time very well from the watch because the dog keeps going around and around, but I like to wear it. One day I am comfortably seated on the train, ensconced in my book, and a very large woman plunks herself down. This woman is quite ample and there really isn't room for her and I grunt, giving her a dirty look. She gives me back a frown. We have this little fight, body checking each other for a minute or two.

. . . .

I go back to my book. But the woman keeps staring at me. She stares and stares and I see she is ready for a fight. So I put my book down and she stares me right in the eyes. Then she asks, "Is that a dog on your watch?"

"Yes, it is."

"Is it your dog?"

I nod.

"Boy," she says wistfully, "I'd sure like to have my dog on my watch."

I think of animals who live underground. Rats (there is supposedly one per person in New York City), moles. I think about dark tunnels, roaring trains, never seeing the light of day. You always know when the train is coming, my daughter says, when the mice scurry away.

I cannot explain this endless fascination I feel. Perhaps because I am an exile myself, having left a home I never wanted to leave. Since I left, my motion seems perpetual. Like all travelers I am filled with anticipation and fear. But for whatever reason I seem to relish it. I hunger for a momentum that will never cease. I am a tunnel gazer, searching for the light on the tracks.

The Panorama Mesdag

. . . .

by
MARK DOTY

A mile or so from the Mauritshaus, which is the serious museum in the Hague, or Den Haag, as the Netherlanders call it, is another museum, a startling and eccentric one.

The Mauritshaus is a seventeenth-century palace, full of Rembrandts, with two splendid Vermeers and one of the only extant paintings of Carl Fabritius, a man who might have been Vermeer's teacher. He died at twenty-three, in Antwerp, when a powder keg exploded, and one of the few things he left behind is this small rectangle of canvas that depicts a goldfinch chained by the ankle to an iron hoop embedded in a wall of soft yellow plaster. Wall and bird are somehow palpably *there,* and distinctly paint as well, so they seem strangely fresh, as ambiguous and fragmentary as they must have the day they were painted, nearly four hundred years ago.

The day we visit, the Mauritshaus is surrounded by scaffolding, all but the windows wrapped in billowing sheets of plastic. The cool, orderly rooms, their walls covered in dark damasks, look out onto a geometry of ponds and the orderly brick courtyards of public buildings, but that day in each window a man in overalls scrapes or paints, and out in the front courtyard two workers pursue the particularly exacting task of gold-leafing the spear points of the wrought-iron fence, one applying mastic, the other lifting thin, ragged sheets of gold into place. They stop when the intermittent rain grows too heavy and resume again as soon as it clears a little, sunlight breaking through onto the courtyard where the iron pickets they've finished gleam with a startling brightness.

No gold and no Vermeers distinguish the Panorama Mesdag, which is

. . . .

found by following street signs from the grander museum through some handsome downtown streets, turning onto a quiet edge of the commercial district. It's a curiosity, only to be visited by people with extra time, perhaps more a folly than a work of art exactly. Though what the guidebooks don't tell you is that Hendrik Willem Mesdag's grand circular extravaganza of a painting is also a parable, a meditation on limit, on what art might and might not achieve. And that, in the strange way that souvenirs of gone ambitions do, it gets under your skin.

If Carl Fabritius is the type of the artistic life truncated—vanished before his abilities could come to full bloom; the tiny goldfinch, alert and sad at once, looking off away from us the calling card of his genius—then Mesdag is the opposite, a man whose long artistic life was fulfilled, complete, conducted in public, attended by honors and an encrustation of professional recognitions, which must have come to encase him like a very solid suit, an armor of reputation and regard. He was the very type of the successful nineteenth-century painter, the artist as businessman, his achievements held in high public regard, not open to doubt; he built his own museum, attached to his own house, in which he planned to display both his own work and the rather murky *fin de siècle* paintings he collected, some of which aren't bad and some of which are completely hilarious, especially a suite of Italian Symbolist pictures, which represent fauns and nymphs caught in moments of candescent desire, leering out from messy swathes of paint. Mesdag had shaky taste, and he wasn't a good painter, either. He had his moments, in horizontal landscapes that seem lit by a love for the Dutch countryside's peculiar horizontality: big flat fields, divided into bands of color, grainfields, bulbfields, bands of canal. Strips of color intricately fitted together, like marquetry, under wide, lively skies in which huge clouds move in from the North Sea, incandescent patches of blue opening between them.

But what made Mesdag famous, unfortunately, were seascapes. The dunes began just outside Den Haag in those days, and they rolled to the adjacent coastal town of Scheveningen, and the painter liked nothing better than portraying the swelling, roiling surface of the sea. He perfected a technique for this that seems to have more to do with an idea of the sea, or a feeling about it, than with observation; my immediate response to his seascapes was to wonder how a painting of waves could be sentimental. Where does that quality reside? But sentimental they are; they make it very clear that Mr. Mesdag felt much more about his briny scene that we do. The paintings have everything to do with his desire to present the sea, or his own virtuosity in representing it, and nothing to do with the sea itself—the performance feels hollow, a quality doubtless enhanced by repetition. And repeat he did, generating for an eager market countless seascapes in ponderous, important gilt frames,

But his Panorama is quite another thing. Unframed, continuous, borderless, the Panorama confounds the powers of description. In a wonderful book on Dutch painting and culture in the seventeeth century called *Still Life with a Bridle,* Zbigniew Herbert points out that language must go to great lengths to accomplish a mere replica of what painting does in an instant; arranging his sentences to describe a canvas, he writes, is like hauling heavy furniture around a room. Mesdag's Panorama, indeed, makes me feel I must now muster a whole household of verbal furnishings—bottom to top, cellar to attic—and lug them about the page in order to give some sense of his project's peculiar presence.

It is housed in a building of its own, designed exclusively for this purpose—a fact that points to the collaborative nature of the thing, in which Sientje Mesdag–van Houten, Mesdag's wife, was also involved, as well as an architect and a number of other Den Haag painters. The Panorama isn't entirely anomalous; there was a bit of a fashion for them, in the late nineteenth century, when they were also called cycloramas—circular, sweeping paintings of large views. They were associated with exhibitions and large fairs; other examples of the form represented Jerusalem and the awesome chasms of Niagara. In truth, the Panorama wasn't Mesdag's idea at all; he was commissioned to paint it by a panorama company, which must have intended to build an attraction rather than a work of art, though just at that moment the distinction between the two may not have been a firm one. It's odd to think of a painter taking on such an immense, flashy commission, agreeing to create a wonder, a tourist attraction. Did Mesdag know from the beginning he'd create something peculiar, enduring, ambiguous?

The building is of gray stone, big and square, and the door leads through entrance galleries full of bad Mesdags and antique Panorama souvenirs displayed in glass cases to the ticket counter, where two kind Dutch ladies and one pleasant, homosexual Dutch gentleman are waiting to take our guilders and provide us with brochures. The patrons trickling in don't seem your usual art museum consumers: mostly families with kids, mostly Dutch themselves; this place isn't high on the foreign traveler's list. Down a flight of stairs, around a narrow curving hallway, painted black,

. . . .

and soon we're on another, spiral stair, which is leading us up into the great chamber of the Panorama itself.

Where to begin? The first impression is of light, cloudy daylight, which is not only coming from above but oddly ambient, in the way light really is at the seashore, reflecting from sand and water. And we *are* at the shore, or at least at a version of it, because the structure into which we have emerged from up the winding stair is a large beach pavilion, of wood, with a conical roof of thatch. Our pavilion—a simple round gazebo—is atop a hill of sand, and from it we look out, 360 degrees, as the sand descends, dotted with dry bits of beach grass and driftwood, to . . . what? A painting, a huge painting, which is wrapped all around us and which represents the North Sea, reaching out to great distances where light breaks through those towering clouds, and the shore, where boats are clustered, and where people walk, and the dunes, and upon them the town of Scheveningen, with its summer houses and its chapels, its pleasure pavilion and hotels and music hall. A world, in other words, in which we are standing at the center. It smells like sand, dry old sand, and there is even a recording of seagulls and distant waves.

It is not a very good painting, it turns out, but it is a very good illusion. Because the bottom of the painting is obscured by sand and grass and bits of flotsam, and is some way away from us as well, it seems to rise seamlessly out of the earth. Because the top is covered by the jutting, vegetable roof of the pavilion in which we stand, the painting *has no edges*. It is unbroken, uninterruptible. And when you take a step forward or back, the experience is nothing like approaching or retreating from a painting hung on a wall; instead, weirdly, you realize instead you are *inside* of something. The "world" around you is a work of art, and you are its center.

That center is strangely, unnervingly unstable, because every way you step your perspective changes a little. Not in the effortless way it does in the world outside; within this strange hothouse of a theater, there's a disorienting little adjustment every time you move; the eyes readjust in relation to a new perspective on an illusion. The focus of your attention shifts: that woman with the white umbrella on the beach (who turns out to be Sientje Mesdag), those sailboats far out in the blue-green shallows. And over it all sky and sky, endless, complicated by grand marine clouds, whole armadas of them. Where is all this light coming from, and why does it keep shifting in these unnerving, subtle ways?

There's an oculus in the ceiling, hidden by the pavilion's roof, that bathes the world in natural light, and because it's a day of rapidly shifting weather, the light inside pulses and changes as those clouds—prototypes of the billows forever frozen in here—hurry overhead, themselves like heavy, graceful ships.

And the effect of all this effort?

A weird sense of being transported into an illusory space, like the dicey three-dimensionality of a stereopticon slide, or the fuzzy depths of a hologram. Something inescapably false about it, and something endearing about that falsity. Something childlike? Quasi-scientific, in a sort of gee-whiz, nineteenth-century way, something that would have earned the admiration of Jules Verne. A sense of a rather comical arrogance, the result of the artist's ambition to get closer and closer to reality? *I'll make a painting that seems as large as the world!* Walt Disney said that his "audioanimatronic" figures—the walking, talking Mr. Lincoln, for instance, a robotic Madame Tussaud manikin—were art's highest achievement, because it was the closest thing art had made yet to the real. There's something endearingly quaint about the notion, provincial as Scheveningen, doomed to failure.

And yet the Panorama Mesdag doesn't fail—not exactly, since it has this odd, unsettling power. Of what sort, exactly?

The Panorama denies the tyranny of the frame. We're used to art held in its place, contained, nailed to the wall, separated from the world by a useful golden boundary, which enhances and imprisons it. What if art refused to stop there, on the museum wall? Wouldn't the result be revolution?

A great ambition, to take us inside, for art to subsume reality.

Fabritius versus Mesdag; the former is tiny, bounded. We are in control. We walk away and turn our attention elsewhere. The painting has edges; the shadow of the finch is headless, jutting out of the frame to the right; the painting doesn't try to include everything. It occupies only its own space, contained, in some way indifferent to us. There it is, whether you look at it or not. It bears its signature proudly, as though it were inscribed in stone: C. Fabritius 1654.

But even that bold signature seems inherently modest in the face of Mesdag's hubris; Carl Fabritius is quite content to represent one bird, and to fill that little feathered vessel with feeling of a decidedly ambiguous, poetic sort. He is deeply concerned with light on a patch of plaster no larger than, say, the Yellow Pages, while Mr. Mesdag requires nothing less

. . . .

than a universe, his only limit the unbanishable edge of the horizon. If he could get rid of the horizon, one guesses, he would.

But how unpressurized art is without its frame—this grand encompassing gesture fails to move. Well, that's not entirely true; it seems that everyone mounting the dark stairs and stepping out into the filtered light of this grand theatrical space feels something: awe, amusement, surprise? But it couldn't make anyone weep, could it, except perhaps at the folly of human pride?

The brochure says after its first hundred years the Panorama was in sorry shape, and a team of experts came to restore it: cleaning, restretching the great canvas on its circle of poles, retouching where necessary. Queen Beatrix was here for the final brush stroke. "We would have lost our beautiful Panorama," the narration says, touchingly including us all in the sad prospect that has been so fortunately averted.

But I confess: I would have loved the Panorama more in disarray; I'd have loved to have seen it with stains of mildew creeping through its skies, or a worry of unraveling the mice had done down in the sands beneath the high dunes of Scheveningen. Then, in the face of time's delicate ruination of human ambition, I would have been moved.

Could he have known his work would become history? At the moment of its conception, when he made his original sketch, then transferred it to a glass cylinder and shone a strong light through it to project the rough sketch onto the great suspended canvas, he was recording how Scheveningen looked—its actual present. It's the action of time, not of the painter, that's made it quaint, historical, an artifact. Look around you, right now, turning in a circle from you sit. Suppose what you see in this circle from your body to your horizon were recorded, on canvas, or in a photograph: in a hundred years it would be a history of your moment, of the daily surround. It would have passed out of the realm of the ordinary, the familiar become not quite imaginable, unreal.

Later, I ask Paul what he thinks the Panorama is about. He says, "Instability, everything in flux. Everywhere you step it all seems to shift, the light looks different. And weather! That looming dark storm hurrying in."

"What storm?" I say. "I don't remember a storm."

"There's a storm," he says, "coming in over the village, and it's terrifically dark."

I find the brochure I've bought, a foldout panorama of the Panorama, which seems to flatten the whole thing out, darken it, and place it more firmly in the nineteenth century. It looks like a big backdrop for an operetta. There's some shading in the clouds, over the buildings the brochure identifies as the Pavilion Von Wied and the Hotel des Galeries, but hardly a storm. "In the original," Paul says, "those clouds are *much* darker."

I say I think the Panorama is about hubris, about the limitless ambitions of art, which here have become a kind of joke. But I then I think, no. A beautiful, poignant joke.

The sweeping novel that contains a world, the epic poem that entirely believes in itself, the house in which every element bears the hallmark of its maker—those things all seem historical. We've lost such ambitions; no one believes in them quite. Either we don't live in a moment that allows for such coherence, or else we're terrified of the broader vision. Are we collectively holding at bay the awareness of a gathering apocalypse and so prefer a poetry of small gestures, a painting safely ironic and self-referential, a fiction of limited means? Should we try to be Mesdags?

On the evidence of this painting, no; the effort partakes too much of the city council, of civic pride, of public ceremonies, a kind of bourgeois boosterism. I imagine Mesdag and company being presented with medallions hung on ribbons while a brass band plays. One misses an art of intimacy, of privacy, of emotional urgency and connection. There's something hollow and flimsy about the great gesture.

And yet. There is something I miss about the scale of the ambition, something lovely about the longing the project represents: *here is the world around me this minute, all of it.*

In fact, the Panorama isn't much like a painting. It's like a poem. It wishes to place you in the center of a moment, wishes to colonize your attention for a while, while a little time passes. A ring whose center is everywhere and whose circumference is nowhere. Well, the painting's circumference is *there*, a fact in space, but it doesn't seem to be—those skyey horizons open on and on. It's an ancient figure for the divine, the circle whose rim we can't find, can't reach, which seems to have no outer limit.

We step outside. It's raining a little more energetically, people pulling out umbrellas or pulling jackets and anoraks up over their heads. I have a plastic bag full of postcards, including my pull-out brochure, which represents the entire Panorama in the form of an antique tinted photograph, seen in the mode of early in the twentieth century. In the bag is also the souvenir Paul's bought—a little plastic TV set with a tiny peephole on the back side; you hold it up to the light and voilà! there's a little 3D view of a portion of the Panorama. Click a button on top and another view slides into place. Like the Panorama itself, this little perspective box seems part and parcel of the Dutch love of illusion, a long-standing fascination with the intricacies of seeing. *Trompe l'oeil* painting, the minute gestures of the painter rendering the silver lip of an opened oyster, the translucent jelly of a ripe gooseberry. Anamorphosis, that peculiar form of painting which is unreadable till reflected in a curving mirror. And the more pragmatic applications of this fascination: lenses, ground and set into microscopes and telescopes. Gifts of vision, without which the disposable contact lenses I wear, curved to the steep pitch of my cornea and weighted so as to correct, in each eye, a different degree of astigmatism, would not exist. Without them, the tricks and subtleties of Mesdag—or Fabritius or Vermeer, for that matter—would be lost on me.

Paul's little aqua blue television set reminds me of Proust's magic lantern—wavery images on the remembered walls, the stuff of legend and daydream. Now the Panorama Mesdag's filtered through another layer of nostalgia: those plastic TV sets were popular in America in the early sixties. I remember buying one at the Grand Canyon; Paul brought them home from junky tourist shops in Florida or the Jersey shore.

Did Mesdag intuit that his subject, no matter what he intended it to be, would become memory? Everyone who enters this pavilion returns to some original, interiorized beach, memory's shoreline: crash and back-suck of wave, sunlight, sudden cool approach of a cloud's shadow, salt scent and foam and bits of shell. Textures of sand, crook of an arm, curve of a shoulder. Layers of memory, narratives made out of the slipstream of impressions in time: this is the circle in which I stood. Sunflower petals rayed around the center's whorls. This is what seemed to radiate around me, this is the world I arranged merely by standing in the center of my life.

Each man or woman or child who mounts the curving stair into Mesdag's dream palace enters something in the collective memory—here is a beach town, just as it was, in 1881. And here is something of how we understood ourselves, in the nineteenth century's twilight, our pleasures and our ambitions. And we understand then, perhaps without saying it to ourselves, that our moment's just as fleeting, just as certain to seem antique and quaintly lit; that we become, in time, one of those figures on the shore, not very detailed, not particularly individual, a representative of our era, when seen from such a distancing perspective. Oddly paradoxical, and oddly moving—to be reminded that we stand at the center of our own lives, and that those lives are historical, and fleeting. What could the effect be, then, but tenderness?

Now we stand on the wet street, Paul and I, in the center of a realm of light and shadow—reflections off wet cars, a Walk sign distorted in a puddle over cobblestone—and any way we step that world shifts around us, an optical paradox. Already I seem to be recognizing that the Panorama is better in memory—less quaint, more profound, more troubling, not a large bad painting but an accomplished chamber of recollection, a parable, something to keep. We're walking back toward the train station, carrying our souvenirs, and even in motion we seem to stand in the center of circle after circle. Having been in a Panorama once, it seems we never entirely leave.

The Body Metallic

. . . .

by

VICTORIA REDEL

Between the ages of fourteen and twenty-one, I had no body. I lost my body after waiting for two hours in a doctor's office until I was ushered into an airtight office where an orthopedic specialist flung my X rays up onto his light box and with a flourish of medical authority declared that I had a spinal disease called scoliosis. I needed, the doctor decreed, to be fitted for a Milwaukee body brace that I was to wear twenty-three hours a day. With regular six-month X rays, I would eventually earn more time out of the brace. But for the indefinite future I would have one hour out of the brace each day to do a half hour's worth of back exercises, and then whatever else I could fit in the remaining half an hour.

Before that day, had I ever really thought about *having* a body? The body was not something found or noticed, only perhaps when it failed—a childhood fever or a knee split in a driveway tumble. Did I revel in its remarkable daily workings and triumphs? Did I marvel at the consistency and comfort I felt? I suppose I noticed my body, that first house, only when its boundary had somehow been trespassed. Even internal shifts needed to be seismic to register. At that same time, with its sudden breasts and bleeding, wasn't my body becoming a stranger?

I was no stranger to scoliosis. Scoliosis, a progressive curvature of the spine, primarily emerges in adolescent girls, often in siblings. My older sister, Jessica, diagnosed a few years earlier, already slept in the Milwaukee brace. Hadn't there been nights I'd wished for scoliosis, annoyed that Jessica was getting too much of our parents' concern? Hadn't there been nights the brace seemed somehow glamorous, with its dramatic encasing of the body? But by the time my diagnosis came, I was fourteen and wanted to be far from my parents' concerned, devoted gaze. While my mother and the doctor discussed details—calculating the exact degrees of my lumbar and thoracic curves, choosing the brace maker—I excused myself and tore into the ladies room. I was fourteen and pissed off. I wanted to storm the office or the waiting room and find someone to blame. If the disease was congenital, I'd have yet another reason to rail against my old-fashioned, immigrant parents. But I'd seen our father fall apart at the dinner table and our mother up through the night reading medical journals where girls with contorted torsos and girls whose organs had been damaged by their skeletal twist stared out, wearing only baggy white underpants. There, in a bathroom stall, I chain-smoked three cigarettes and, with each fierce teenage inhalation, I swore to myself that if I had to wear a fucking brace I would do in the fucking brace every fucking thing and any fucking thing I would have done out of the fucking brace.

■ ■ ■

The brace maker's workshop was in the basement of a ranch house, mid-block on a lane of family homes. I was positioned, sheathed in a gauze body suit, instructed to hold a pelvic tilt while grasping onto an overhead bar. Wet plaster strips were smoothed against the fixed dangle of my body. Above my head, I heard kids running through the rooms of his home and tried to guess their ages. When the mummy casing was dry, the brace maker slit the mold off of me. Seeing the cast of my torso—neck to mid-thigh—I looked for the twist, the wrongness of my form. What I saw was my body as a landscape, a place being taken from me. I went back to that basement for four fittings. Two days before my birthday, I received the fifteen-pound body brace that would, according to the experts, not only keep my spine from buckling but would also slowly yank it straight.

That first night, my sister stood with me in front of a mirror giving instructions. Pull open the back bars and slip sideways, entering with the right arm through the arm straps while pulling the plastic bodice first around the right hip. Then left arm in. Like this, she showed me to how to get my body inside the metal casing, my new housing for the next seven years.

The brace bracketed me from my chin down to my pelvis, from the back of my skull to the middle of my ass. I was a stretch of metal bars— two running the length of my back and one in front that ran from a plastic chin pad down between my breasts to the molded plastic girdle, which looked like a comic-book chastity harness. There were straps and pads strategically placed to keep my S-shaped spine from snaking anymore. I practiced in front of the mirror until I'd mastered the final step: to reach behind and pull a strap that cinched the brace tighter and tighter until I'd hear the plastic click of the two sides of the girdle meeting.

I'm sure in those first weeks I only felt pity for myself. And discomfort. Impossible to find the right position to sleep. Hard to get in and out of a car when there is no turn or bend of the neck or torso. And, no denying it, I looked awful. I needed clothes two sizes larger. I wore overalls to hide the jut of the bars and the bodice's exaggerated form. But overalls didn't hide the plastic chin support, which poked off the front bar, or the metal prongs that held the back of my skull in a fixed, correct position. No clothes hid how the brace limited movement. I could not slouch or bend. What for other kids was a simple glance left to look at where the teacher was pointing, involved me propping myself with one hand and levering my whole body left to get a look. My head and body were one rigid block. I had to relearn the simplest tasks—tying shoelaces without bending over, rolling from my back to my side in my bed at night, even sneezing had a new limited movement to avoid catching my throat on the chin bar. By that first spring, all the gadgetry of the brace had rubbed and worn down my skin until I was a patchwork of purple skin and bleeding sores. Luckily my grandmother—who, given the chance, might fix the world with a needle and thread—slit and tapered men's undershirts so that they were a thin skintight cotton protection over my bleeding waist and bruised hipbones.

With the final closure of the brace, the space I inhabited had altered. We assume the body. It is our comfortable home. And our transport. But when the body is no longer a place we fully inhabit, then how we inhabit other spaces is called into question. But what even was my body? Where did the old body go inside the new framed body? Enclosed. My body had doubled. I was double. An equation of what? The real and the fake? The damaged and the corrective? Inside and outside? Gaston Bachelard says, "If there exists a border-line surface between such an inside and outside, this surface is painful on both sides." The body inside the frame was rendered useless. The body became the non-body held in the cavity of the metal body. The old body was something I was going to have to earn back. Earn back? How? By not letting it grow unwieldy. By correction. I adopted strictness. No complaints. Do everything. And I vowed not to cheat, never sneaking hours out of the brace for important events. Perhaps I believed that following the rules would really halt the spine's progression. More likely I understood that at fifteen, at seventeen, when just going with friends to buy a pack of cigarettes is a major social moment, an opportunity for *everything,* I'd be lost trying to evaluate special events.

From this place of retrospect, I see that in those gangly years, where the body's sudden changes make for daily negotiations, daily ways to proclaim, *Really I'm cool; I'm part of the crowd,* I was a billboard for strangeness. When all tie-dyed, ripped-jean efforts were toward blending in, I was a freak, the metallic quirk. Strangers—from storekeepers to garbage men—asked what was wrong with me. I told lies. I learned that no one was eager to hear about a spinal disease. I invented wild boys and motorcycle accidents. I invented faulty parachutes. There was always blood and an ambulance. I got off on the horrified pleasure of strangers when I described the avalanche. But there were also assumptions about who and what I was. In eleventh grade, I joined one of the rap groups that were all the seventies' rage. In a room with lots of soft pillows, the other rap members slouched fashionably, their limbs overlapping one another with communion and deep connection. I was stuck straight up, shifting from cross-legged onto my knees just trying to find a comfortable position. The first day of group, the leader, a trained therapist, went around the room, assigning each member three adjectives that spoke to his or her character. When it came to me, the group leader assigned me the words "rigid," "distant," and "uptight."

But wasn't I also relieved? Relieved to be rid of the body? Relieved of how to manage certain concerns? The very concerns I obviously envied. I envied the midnight trysts with a Jeff and a Jack and a Gary. I envied the way boys looked at my girlfriends. I envied heartbreak. Sometimes, leaving a party to get into my brace, I'd joke with my friends that I was going home to get it on with my all-night lover. I was exempt from competition about who looked the best. I was exempt from worrying about how good I looked in tapered jeans. Truth was, when it came to me in the new body, everyone looked better. Truth was, I was not a contender. And in that there was relief.

■ ■ ■

But here's a snag in the story. Or the story's built-in irony. I came from a family where bodies mattered. Mattered supremely. Our mother ran the Ballet Guild, a well-respected regional ballet school. Ballet class was where I spent four afternoons a week. Continuing ballet was never in question. My mother made a case that the ballet's development of musculature was the essential thing that kept her daughters' spines from entirely collapsing. The doctor even permitted extended hours out of the brace on days when I took class. I was in training. Perhaps for a professional dance life. At the very least it was the center of our family's life. Jessica, just prior to her scoliosis diagnosis at fifteen, had begun dancing with the Philadelphia Lyric Opera. Even with her curvature, Jessica went on to join the New York City Opera, where she danced until, at twenty-two, she underwent her first full spinal fusion (becoming for the next twenty years the ballet mistress and resident choreographer at the New York City Opera.)

Not to waste time out of the brace, I wore the brace over a leotard and tights until ten minutes before class. Then I took it off, leaned it against a wall in the girls' dressing room, and began trying to limber up. Barre was always painful. Stretching back in *port de bras* was nearly impossible after a day in the brace. I'd been rigid and now I was focused on fluid movement. Like any dancer, I concentrated on locating small muscle groupings, identifying inside and outside leg muscles as I moved through *passé* and into *développé à la seconde*. I worked on the alignment of my hips.

The body, my body, was being called upon with intense particularity. My body.

The lost body, the pliable clay of limbs, regained.

During the hour and a half of class, the captive landscape was loose, loosening in motion. I liked the adagio, with its attenuated movement, the careful angles—*effacé* and *écarté*—stressed in adagio, the arm and leg extension, the elongations into *penché*. But joy was in speed and burst. I loved the mazurkas, the high, bright waltzes where my mother demanded in Russian to the pianist that he pick up the tempo. She shouted that our *grand jeté* should have real lift. It was verticality and ground I wanted to lose. I leapt through space. Higher. Those afternoons, not only did I get a chance to move, I made a measure of art with my body. How odd—how fortuitous—that the incorrect, the defective body let loose brought such joy. And, for the duration of class, I inhabited every muscle and tendon of that body. Ballet class was a crazy, secret place where all my wrongness was for the span of the hour and a half made right. The inside world was like a ramshackle cottage, perfect in full summer bloom. And I'd returned for a brief, thrilling visit.

Then I'd go home, shower, put on a fresh undershirt, and slip, right arm first, into the inflexible body that was my brace. I'd kneel, angled by my bed, not to pray, but because that was the only comfortable position I could find to do homework or read a book.

I read books. A lot of books. With or without a brace, I would have been a voracious reader. But I also think that like other people with handicaps—temporary or permanent—I found the world of the imagination, of literature, of art, a sacred and safe world. At night, while friends defied their curfews, or came home chap lipped and in love, I came home from parties, knelt by my bed, a stretch of metal, and read every book I could find. I had a life in books that was dense with intrigue and bodies and love.

Actually, after hours out of the brace, it felt good to pull the brace around me. I was tired, and it felt good to let the array of pads and straps do the work of holding me straight. After a few years, the inflexible casing felt like my true body and my actual body felt like an accessory, something I was allowed to put on for a few hours each day.

Maybe it is not that I had no body, but that I had two bodies.

My body on: that is how I had come to see my body. Even if being inside the brace felt closed, it felt right. My actual body was something foreign to me, as much a disguise as I had first felt the brace to be. I recall a day of my first spring in college, walking across the green. It was the great warm relief one feels in New Hampshire when winter and all of the false muddy springs have passed. By then I spent four hours a day out of the brace. I had my hands shoved way in the back pockets of my jeans. I loved feeling the spring warmth and the workings of my body as I moved. The movement felt good. My hands against my ass felt good. But I was unsure. I felt conspicuous, as if, somehow, having a body that moved naturally, without any restriction, was a flaunting. As if just moving as freely as everyone else moved was almost a promiscuity.

Having a body was almost more, at that point, than I could handle.

By then I had a boyfriend. At night, in his dormitory single, we listened to albums, used highlighters, and made our first forays into making love, the brace propped against the wooden door. He had the grace and generosity to ignore all of the discolored skin and the funny marks the brace made. He seemed, actually, to barely notice the brace on or off of me. After making love, I pulled on my grandmother's sewn undershirts, put on

. . . .

the brace, and he'd spoon behind me, grasping the back steel bars until we both fell asleep.

By twenty-one, I had gained so much freedom that I only slept in the brace. By day, out in the world, I was now like everyone else. People I met commented on my terrific posture (it hurt to slump). People I had known while I was in the brace rarely noticed that I wasn't wearing it but asked if I had lost a bunch of weight. I was unencumbered but found that I identified with the people on the street who limped or labored through the world with crutches or false limbs. It was not that I considered myself handicapped. God forbid! Given my pledge to do everything (damn it, I'd hiked across the Great Divide, white-water canoed, all in the brace!), handicapped was not an identity that I had included myself in. Yet I was still not living in my body. I was a visitor. I knew that this body which people accepted as regular was a fraud. I may have been corrected, but I still lived in the frame. When I walked into a room wearing the skimpiest dress (after all those years of overalls!), part of me walked in, like the Tin Man, all clanging metal, in oversized overalls.

"How can secret rooms, rooms that have disappeared, become abodes for an unforgettable past?" asks Bachelard. I love that question. But for me, the question is how to understand what new world is made in the landscape of the lost body, of the double body, of the wrong and righted body. That other body, the exterior frame, the enclosing otherness, was my otherness. If my wrongness was internal, a skeletal disease, wearing the corrective bulk externally those seven years was a way of announcing—mostly to myself—my otherness. Lose the double self, the exterior frame, and I still wanted my strangeness, my asymmetry.

A few years ago, my family sold the house where I'd grown up. We spent a couple of weekends up at the house sorting, claiming, and throwing out what remained. Up in the attic was a jumble of cartons—recital costumes, all the shoes my sisters and I had ever worn, our school reports, all saved in great sentimental heaps. Among the years of family clutter, leaning against an attic post, was my brace. I picked it up. It seemed impossibly heavy to me. It seemed like something I could not manage to walk two steps in. I picked it up, stretched it open, and instinctively pulled it on—first the right arm and side and then the left—as I had for those seven years. I closed the brace, hearing the plastic click of the girdle.

The brace still fit. But I felt I would die if I had to wear the brace for one hour, let alone one day or seven years.

I called my soon-to-be husband up to the hot attic. Like a strange mechanical model, in the dusty light of the attic, I turned in a full circle for him to see the brace's configuration of straps and buckles, screws and pads. What I felt I wanted then was exactly what I had spurned those seven years: I wanted to be looked at. I wanted to be seen in the brace. I wanted him to look closely at how it limited me. Then—God bless him— I asked that he hold me by my steel brace bars for a grand waltz through the disorder.

．　．　．　．　．　．　．　．　．　．

ANDREA BARRETT's most recent books are *Ship Fever*, which received the National Book Award, *The Voyage of the Narwhal*, and *Servants of the Map*. She teaches at the M.F.A. Program for Writers at Warren Wilson College and recently completed a fellowship at the Center for Scholars and Writers of the New York Public Library.

CARMEN BOULLOSA was born in Mexico City. She has published novels, plays, and volumes of poetry and essays. In 1990 she received the prestigious Xavier Villaurrutia Prize, in 1997 the Liberaturpreis of Frankfurt for one of her novels translated into German *(die Wündertäterin)*, and in 1998 the Anna Seghers Prize of the Berlin Arts Academy. A Guggenheim fellow, she has published two novels in the U.S. from Grove Press, *Leaving Tabasco* and *They're Cows, We're Pigs*. She lives with her two children in Brooklyn.

KAREN BRENNAN's memoir, *Being with Rachel: A Story of Memory and Survival*, was published by W. W. Norton in 2002. She is also the author of a volume of poems, *Here on Earth*, and a collection of short stories, *Wild Desire*. She teaches at the University of Utah and at the M.F.A. Program for Writers at Warren Wilson College.

DERICK BURLESON's first book, *Ejo: Poems, Rwanda 1991–94*, won the 2000 Felix Pollak Prize in Poetry. He teaches in the Creative Writing Program at the University of Alaska—Fairbanks.

KATHLEEN CAMBOR's most recent novel is *In Sunlight, in a Beautiful Garden*. A recent Guggenheim fellow, she is currently working on a book set in eighteenth-century Peru. *The Book of Mercy* was a finalist for the

PEN/Faulkner Prize, and was awarded the Janet Heidinger Kafka Prize for Excellence in Fiction by an American Woman.

RAFAEL CAMPO teaches and practices medicine at Harvard Medical School and Beth Israel Deaconess Medical Center. His most recent books are a collection of poetry, *Landscape with Human Figure* (Duke, 2002), and a volume of essays, *The Healing Art: A Doctor's Black Bag of Poetry* (Norton, 2003).

BERNARD COOPER's most recent book is *Guess Again,* a collection of stories from Simon & Schuster. Cooper's work is included in *The Best American Essays 2002.* He is the art critic for *Los Angeles* magazine.

MARK DOTY is the author of six books of poetry and three volumes of nonfiction prose. His work has been honored by the National Book Critics Circle Award, the PEN/Martha Albrand Prize for Nonfiction, and a Whiting Writers Award; he's the only American poet to have won Britain's T. S. Eliot Prize. He teaches at the University of Houston and divides his time between Houston, New York City, and Provincetown.

MICHAEL JOSEPH GROSS has written for the *New York Times Magazine,* the *Atlantic Monthly,* and many other magazines and newspapers. His first book, *In Person,* about the relationships between stars and fans in Hollywood, will be published by Bloomsbury USA. He lives in Los Angeles.

BARBARA HURD is the author of *Stirring the Mud: On Swamps, Bogs, and Human Imagination* (Beacon); *Entering the Stone: On Caves and Feeling through the Dark,* forthcoming from Houghton Mifflin; and numerous essays, including ones that appeared in the 1999 and 2001 volumes of *Best American Essays.* A recipient of a 2002 N.E.A. Fellowship, she is the Wilson H. Elkins Professor at Frostburg State University.

PAUL LISICKY is the author of *Lawnboy* (Turtle Point, 1999) and *Famous Builder* (Graywolf, 2002). A recipient of awards from the National Endowment for the Arts, the Michener/Copernicus Society, and the Fine Arts Work Center in Provincetown, he teaches writing at Sarah Lawrence College.

DEBORAH A. LOTT is the author of *In Session.* She received her M.F.A. from Antioch University. Her work has appeared in *Salon.com, Lear's, Psychiatric Times, Psychology Today,* and the *Los Angeles Times.*

ELIZABETH MCCRACKEN is the author of a collection of short stories, *Here's Your Hat What's Your Hurry,* and two novels, *The Giant's House* and *Niagara Falls Over Again.* A National Book Award finalist, she won the Harold Vursell Award from the American Academy of Arts and Letters.

HONOR MOORE's most recent books are *Darling* (poems) and *The White Blackbird: A Life of the Painter Margarett Sargent by Her Granddaughter.* She lives in New York and teaches in the graduate writing programs at Columbia University and the New School.

MARY MORRIS is the author of twelve books including the novels, *House Arrest* and *Acts of God* and the travel memoir, *Nothing to Declare: Memoirs of a Woman Traveling Alone.* The recipient of the Rome Prize in Literature, Morris teaches writing at Sarah Lawrence College.

A seventh collection of poems by CAROL MUSKE-DUKES, *Sparrow,* was published by Random House in 2003; her most recent collection of essays is *Married to the Icepick Killer: A Poet in Hollywood* (Random House). The recipient of numerous awards including N.E.A. and Guggenheim fellowships, she is professor of English / Creative Writing and Director of the Graduate Program in Creative Writing and Literature at the University of Southern California.

VICTORIA REDEL is the author of *Loverboy,* a novel; *Already the World,* a collection of poems; and *Where the Road Bottoms Out,* a volume of short fiction. She has been the recipient of several awards, including the Sister Mariella Gable Prize, the Wick Poetry Prize, and an N.E.A. fellowship in poetry. She currently teaches at Sarah Lawrence College, Columbia University, and in the low-residency M.F.A program at Vermont College.

REGINALD SHEPHERD's fourth book of poems, *Otherhood,* is forthcoming from University of Pittsburgh Press in 2003. His other books are *Some Are Drowning* (1993 AWP Award), *Angel, Interrupted,* and *Wrong.* He lives in Pensacola, Florida, where magnolias and live oaks are evergreens.

TERRY TEMPEST WILLIAMS is the author of *Refuge, Leap,* and most recently, *Red: Passion and Patience in the Desert.* She is the recipient of a Guggenheim and a Lannan Literary fellowship. A major American environmental activist, she lives in Castle Valley, Utah.

Graywolf Press is a not-for-profit, independent press. The books we publish include poetry, literary fiction, essays, and cultural criticism. We are less interested in best-sellers than in talented writers who display a freshness of voice coupled with a distinct vision. We believe these are the very qualities essential to shape a vital and diverse culture.

Thankfully, many of our readers feel the same way. They have shown this through their desire to buy books by Graywolf writers; they have told us this themselves through their e-mail notes and at author events; and they have reinforced their commitment by contributing financial support, in small amounts and in large amounts, and joining the "Friends of Graywolf."

If you enjoyed this book and wish to learn more about Graywolf Press, we invite you to ask your bookseller or librarian about further Graywolf titles; or to contact us for a free catalog; or to visit our award-winning web site that features information about our forthcoming books.

We would also like to invite you to consider joining the hundreds of individuals who are already "Friends of Graywolf" by contributing to our membership program. Individual donations of any size are significant to us: they tell us that you believe that the kind of publishing we do *matters*. Our web site gives you many more details about the benefits you will enjoy as a "Friend of Graywolf"; but if you do not have online access, we urge you to contact us for a copy of our membership brochure.

www.graywolfpress.org

Graywolf Press
2402 University Avenue, Suite 203
Saint Paul, MN 55114
Phone: (651) 641-0077
Fax: (651) 641-0036
E-mail: wolves@graywolfpress.org

This book was designed by Will Powers. It is set in Sabon and Formata type by Stanton Publication Services, Inc. and manufactured by Maple Vail Book Manufacturing on acid-free paper.